PRAISE FOR TOXIC FAITH

"Steve Arterburn plows new ground with this book."

—BILL HYBELS, pastor of Willow Creek Community Church,

author of *Too Busy Not to Pray*

"The hot topic! The urgent issue! All tackled by the right man for a GREAT book."

—DR. ROBERT SCHULLER, pastor

"This man…speaks with wisdom. He is one of the most relevant voices addressing the inner pains of both youth and adults."

—DR. TONY CAMPOLO, professor of sociology, Eastern College

"A bold confrontation… Integrating the principles in this book will be a major step in restoring spiritual and emotional health."

—DAVID A. STOOP, PH.D., clinical psychologist

"With the utmost clarity Stephen Arterburn and Jack Felton expose the hazards of a 'toxic faith'…and point us back to a real faith."

—DR. ARCHIBALD HART, author of *Healing Life's Hidden Addictions*

TOXIC
FAITH

TOXIC
FAITH

Experiencing Healing *from* Painful Spiritual Abuse

Stephen Arterburn & Jack Felton

SHAW

WATERBROOK
PRESS

Toxic Faith
A Shaw Book
Published by WaterBrook Press
2375 Telstar Drive, Suite 160
Colorado Springs, Colorado 80920
A division of Random House, Inc.

Some of the stories in this book are composites of several different situations;
details and names have been changed to protect identities.

Scripture taken from the *New King James Version.* Copyright © 1982 by Thomas Nelson, Inc.
Used by permission. All rights reserved.

ISBN 0-87788-825-6 (formerly 0-84079-115-1)

Library of Congress Cataloging-in-Publication Data
Arterburn, Stephen, 1953–
   Toxic faith : understanding and overcoming religious addiction / Stephen
   Arterburn and Jack Felton.
      p.   cm.
   Originally published: Nashville : Oliver-Nelson, ©1991.
   Includes bibliographical references.
   ISBN 0-87788-825-6
   1. Religious addiction—Christianity. 2. Christian life. I. Felton, Jack, 1953–
   II. Title.

BR114 .A77 2001
248.2—dc21

                                  00-047700

Printed in the United States of America
2001

10 9 8 7 6 5 4 3

I would like to dedicate this book to Denny Bellesi,
pastor of Coast Hills Community Church in Aliso Viejo, California.
After a very toxic church experience, you asked me
to do nothing but heal in your church.
You were my first real pastor, and I did heal.
Thank you for your heart and integrity that restored my faith
and led to the creation of this book.
S. A.

———————————

Dedicated to my wife and children, Robin, Jack, and Christy
who make my life so enjoyable and helped me realize
the importance of healthy faith in my life.
J. F.

Contents

Preface

In 1989 Victor Oliver, my publisher with Thomas Nelson, called me with an idea for a book. Several authors already had turned him down, but he thought I might be interested. He suggested that I create a book to help men and women stuck in sick churches, to throw out a lifeline to hurting believers who had been used and abused and robbed of their relationship with God.

Victor knew that many believers struggle to find a real relationship with God because their group's rules, regulations, and religious rituals become the main forces in their lives, displacing a powerful and personal God. They grow blind to practices that misplace faith in faith, structure, false leaders, good works, and many other spiritual substitutes. Such false practices have the scent and feel of God, but they lack his holy presence. Victor knew that many religious folks are good people doing some very good and right things but for all the wrong reasons—resulting in a paradoxical separation from God rather than intimacy with God.

The discussion with Victor ended with my commitment to consider the project and pray about it. The authors he had contacted first had not wanted to write the book because of its negative topic, and negative topics do not produce bestsellers—or so they thought.

But I knew a book like this needed to be written. I knew it because I had discovered that some of my own problems with the church (and by no means all) were not really my problems. That may sound smug, but I had come to realize that some of my thoughts and feelings about manipulative church leaders and practices were accurate, and that realization freed me to develop a real and authentic relationship with God.

Although I knew such a book could be vitally important for the body of Christ, I also knew that by myself I could not do justice to the subject.

Therefore I turned to a counselor and theologian, Jack Felton. Jack not only supplied the information that I lacked, but he also came up with the title for our joint project: *Toxic Faith*. I suspected the bruised and broken would connect immediately with the title just as I did.

Toxic Faith was first released in 1991. To our surprise (and that of many others), it quickly grabbed a spot on the bestseller list. *Publisher's Weekly* called it a future "Christian Classic." Soon I received invitations to appear on television shows such as *Oprah, Geraldo, Jenny Jones, Sally Jesse Raphael,* and many others—golden opportunities to share my faith with hundreds of millions of viewers. What a privilege to declare that the extremes of toxic faith featured in the media did not represent authentic faith or a focus on a real God!

Letters came pouring in from wounded readers (this was before the advent of the Internet)—heartbreaking stories that ended with hope. I read story after story of leaders, husbands, family members, and pastors who used Scripture erroneously to grab or maintain control of others' lives. Hundreds told us the book literally saved their lives. God had led them to the book just before a suicide attempt or after they had abandoned God altogether. Many days I cried over the long-term grief and newfound joy described in these letters. For the first time, these individuals realized that God loved *them,* no matter how someone in power had misrepresented God or used the Lord's name to control and manipulate them. The book had encouraged these readers to refuse to judge God or the church on the basis of the toxic behavior of people who did not really know God and were not close to what God wanted the church to be. Freedom, healing, strength, and hope replaced bondage, shame, fear, and despair. We had cut in on the dance of self-deception and introduced tired dancers to a God who could not be manipulated and whose love could not be earned.

To this day, people still tell me stories of how the book changed their life and their relationship with God. To date I have published thirty-five books—and *Toxic Faith* is by far the most important and fulfilling of them all. If I could have published only one book, it would have been *Toxic Faith*.

Some time after the hardback edition of *Toxic Faith* came out, the publisher issued a paperback version under the title *Faith That Hurts, Faith That Heals.* "Why the title change?" many asked. The reason was simple. Some bookstore owners did not like the original title, even though it drew thousands of struggling believers to it. In order to reach a wider audience through the stores that never carried *Toxic Faith*, we changed the title to something milder. Amazingly, the paperback received a stronger reaction than did the hardback! It reached deeper into the Christian community than *Toxic Faith*—and once again I was humbled at the privilege of delivering God's truth to some severely hurting Christians.

Eventually *Faith That Hurts, Faith That Heals* went out of print. WaterBrook Press recognized the need for a book that described healthy faith—the flip side to *Toxic Faith*—and in 2000 it published my book *More Jesus, Less Religion.* In addition to selling in Christian bookstores, Crossings Book Club offered this book in a hardback edition, selling thousands of copies to men and women looking for a closer relationship with Jesus. This time, e-mails came pouring in, telling us that readers had found exactly what they were searching for. Amazingly, almost everyone wanted to read *Toxic Faith*—but they could not find it. The requests multiplied so fast that WaterBrook decided it had to publish a slightly revised and updated paperback version of the original *Toxic Faith.* I am forever indebted to Dan Rich and the quality folks at WaterBrook for rereleasing my favorite book, under their Harold Shaw imprint.

I don't know how you came to pick up this edition, but I hope and pray that God will use it in a mighty way to renew or restore your faith. If he does so, please let us know your story. You can email us at Sarterburn @newlife.com. When you write, I will read your note and respond to you. I'd even like to hear from you if you don't find the book all that helpful.

Blessings to you from all of us who had a hand in this project!

Gratefully,

Stephen Arterburn

P.S. We would feel greatly honored if you would pass on this book to someone who might receive help from it.

Acknowledgments

Thanks to Dan Rich and the WaterBrook team who worked to bring this book to completion. You are a joy to work with because you are big thinkers who actually care.

Introduction

My grandmother died in 1989. If there were ever a person of strong faith and conviction, it was Nany. All alone she reared her three children, including my mother, after the suicide of my grandfather. She never gave up, never stopped believing, never lost faith. For her, death was merely a step into a better place. She didn't fear it. Her faith kept her at peace, motivated her to care, and provided constant hope. She was always actively doing her part while she trusted God to do his. God's love seeped through every pore of that marvelous woman, who cheered up just about everyone she touched. Much of my own faith came from watching her and hearing her talk about a loving God who loves his children.

At Nany's funeral, the minister told of one of the frustrations my grandmother had to endure: an audit by the Internal Revenue Service. The IRS went to a lot of trouble to make sure that someone who made every bit of eight thousand dollars a year paid her fair share of income taxes. While others were hiding millions of dollars from the federal government, special agents were hard at work on the case of Pearl Russell, making sure the country would not be shorted a few hundred dollars by a sweet old lady in Athens, Texas.

At issue was Nany's large deduction for charitable contributions. The government could not believe that a woman making so little could give 35, and some years 40, percent to the church and still have enough money left over to pay her bills. The IRS finally backed off when she dug out of the attic all the canceled checks to television ministers, radio preachers, and her local church. Agents did not understand it, but they were convinced that she had given every penny she deducted.

My grandmother not only gave away almost half of her income, she paid off her car loans early, paid off her mortgage, and still had enough money left over to bake her special pies for hurting people. Nany was an amazing woman of faith; it seemed that no matter how much she gave away, she still was provided with enough to live comfortably. What little she could do for God, she did. She did it because of a real faith in God, not a faith motivated by the idea that if she gave she would become rich. She knew she would *never* have a lot of money. Neither did she give because she hoped to buy her way to heaven. She had taken care of her place in eternity years ago. No, she gave because she wanted to give back to God a portion of all he had given her. Her pure motives set a great example for all who had the privilege to watch her.

There was nothing toxic about Nany's faith. She never gave to a particular minister, but always to the ministry, such as to a children's home or to a project to feed the homeless. When she gave a dollar, she knew how that minister was going to spend it.

At least she thought she did.

Some of the individuals to whom she gave her money were not so admirable. Their toxic faith robbed my grandmother of the great blessing of knowing her money had been used to further the kingdom of God. They took her money and spent it on themselves and their big plans, schemes that had nothing to do with my grandmother's desire to tell the world about God's love or to feed and clothe orphans. Some of those ministers that she so faithfully supported wound up in jail, divorced their wives, were arrested for indecent exposure, or fell into other public sin. They proclaimed a faith on television or over the radio, but they lived something else. They didn't shrink from asking my grandmother and others like her to sacrifice their food money so they could buy jet fuel to fly to Palm Springs for a weekend getaway. What they did was dishonest, unfair—and very human. The kind of faith they lived looked radically different from the one they proclaimed on the public airwaves.

These unfaithful men and women who spent Nany's money put more faith in themselves than they did in God. They relied more on their manipulations than on God's providence. They were more concerned about their own comforts than they were for the people who gave them money or for those whom the donations were intended to help. They built big empires for themselves while my grandmother turned off her heater at night so she might be able to save a few dollars and therefore give more. Their faith was *toxic*. It poisoned many who trusted them, and it distorted the view of God held by many who watched as these media ministers fell from grace. As a result, many today believe *all* ministers are charlatans and out to fleece the flock. These cynics have derived a toxic, unhealthy view of faith from the toxic examples they saw in the media.

Unfortunately, media ministers are not the only ones who poison faith. Faith can be tainted from many other sources. Perhaps the loss of a child causes a mother to abandon her trust in God, since she thought he would protect her baby from the evils of the world. Maybe the early loss of a parent left someone feeling abandoned and desperately searching for the care and nurture they believe an uncaring God robbed from them. A business failure, a broken relationship, the death of a wonderful friend—all can change the way hurting people view God. Roots of bitterness and unresolved anger are allowed to poison their faith, causing them to turn away from God and never return.

Still others manifest their toxic faith in more obvious ways. Feeling unloved by God—maybe due to an early incident of child abuse—they try to earn God's love. They believe that if they work hard and put in enough effort so that everyone notices their dedication, they might win favor with God. Of course, it is not a conscious effort to win God's favor. They believe they are doing what any godly person would do. When the church doors open, they are there—not because they want to be there, but because they are driven and feel extreme guilt if they don't sacrifice family, friends, and themselves in service of the church. Their faith is toxic, poisoned by trauma or a desire to work their way to heaven. And so what should be a source of strength and hope becomes an addiction, trapping the toxic believer in painful obsessions and compulsions.

The toxic faith of others is used to avoid the realities of life. These individuals expect God to work miracles at their beck and call, as if he were a genie. They seek a personal magician, not the Creator of the universe. Rather than face up to the needs of a sick child who needs extensive (and expensive) medical care, they insist on healing prayer alone…and allow the child to die. Others spend long hours in prayer for a failing marriage, while steadfastly refusing to seek counseling aimed at mending marital wounds. They expect God to do for them what God may be waiting for them to do for themselves. In fact, they are not looking for God, but rather are searching for relief and a means to avoid the pain they need to face. They are addicted to a toxic religion that allows them to live in a fantasy world of quick fixes and easy solutions. Rather than growing deep in their faith, they grow weak in their ability to cope. Always looking for the religious high, these wounded faithful are not far from functioning like heroin addicts searching frantically for their next fix.

Those who possess a toxic faith have stepped across the line from a balanced perspective of God to an unbalanced faith in a weak, powerless, or uncaring God. They seek a God to fix every mess, prevent every hurt, and mend every conflict. They and others like them need to answer the following questions:

- Where is the balance between an ungodly independence that leaves a person overwhelmed from the need to be self-sufficient and an ungodly passivity that leaves someone doing nothing unless "God has spoken" with audible, personal direction?
- Where is the line between conviction to help people out of a love for God and addiction to compulsive work and striving to please God?
- What is the difference between giving money to honor God and giving to buy God's favor?
- When does growing in faith become a futile attempt to be perfect?
- When does dependence on God become a cop-out, a way to avoid dealing with tough life situations?
- At what point does faith turn into something ugly, void of a loving God, toxic to the believer, and toxic to those who are near?
- How can a person determine when it is right to follow a leader and when it is dangerous?
- How does one recover from a toxic faith to grow in the grace and knowledge of God?

These are the issues for *Toxic Faith*. Most likely, you have dealt with at least one of these issues in your search for truth about life and the God who created it. You may have grown frustrated in your search and now claim there is no God. Your faith may have become so poisoned that you felt you had to get away from it altogether just to survive. You may be left wondering if God exists, and if he does, what real faith in a real God would be like. It is my desire that you find answers here. I want you to find hope for a return to faith that can add meaning to your life. I especially hope that you will find the reality of true faith and be able to separate that from those who model only a caricature of faith. I want to help you throw out that toxic faith and bring you back to the real thing.

My grandmother had the real thing. I'm grateful for her example of trust in God through the tough times and the good times. She exemplified God's love, not just when it was convenient, but when she did anything. The moment she died, Pearl Russell was able to walk through the Pearly Gates because of a faith that would not be distorted by events, circumstances, pain, or false teaching. She made it to a place where toxic faith does not exist.

I pray that, like her, you will be able to sift through your pain, circumstances, and our cruel world to find the God who meant so much to my grandmother and now to me.

Good and Bad Spirituality

If I were asked for a yardstick to discern good from bad spirituality, I would suggest three criteria to be detached from: material gain, self-importance, and the urge to dominate others. Unfortunately, much of what is labeled spirituality in America today moves in the opposite direction. It means using the names of God and Christ to promote one's own importance, material gain, and right to oppress others.[1]

— ROSEMARY RADFORD RUETHER, PROFESSOR OF THEOLOGY

Beware lest anyone cheat you through philoso-
phy and empty deceit, according to the tradi-
tion of men, according to the basic principles
of the world, and not according to Christ....

Let no one defraud you of your reward....
[W]hy, as though living in the world, do you
subject yourselves to regulations—"Do not
touch, do not taste, do not handle," which all
concern things which perish with the using—
according to the commandments and doc-
trines of men? These things indeed have an
appearance of wisdom in self-imposed reli-
gion, false humility, and neglect of the body,
but are of no value against the indulgence of
the flesh....

Set your mind on things above, not
on things on the earth.

COLOSSIANS 2:8,18,20-23; 3:2

CHAPTER 1

The Extremes of Toxic Faith

Rebecca Grant had lived a hard life in the hot desert town of Barstow, California. Her father died when she was very young and her mother struggled to keep her and her sister in clothes. During the day, her mother sold tickets at the Greyhound bus depot; at night she sold tickets at the theater. On her days off she cleaned their small, rented house and did chores. It wasn't a wonderful existence, but her persevering spirit kept the family going.

Rebecca loved her mother and knew how hard she worked to provide the basics. Some of Rebecca's friends teased her because she didn't have a dad and her mother had to work so much. Their comments stung, but they also caused her to respect her mother all the more.

At fourteen, Rebecca began to work. All the money she earned went into a bowl, along with her mother's money. They took out only what they needed for the essentials. Rebecca's mother put the rest in a passbook account at the savings and loan for the days when Rebecca and her sister would need help with college fees.

Rebecca's mother was a woman of faith, a Christian who believed that God had a plan for her life. If she remained faithful, she believed she would see that plan and God would bless her faithfulness. She didn't waver from her beliefs. In the toughest of times she didn't doubt God's love for her. She trusted him to take care of her and her two daughters. She would do all she could do to provide for her family, and she would leave the rest up to God. She never worked on Sunday and always took the girls to church where they prayed and sang together.

Rebecca was close to her mother, but not to her mother's God. She enjoyed going to church because of the people there; it was something out of the ordinary routine of the week. She liked it, but she didn't become a Christian. She doubted there was a God, and if he did exist, she felt distant from him. He had never spoken to her or shown himself to her, and he certainly hadn't made life easy for her. She wanted to believe, but she rejected what she heard in church.

Rebecca heard a contorted gospel that continues to be preached from many pulpits—a distortion of truth, oftentimes manipulative. She heard that if a person becomes a Christian, life will become easy. God will take care of everything. Miracles will occur and all problems will vanish. She was told that true believers in Christ are protected from the evil of the world. Faith in Christ was presented as an insurance policy against any pain in the present.

But Rebecca had a question: If God is so loving, then why does he allow my life to be so hard, and why does he force my mother to struggle so much? If there really were a God, he would help us.

The expectation of a problem-free life brought about by trust in God led Rebecca into a toxic faith. Her distorted view of what God should and should not do caused her to abandon the search for truth and latch on to anything that would bring relief from her misery and pain. She turned first to alcohol. Then it was drugs. Finally, she became promiscuous and contracted incurable genital herpes. Her suffering seemed to provide more proof that God either did not exist or was not interested in her. Her toxic faith pushed her behavior to become increasingly destructive.

THE PROMISE OF PROBLEM-FREE LIVING

I wish I could say Rebecca's faith experience is uncommon, but it isn't. More agnostics and atheists have been created by a false expectation of an easy life from God than from any other false belief. When many men and women find that a faithful life does not free them from pain and discomfort, they turn from God.

Preachers who don't fully explain the life of faith are partly to blame for these spiritual defections. They ought to make it plain that a biblical faith in God changes the believer's perspective so much that the pains of life hit with less impact. God can use each hardship to bring greater faith and deeper peace from trusting that he is in control.

It simply is not true that acceptance of Christ or belief in God will cause all problems to vanish. All difficulties do not go away simply because you turn your life over to God. In fact, just the opposite may occur!

When I first turned my life over to God, problems that I never knew existed seemed to cling to me like leeches. If I had been motivated to live for God by the promise of an easy life, I would have made a serious error! If I didn't believe God had set a standard for my life, I could have given in to every temptation without guilt or shame. But because I believed in God, I had a strong desire to fight the lure of sin that tempted me to stray from the will of God. At times it seemed as if some new temptations had been developed just to taunt me! It didn't take me long to discover that the life of faith is not sugarcoated or pain free.

Although Rebecca heard of an easy life through faith in God, like everyone else, believer and nonbeliever alike, she was forced to endure tragedies and hardships. False expectations of God frequently lead to a toxic faith—or the extermination of faith entirely.

NAIVE FAITH

My mother grew up with a version of this toxic faith. She believed that dedicating her sons to God would spare them the heartache other children would have to endure. She thought that somehow her prayers and faith vaccinated us against evil and that temptations would not likely come our way—but if they did, we would not succumb.

The first blow to her toxic faith came when her father committed suicide. It hit her much harder than it would most others because she thought she and her family were protected. Even so, she didn't give up her belief in a God who would prevent the natural course of nature or evil from harming her family.

When my brother contracted AIDS and eventually died,[1] my mother was confronted in a most painful way with the fact that her faith, the faith of her family, did not supernaturally vaccinate us from terrible events. She struggled with his illness and with her faith at the same time. She sank into a deep depression, and at times I didn't know if she would return to being the wonderful lady she had been all her life.

Fortunately, she did return to being that person. She made it out of her depression and back to reality. How? By dealing with her confusing ideas about faith and God. She yelled at God. She told him it wasn't fair. She admitted she had come to her faith as a way of making life easier. As she shared her anger and frustration with a God who did not do things according to her fondest wishes and expectations, she recovered from the death of her son. In the process she also recovered her faith. It is no longer toxic; it is whole. It has brought her into a new understanding of who God is and how he works. She is more deeply committed to God than ever before and is better equipped to help others looking for someone who understands.

TOXIC-FAITH HEADLINES

Our fast-paced, push-button society spawns many variations of toxic faith. Men and women traveling the narcissistic roller coaster, searching for the next thrill or quick fix, seem interested only in a God who can make things easier or less painful.

Many members of this generation refuse to cling to a God who allows pain. They don't walk in faith long enough to discover that God actually lightens the burden and eases the pain. Of course, such a reduction in discomfort doesn't come overnight; it comes slowly, as a relationship with God grows stronger and deeper. As a person studies the attributes of God and understands how he really works, events that once would have brought disaster now become an opportunity for growth. Character blossoms out of the inconveniences.

Sadly, it's not hard to find many variations of toxic faith far more bizarre than the concept of a God who makes life easy. Almost every day in newspapers and magazines across our land, tragic stories illustrate poisonous belief. These are true-life examples of toxic faith that degenerate into deadly religious addiction. Consider just a few instances in which toxic faith has destroyed lives, fortunes, and families.

Headline: Baptist Couple Convicted of Kidnapping, Abuse

A Baptist pastor and his wife from Bristol, Tennessee, were convicted in early 2000 of kidnapping and abusing a girl they took from an orphanage. The Reverend and Mrs. Joseph Combs of Emmanuel Baptist Church were sentenced in March, while the Reverend Combs has yet to be tried on charges of rape.

The kidnapped child, Esther, now twenty-two years old, was reared as a family servant. She testified at the trial that Mrs. Combs beat her with baseball bats, burned her with a curling iron, and pulled out chunks of her flesh with pliers—leaving more than four hundred scars on her body. Esther said she was denied an education, forced to do all the chores, and required to wear clothing that covered her scars.

The young woman now lives in another state under a different name.[2]

Headline: Nude Pentecostals Crash into Tree While Fleeing Satan

Two self-professed Pentecostal preachers and eighteen members of their families escaped serious injury in Vinton, Louisiana, after crashing into a tree while attempting to elude police. The chase occurred after officers responded to a call for help at a local campground, but the story begins long before that.

Floydada, Texas, Police Chief James Hale said he had been looking for the Rodriguez family since Tuesday night, when relatives reported them missing. "They made statements like the devil was after them and Floydada was going to be destroyed if they stayed here," Hale said. Floydada lies in the Texas Panhandle, about 550 miles from Vinton.

The family started out in five cars on August 17, 1993, with whatever they could carry. As the cars broke down or ran out of gas, they were abandoned. One vehicle was left behind in Lubbock and a second in San Angelo. As the group neared San Antonio, Danny Rodriguez said the Lord told him that their clothes had been cursed by the devil. "The word that we had received said that everything we needed would be provided for us as soon as we reached Louisiana," he said. Police found a third car in Galveston, along with the family's clothes, pocketbooks, wallets, and other belongings. After the fourth car stopped working, the children climbed into the trunk of the last remaining vehicle, a 1990 Grand Am. Adults propped open the trunk with a hanger to let in air.

When the family rolled into Vinton and saw the KOA Kampground, they drove in, believing the Lord had provided a recreational vehicle filled with all the money, food, and clothes they needed to get to Florida. "We pulled up next to an RV, thinking it was unoccupied and waiting for us, but people were in it," Danny Rodriguez said.

In an effort to "claim" the RV, the family sent a towel-clad fourteen-year-old male into the vehicle to instruct its occupant to leave, since God had given the RV to his family. When eight adult members of the Rodriguez family started rocking the RV, its frightened owner, who had been taking a shower, laid on the horn. A neighbor saw the disturbance and called the owner of the campground, who phoned police. By that time the Rodriguez clan had piled back in their car and sped away. A Calcasieu Parish deputy stopped their car moments later, and a man wearing only a towel got out.

"When the officer went to ask what was going on, he jumped back in and took off," said Vinton Police Chief Dennis Drouillard. The Grand Am sped down Vinton's main street until it hit a tree at the end of town. Five children and fifteen adults—one as old as sixty-three—piled out of the totaled vehicle. None suffered more than minor injuries.

"And they were completely nude," Drouillard said. "All twenty of them. Didn't have a stitch of clothes on. I mean, no socks, no underwear, no nothin'."

Sammy Rodriguez was booked for reckless driving, flight from an officer, property damage, and several minor traffic violations. He pleaded guilty and was allowed to leave town.[3]

Headline: Football Star's Pastor Sentenced in Drug Case
Forty-five-year-old Jerry Upton, a close friend of NFL superstar Reggie White, was sentenced in March 2000 to ten years in federal prison on

cocaine trafficking and gun charges. Upton was a minister and key church leader at White's inner-city church in Tennessee. In his autobiography White described Upton as his pastor and best friend.

Upton ran a multimillion-dollar cocaine ring out of one arm of the church, using a white Mercedes owned by the church to make trips to Florida to complete drug deals.

The church burned in a mysterious arson fire in 1996. Donations and insurance money totaling more than $900,000 poured in from across the country after the blaze was publicized, but no one knows where the money went. Upton claims the funds were spent legitimately but is unable to prove his claim. One federal prosecutor described Upton at his sentencing as a "dangerous, devious manipulator" who hid behind God.

The church no longer exists.[4]

Headline: Priest Embezzles $1.35 Million from Collection Plate, Then Dies

The Reverend Walter J. Benz, seventy-two years old, died two hours after somebody crept into his room at a Catholic nursing home near Pittsburgh and plucked the oxygen tube catheter from his nose and the IV needle from his arm.

Benz had slipped into a coma just weeks after admitting to police and church officials that he had been living lavishly with a lady friend and amassing six-figure gambling losses in Atlantic City. He also had collected a house in the suburbs, a condo in Florida, a cache of precious coins, a Cadillac, a collection of twenty-seven handguns, stylish Japanese furniture, and a statue of Buddha.

Benz confessed that he began dipping into the offering plate in the early 1970s, estimating that he took a thousand dollars a week for twenty-six years at two churches, for a rough total of $1.35 million. Even the votive light fund at Saint Mary Assumption Church, the parish just north of Pittsburgh where Benz had served since 1992, was being tapped for up to five hundred dollars a month.

Police discovered that for three years prior to his death, Benz had been living with Mary Anne Albaugh, age fifty-one, a parishioner from a former church. When Benz was transferred to Saint Mary, Albaugh joined him on the payroll as driver, cook, and eventually church secretary. The couple often took trips to glitzy gambling places such as the Showboat, the Tropicana, and the Taj Mahal.

Almost as soon as he admitted his embezzlement, Benz was diagnosed with a fatal brain fever that causes rapidly escalating dementia and had to be admitted to a nursing home. The day police arrived at the home to arraign Benz on theft, forgery, and conspiracy felony charges, the priest slipped into a coma. A few days later some unknown person disconnected him from life support and he died.

Parishioners said the priest was personally distant, chronically unavailable outside of Mass, and constantly complaining about church finances. He was always putting the pinch on parishioners. "Every time people met him, he said, 'You have to give more,'" said Barbara Hartmann. "Now we know why. Your faith really takes a knock when something like this happens."[5]

Headline: Faith Healer Threatens Children into Having Sex

Forty-nine-year-old Carlos Catalan, a faith healer with no known religious affiliation, in May 2000 was jailed on fifteen counts of rape, two counts of sodomy, and multiple other charges.

Police said Catalan would tell young women that having sex with him would lead to healing for family members. He allegedly told a sixteen-year-old woman that unless she sacrificed her virginity to a saint channeled through him, her father would die.[6]

Headline: Loyola Marymount Grad Helps Direct Worst Cult-Related Mass Murder in History

By late April 2000, Ugandan police had uncovered 979 mutilated bodies belonging to members of the Movement for the Restoration of the Ten Commandments of God, thus surpassing the 1978 Jonestown tragedy in which 913 individuals died. The Uganda deaths now rank as the worst modern-day cult-related mass killing in history.

Dominic Kataribabo, aged sixty-three, an excommunicated priest who studied theology at Loyola Marymount University in Los Angeles from 1985 to 1987, is one of six Ugandans wanted in connection with the murders. Kataribabo came to California in the fall of 1985 to enroll in a graduate program at Loyola Marymount as a student priest. He received one of the school's presidential scholarships for Third World priests, and while living at Saint Anthony parish in El Segundo, he was granted sacramental ministry to celebrate Mass and weddings. After earning a master's degree in August 1987, he returned to Uganda. Officials believe the cult began in 1991.

Kataribabo is thought to have been third in command of the cult, which preached that the world would end on December 31, 1999. The cult drew largely on disaffected Roman Catholics, encouraging members to give up their land and worldly possessions to take up a strict doctrine of fasting, silence, and prayer. When the December date passed uneventfully, some members began asking for their goods back.

A gasoline-fueled fire on March 17, 2000, inside the cult's sealed chapel in the town of Kanungu burned to death more than 500 members of the group—perhaps including Kataribabo. At Kataribabo's home, police found 155 additional bodies. Of those, 81 had been buried beneath the floor, some strangled with knotted cloth, and others poisoned. An additional 74 corpses were found in his garden and another 55, mostly women and children, under a garage he had rented.

Police said they did not have enough investigative resources to exhume any more bodies and appealed to the international community for help. Meanwhile they continued to check for more gravesites, guarding them until a plan could be prepared on a way to proceed.[7]

The examples cited here are the extremes. Most people do not practice faith in these ways; that is why these tragic stories made headlines. It is the very nature of reporting to find the exceptions and the extremes. Naive critics of faith in God accept these bizarre exceptions as the norm, using them to push people away from God.

Yet these extremes do provide a perspective on more subtle forms of toxic faith. In each experience, whether extreme or closer to the norm, faith becomes toxic when individuals use God or religion for profit, power, pleasure, and/or prestige. These four preoccupations are the foundation of any addiction—and they must be excised from faith. Each time they are allowed to distort or minimize true faith, people are hurt, some are killed, and many are left to suffer alone.

Such headlines shock us with the reality that even the people next door can become involved in strange, addictive practices of faith. And they prompt a question: Shouldn't rational people be able to spot and steer clear of such shocking activities? It seems impossible for any sane believer to be led away from a powerful God into a faulty ideology of life. But this never happens overnight. The believer gradually drifts into an unreal world of false belief until the victim is completely blinded to the true God and true faith.

And don't kid yourself! Within us all are poisonous beliefs that need to be neutralized. Our faith cannot help being soiled in a drug-filled, self-obsessed world such as ours. We may never turn our backs on God, join a cult, or handle a snake, but we are all victims of poisonous ideas that distort the image of God and negate our faith. Though we tell ourselves we would certainly be able to escape the most toxic levels of faith, we would do well to remember that the headlines often describe people "just like us" who thought they were in touch with reality—but who ended up with a compulsive addiction to a false and hurtful religion.

CHAPTER 2

What Are Toxic Faith and Religious Addiction?

Toxic faith is a destructive and dangerous involvement in a religion that allows the religion, not a relationship with God, to control a person's life. People broken by various experiences, people from dysfunctional families, people with unrealistic expectations, and people out for their own gain or comfort seem especially prone to it. It is a defective faith with an incomplete or tainted view of God. It is abusive and manipulative and can become addictive. It becomes so central to a person's life that family and friends become insignificant compared with the need to uphold the false beliefs.

Those with toxic faith use it to avoid reality and responsibility. It often results in perfectionism; people are driven to perform and work in an attempt to earn their way to heaven or at least to gain favor with God. Like other addictions, it causes great damage, but the addicted continue to pursue it.

Toxic faith has nothing to do with God and everything to do with men and women who want to concoct a god or faith that serves self rather than honors God. In short, toxic faith is an excuse. It is an excuse for an abusive husband to mistreat his wife because he believes God would want her to submit to him as if he were God. It is an excuse to put off dealing with the pain in life. It is an excuse to wait for God to do what he wants you to do. It provides a distraction through compulsive "church-aholism" or religious ritual.

Toxic faith is also a counterfeit for the spiritual growth that can occur through a genuine relationship with God. The toxic faithful find a replacement for God. How they look becomes more important than who God is. Acts of religion replace steps of growth. A facade is substituted for a heart longing to know God. The facade forms a barrier between the believer and God, leaving the believer to survive with only a destructive addiction to religion.

CHARACTERISTICS OF RELIGIOUS ADDICTS

Plenty of people are susceptible to religious addiction. Their brokenness, misery, and conflict leave them open to becoming hooked on working hard to win God's favor or believing any doctrine that promises to make life easier. They develop toxic-faith practices that become every bit as addictive as heroin. Out of a desire to delay or deny pain, they develop their own toxic beliefs. There are many variations of religious addicts.

Common Characteristics of Religious Addicts

- Rigid parents
- Experience of disappointment
- Low self-worth
- Victims of abuse

Rigid Parents
As strange as it may seem, the child who grew up with a rigid parent (or parents) enters adulthood attracted to those who serve up any form of rigidity. One might think that, once freed from the rigidity, the adult child would avoid it. Instead the individual is often drawn to it, which makes the person highly susceptible to an addictive religious system or to follow a toxic-faith leader. Why is this so? One explanation is that human beings are creatures of habit; we are comfortable with what we know. Or perhaps people are drawn toward a rigid system because they have a

hidden desire to fix it, to loosen themselves up and free themselves to enjoy life—something they were unable to achieve with their parents.

One boy grew up in a very rigid family in which it was difficult for him to express who he was or what he wanted. His father communicated with directives, offering no reasons for his demands, just expecting compliance. The boy rebelled forcefully. He became a heavy drug user and at age eighteen quit school and moved in with several other drug addicts. Eventually his addiction put him out of work, and he found himself at the bottom with no hope.

When a cult follower befriended him, he responded. He felt love and support and a genuine offer for help. Inside the cult he was confronted with a controlling leader who dictated every decision of the group. He had found home. He had come full circle, back to a variation of his original situation. He became a faithful follower, unwilling to question the validity of the group, its rules, or the demands it placed on him.

Experience of Disappointment

A deep wound from a major disappointment lies in the background of most religious addicts. It might have been the early loss of a parent or a parental divorce. It could have been their own divorce or abandonment in later life. The loss and the disappointment cause a tremendous fear of yet another abandonment. Addicts become attracted to and attached to any group that promises acceptance without risk. Often the group promises instant relief or gratification. Feeling the pain from their disappointment, religious addicts want relief, especially if it does not require effort on their part.

I worked with a vulnerable woman who was devastated by the loss of her parents and her own nasty divorce. Somehow she felt she could have done something different to prevent the tragedies. Seeking relief, she began a dating spree that included frequent sexual intercourse. In addition to her grief over the loss of her parents and her divorce, she began to believe God was going to punish her for having sex outside of marriage. She was filled with guilt. She knew God didn't want her to have sex with everyone she dated, but she succumbed frequently. She was convinced that God was going to punish her by giving her the AIDS virus.

She became obsessed with God's wrath and the idea of his swooping down on her to wipe her out. Each month she would have another AIDS test—but she didn't change her behavior or use precautions in her sexual relationships. She went on trying to say no, giving in, and then waiting for God to deliver the death sentence. Her disappointments with death and divorce led her to abandon God for quick sexual relief from her pain. Her chosen source of "relief," however, only increased her pain.

Low Self-Worth

We all know that peer pressure helps to destroy many young people. But we seem to forget it is just as powerful among adults. If people do not value themselves or have their own beliefs, they will fall victim to the pressures to conform. They cross over a line from rational to irrational belief. Distrusting their ability to discern truth from manipulation, they go along with the group consensus, even if it invalidates everything they have been taught.

Persons with low self-worth feel alienated and isolated. They want to belong and be accepted. Toxic-faith leaders know this. They can pick out wounded followers who are looking for someone to make them feel important. Under the guise of ministry they cater to people's weaknesses until those people believe they are receiving genuine caring. Thus, the religious group gets new members, potentially forever.

This "care con game" is similar to one of the oldest money tricks among scam artists. First they ask you to trust them with a little money. When you do so, you get a large return. Maybe they tell you to give them one dollar, and in a few days or weeks they give you ten dollars back. Now convinced of a real return on your money, you increase your investment to one hundred dollars...and the thieves are never heard from again.

Toxic-faith practitioners seek out those with low self-worth and minimal boundaries. They ask them to trust just a little. With that first step of trust, the targets are flooded with affirmation and love. Every need is met. Childhood trauma is soon forgotten in the euphoria prompted by so much affection. The ones being manipulated then place greater trust in the leader, sometimes selling all of their possessions to belong to the group. At this stage they often reinforce their radical decision by making justifications for their behavior.

Even when they notice exploitation, the new followers don't turn away, because they continue to reinforce their decisions. They feel bad about themselves already, and admitting they had been duped would seem devastating. Their minds block out the reality of the toxic beliefs, and they become faithful followers under an exploitative leader.

If they had felt self-worthy in the beginning, they would have discerned the unhealthiness of the group and refused to be part of it. But their addiction moves them to believe the unbelievable if it will provide at least a moment of relief. They don't see the exploitation—or at least, they refuse to acknowledge it—because their low self-worth has allowed them to be exploited all their lives. It seems almost normal.

Victims of Abuse

Childhood abuse, whether sexual, physical, or emotional, often leads to further victimization in adulthood. The abused feel detached and unloved. They function with a continual feeling of loss. Often they go to great extremes to fill the void left by abusive parents. Their faith is almost always poisoned by these early incidents. Some forsake God, blaming him for the abuse. Others believe in God but consider him to be detached and uncaring about individuals in pain. Still others replace God with a human being.

Attention from an adult friend, especially a father replacement, can set off a craving for more attention and a vulnerability to be victimized again. Seeking a savior, the adult child of abuse repeats being the victim. When the "savior" turns out to be yet another victimizer, the act is so horrifying and degrading that there is often a complete break with reality. The victim blindly complies with the victimizer as the poisonous faith continues to grow.

Susceptible people have something in common with those who are not susceptible: They all hurt. All of us are hurting people; we all struggle with pain and disappointment. Religious addicts, however, believe they are the only ones who hurt. They think no one else cares or has to endure their kind of pain. When a practitioner of toxic faith arrives with what appears to be a heart of gold and a simple plan for an easy life, the followers are quick to sign up.

FORMS AND VARIATIONS OF TOXIC FAITH

No religious addict professes a cookie-cutter faith. Such toxic faith has many variations—some Christian, some atheistic, and some affiliated with other world religions. The following are the most common ways it is manifested:

Forms and Variations of Toxic Faith

- Compulsive religious activity
- Laziness
- Giving to get
- Self-obsession
- Extreme intolerance
- Addiction to a religious high

Compulsive Religious Activity

Compulsive religious addicts are driven by guilt and a desire to earn favor from God. They work hard in hopes of a day when God will look down on their efforts and change reality for them. They hope he will see their hard work and decide to relieve their pain or magically make life easier for them. They have an "earn as you go" mentality that places their future in the hands of their ability to achieve, accomplish, and sacrifice.

Years ago my wife and I visited Thailand, where we observed Buddhists practicing their faith. We saw hundreds of temples and thousands of worshipers. I was overwhelmed by their dedication to their gods, those they said were alive and those who had died. I watched as they bought gold filament and pressed it into a Buddha statue to the point of causing pain to their own bodies.

These worshipers sought relief through their religious activity. We were often confronted with requests to do something for Buddha. They wanted us to buy a bird and set it free. They asked us to give money to restore the temples. We were also invited to buy lotus blossoms. All of those things, we were told, would bring us "good luck." They constantly suggested new ways for us to please Buddha and obtain favor with him. A person just couldn't do enough in that land where faith was replaced by hard work.

Sadly, it is not much different here in the United States. Many feel compelled to serve on every church committee or represent the church on every possible community council. The family comes in second to the flurry of activity surrounding the church. Underlying this frenzy of activity is the belief that work will gain favor. But another dynamic is also at work, and like every other addiction, it involves running from pain. If these people can stay busy enough, they will not have to resolve their pain. So they work hard and run fast to stay one step ahead of the hurt. But the pain already has incapacitated them. It has driven them to work and drive and try harder to please God.

Laziness

Some people with toxic faith are lazy. Laziness is their most common form of self-defeating behavior. Their faith dumps responsibility for everything that happens on God. Rather than work to heal a marriage, for example, they want God to fix it instantly. Rather than make an appointment with a counselor, they pray for a miracle, asking God to do for them what God probably wants them to do for themselves. It is inconvenient to go to a marriage counselor; it is expensive, too. So rather than do the responsible thing, the lazy believe that if they just pray, God will take care of their marriage. Certainly marriage counseling is a painful growth process. And yet God may want these lazy believers to go through it.

Two girls were on their way to school—behind schedule once again. The moment for the bell to ring grew closer and closer. This pair had been late several times, and they knew there would be grave consequences if they repeated the offense. One girl suggested they crawl down in the nearest ditch to pray to God that they would not be late. The other little girl made the more realistic suggestion: They should pray *and run.*

Thousands of religious addicts have crawled down into the ditches of unreality. They have retreated into a lazy world where they want everything worked out for them in a magical, mysterious way. They want a servant god; they don't want to serve God. They want a god drug that will wipe out consequences and quickly ease all hurts.

That view of God is toxic and addictive. It is irresponsible and leaves believers stagnant, full of false hope and unrealistic expectations. I think God might be watching, hoping such believers will crawl out of the ditches and continue to grow through facing their difficulties one at a time.

Giving to Get

I believe my grandmother gave her money because she thought it was a way to give back to God some of what he had given to her. Others do not possess similar motives. They give out of a belief that the more they give, the more they will get. Their giving is more like a materialistic investment than a spiritual act of worship. Such believers hope their affluence will increase as they give more to a ministry.

Of course, God does promise to bless his people for faithful stewardship—but that blessing is not necessarily in the form of cold, hard cash. I don't know of many people who give 35 to 40 percent of their money, like my grandmother did. So, if anyone would be rewarded materially, she would be a likely candidate. But though she never had to struggle, she grew no wealthier after ten years of sacrificial giving. The hope of wealth was never her motive, and material wealth was not her reward.

I have heard some fund-raisers ask people to "claim" their material blessings. Supporters are told to claim the Rolls Royce they want, to trust God to provide it, to give money to secure it, and it will come. Some charlatans arrange for the unsuspecting to receive the automobile they "claimed." These hucksters go out and buy a car, deliver it, and then write up the "miracle" in a newsletter to inform all the other faithful (whose automobiles have not yet arrived). They are told that if they have more faith and give more money, they will receive the material possessions they want. With this "proof" before them, the duped shell out more money, hoping God will give them what they believe they deserve.

God cannot be bribed or bought, but the actions of many individuals appear to be attempts to do just that. Their money might be better spent in Las Vegas where luck, not God, is the rewarder of money. This form of religious addict has more in common with a compulsive gambler than with a faithful follower of God.

Self-Obsession

Self-obsession leads to the practice of toxic faith, religious addiction, and all other addictions. Poisoned by their constant focus on their own needs, hurts, and desire for relief, the self-obsessed have little room left for worshiping God or meeting the needs of others. It is no wonder that people living in such a selfish state have sky-high expectations of God.

Yet Christ is quoted as telling Peter to show his love by feeding his sheep (i.e., meeting the needs of others). The self-obsessed are not interested in feeding anyone else's sheep or helping others in any way. They concentrate on how others can meet their needs, especially how God can relieve them of their burdens.

Of course, God *does* relieve burdens. He *does* bless. He meets needs in miraculous ways. He brings babies to infertile couples. At times he will heal or reverse a terminal disease. Evidences of divine intervention abound; we call them miracles. But the reason they are called miracles is that they rarely happen. To have faith in God because he is bound to perform miracles is to have faith in miracles more than in God. True faith in God is not focused only on what God can miraculously do or provide; it is focused on what the individual can do for God. Additionally, the individual must make an effort to care for those God loves, his sheep, one's neighbors.

In a discussion with a psychiatrist friend on how faith can become self-serving, he described another friend's habits, the qualities of a person after God's heart. He said the man's motivation for everything he did was to please God and serve him. He worked with people not to make money but to serve God. He was dedicated to the needs of others and derived joy from meeting those needs. This selfless man had a faith that went beyond his own needs and self-obsession.

It is a rare faith. More often today people proclaim faith in God as long as that faith will increase the bottom line and make life better. There is no greater sin than self-obsession, and no greater poison of faith.

Extreme Intolerance

Religious addicts are extremely intolerant of varying opinions or expressions of faith. Either walk their way or be out of step. Rather than accept other believers, their rigidity rejects them. They routinely judge others and find the negative in everyone else's life. From a position of superiority, they put down others for what they believe and how they manifest their faith. They want to control the lives of others, especially what they believe.

One gentleman, a member of a conservative group, was fearful that his sons would veer into a more liberal faith or that they would end up with no faith at all. He believed that one of the most beautiful pictures to God was of a family going to church together. He took his family to church twice every Sunday and also on Wednesday nights. If the church doors were open, he walked through them with his family.

His oldest son had some friends who attended another church on the edge of town. He developed good friends there and liked it much better than his father's church. He asked to leave his parents' church to attend the one on the edge of town. Now, it was not a strange religion or cult; both churches were part of the same denomination. But the father couldn't handle it. He told his son he had to stop going to the other church. He wanted the entire family to attend church together, and nothing would stand in the way of achieving that goal. He was intolerant of his son's expressions of faith and of the other church and its members.

His demands caused a deep split between him and his son. It was not their first problem, but it was the biggest. Tremendous bitterness and resentment grew from it and destroyed their ability to relate to each other.

This kind of intolerance is common among those with toxic faith. They will sacrifice relationships with family and friends to uphold a standard or ideal of their own faith. As long as they believe they are doing what God would have them do, they won't hesitate to push their ideas on others and judge them as less faithful and less in touch with the way things should be done. Certain they are upholding God's standards, they control others by demeaning their beliefs and practice of faith. They create a fake faith and a legalistic caricature of what faith is. Their children, resisting this intolerance, flee from their parents' faith and often never again seek a relationship with God.

Addiction to a Religious High

The practice of faith can provide tremendous relief from the pain and frustrations of life. When a person trusts in God, he or she no longer feels overwhelmed with problems or burdened from believing all problems must be resolved alone. This is a natural result of placing faith in a God who promises that his burden is light. But there is another kind of relief, an emotional frenzy that becomes an addiction and robs the individual of real faith.

I was on a Christian talk show and afterward had the pleasure of going to lunch with the staff. They related stories of the variations of faith and the strange incidents that develop when faith becomes unbalanced.

One story particularly intrigued me. The program had sponsored a tour to Israel, and about five hundred people signed up to visit the Holy Land. A woman traveling with the group had felt led to become a nun. Unable to find an order to accept her, she established her own order of one and wore the attire of a traditional nun. Each time she visited a site, she worked herself into a frenzy, chanted loudly, then passed out, claiming to be slain in the Spirit. Although most people on the tour were charismatic Christians, they were not impressed with her performance.

Each time they approached a monument, they stood back and waited for the show to begin.

The development of her own order of one was the woman's first major leap from reality. Her repeated frenzies were further steps of escape. She was addicted to the self-manufactured highs supposed to be religious experiences.

Many other gradations of such extreme religious intoxication exist. Often the toxic faithful become so enthralled with the religious experience that they reduce God to secondary importance.

Anyone who has ever been to a church camp knows what it is like to have a religious high, commonly called a mountaintop experience. When the kids leave camp, they are warned that the wonderful emotions they feel will go away. An eventual "downer" experience will come when the emotions of the mountaintop wear away. The kids must learn to adjust to reality where everyone is not as supportive and loving as the kids and staff at camp.

Yet some people cannot or will not handle the downs after a marvelous spiritual experience. Rather than deal with reality, they manufacture a pseudoreligious experience or a spiritual frenzy. The adrenaline rush energizes and stimulates them, alters their mood, and provides relief from real pain. The hysteria is repeated anytime they need to escape or feel differently. These "instant religious experience" practitioners might as well take a drink, swallow a pill, or inject a drug. The intent is not to worship God but to alter their perception of reality. They are religious junkies, obsessed with mood alteration and a quick fix to face life.

These variations of toxic faith and religious addiction never bring people closer to God. In fact, they form barriers between individuals and God, which allow the deceived to stay busy and active in every way except for a true worship experience. With barriers to God and others in place, the toxic faithful are left with many more painful feelings to compound the original pain at the core of their toxic faith.

Every addiction ultimately destroys intimacy with family, friends, and God. The addicted loathe placing themselves in a vulnerable position of trust with another. Toxic faith is no different. Those with toxic faith cannot or will not trust God. Faith has been eroded, and as individuals place distance between themselves and God, the chasm formed is filled with compulsion, activity, addiction, manipulation, control, and extreme effort. The work is never done and the heart is never at rest. Faith has become toxic.

A Paradox of Toxic Faith

One paradox of toxic faith sets it apart from any other compulsion or addiction: the issue of moderation.

In alcohol consumption, the goal is abstinence or moderation. When a person moves beyond moderation, evidence of addiction mounts as the level of consumption increases. Eating works the same way. Compulsive overeaters must learn to eat less and find fulfillment in less consumption.

Faith is not this way. True faith, real and pure faith, cannot be practiced in moderation. One cannot trust God too much or seek God too much. Persons whose faith has grown to encompass every aspect of life are spiritual giants to be modeled. On the other hand, a little faith—a faith that knows only a bit about God—is a form of toxic faith. It pays a small tribute to God instead of developing a strong relationship with God. As poisonous as these varieties of toxic faith are, they are minimal compared to the most toxic faith: no faith at all.

Once faith is poisoned, it is a complex process to detoxify the individual and restore a pure faith. Identifying the toxic elements is the beginning of hope. To see toxic beliefs and practices for what they are can allow men and women to plunge deeply into true faith and to know and serve God, rather than to walk on the deadly fringes.

Herein lies the most formidable challenge: to look within oneself and find the toxic elements of faith and remove them. Some people are so self-obsessed, so sold on faith in themselves, that it is difficult for them to break through denial and see what is sick at their core and how that sickness has damaged their relationships, including the one with God.

Yet it is not impossible to break through the denial and clean up faith. Individuals willing to take a second look at God and faith and why they have messed up the relationship so badly are in for a painful experience. But be assured, this pain is less than that experienced in continuing to use God rather than relate to God! It is less painful than realizing one is afraid and continuing to live with that knowledge. By making the effort to detoxify faith, one will go through some difficult times before finding what God designed for a relationship with himself. But in the end, a relationship based on pure faith leads to complete contentment and joy.

CHAPTER 3

Twenty-One Beliefs of a Toxic Faith

Faith is slowly poisoned as lies and false ideas are integrated into a person's beliefs about God. For some, this occurs after a major disappointment in adult life. The faith of others is distorted from early years, by watching parents practice a faith with little truth and hope.

Toxic beliefs are tough to counter. At first glance they make such good sense. And plenty of people support the distorted beliefs that have been around for thousands of years.

Once persons are deceived, they vigorously resist changing their beliefs. Since they are so self-obsessed, they want to believe that they are right and are incapable of serious error. Additionally, these people invest much time, money, and energy in toxic beliefs, which they hold more sacred than God. Whether handed down, learned later in life, supported by others, or reinforced by denial, toxic beliefs take root and spoil the relationship with God. These beliefs must be countered and replaced with truth.

Melody illustrates the challenge. Years of pain stemmed from a set of toxic beliefs that took root when Melody was a child. At one point in her growing-up years, her minister father became obsessed by her beauty and form. He fought the temptation to touch her for two years. Finally, on an overnight outing, he went to her sleeping bag and, while she slept, he molested her. He unbuttoned her shirt to see her breasts. When she awoke, he was sitting beside her, staring at her.

She was horrified but didn't scream. He took that as an invitation to come closer, and he lay down beside her and fondled her. She cried silently the whole time. When he was finished, he buttoned her shirt and returned to his sleeping bag.

Melody didn't sleep the rest of the night. As she lay awake, the nucleus of a lifetime of toxic beliefs began to form. She wondered why God had allowed this to happen. She thought that she must be bad or this bad thing wouldn't have happened. She felt this must be some kind of punishment for something she had done. Her faith shattered. *Since my father is a fake,* she thought, *all believers must be fakes also.*

Melody kept the secret. And although her father never touched her again, his relationship with her changed dramatically after this incident. No more sexual abuse occurred, but the emotional abuse was just as destructive. He became negative with her and very critical. It was as if he blamed her for what had happened. She never again felt an ounce of love from her father.

Over the course of the next year, Melody became a drug and alcohol abuser and a compulsive eater. Hoping to resolve the pain, she decided to tell her mother what had happened. Melody's mother could not believe it and accused Melody of lying. The revelation destroyed her relationship with her mother. She felt isolated and abandoned by her father, her mother, and her God. In a deep depression, she slit her wrists and hoped to die. However, her mother found her in time and saved her life.

The suicide attempt forced Melody's mother to find treatment for her, and she found it with us at New Life Treatment Centers. Through the program and staff, the molestation was verified, and the father was arrested after the authorities were notified. No legal consequences emerged from the incident, but he lost his church and his family.

Melody grew bitter and angry. She felt guilty about the molestation, guilty that she had not told her mother sooner, and guilty that her father had lost his job. She took all of the burdens of the molestation on herself. Yet she also blamed God for deserting her when she most needed him. She had no place for a God who could not be counted on or who must be punishing her for some long-forgotten sin.

Treatment did not restore Melody's faith immediately, but it did restore her to spiritual and emotional health. Through hard hours of therapy, Bible study, and prayer, she worked through her self-deprecating feelings and emerged with a new sense of self-worth. She found tremendous support from the staff and other patients to see herself in a new way. As each day passed, she grew more and more in her quest for peace.

Before leaving treatment, Melody began to work on an aftercare plan. One question concerned church attendance. She stated that she had no plans to attend church, that she needed more time to heal before facing another male minister in a church setting. Her plan seemed very realistic; she did need more time. She might have been devastated by returning to a church too soon; the experience might stir up much of what she could not yet manage emotionally. The counselor expressed approval of Melody's plan. She asked Melody to describe her feelings about God. Melody slowly responded, "I believe he is there. I believe he is real. But I believe he is tougher than I could have ever imagined."

Melody had come a long way in her short stay with us. It is a long journey from belief in an uncaring God to belief in a God who is interested in each life. By saying God is real and he is there, Melody was on the verge of realizing that he cares about *her* and loves *her*.

Destroying the roots of toxic faith takes time and effort. It requires vulnerability and the admission that life and God can be viewed incorrectly. The first step toward spiritual health is to identify the incorrect beliefs. Once identified, they can be changed and a real faith in God restored.

Melody's molestation was at the core of the toxic beliefs she developed. Her faith soured as she struggled alone to figure out who she was and who God was in light of the molestation. Through treatment, she identified some of those toxic beliefs: she felt that she must have been bad and that God was punishing her; she believed if she had been better, it would not have happened; she believed her behavior determined how much God would love her; she thought God should have protected her from a terrible incident; and she found her father was a fake, so she came to believe all Christians were fake. Melody came to see how one incident affected her whole concept of God, life, and her future.

Such toxic beliefs are not unique to Melody. Millions share them. The following are the most common beliefs of a toxic faith.

CONDITIONAL LOVE

Toxic Belief #1: *God's love and favor depend on my behavior.*

The central theme of the Bible is that God is love. But individuals plagued with toxic faith neglect that fact. They see God as a critical parent, waiting to say, "It's not good enough. Try harder. You could do better." Their faith is so toxic that they turn to a faith in self rather than a faith in God. They depend on their performance, not God's wondrous love.

A young man came to me who had heard of my problems in the past. He felt extreme guilt over paying for a girlfriend's abortion. Before that event, he believed he had a great future and that God wanted to use him. After the abortion, however, he doubted God had a place for him. He felt like a complete reject. He began to focus on his behavior rather than on God's love. He worked and worked to resume a place of favor. But no matter how hard he tried, it was never good enough. He kept coming up short. He asked me, "Will I ever know God's love and acceptance again?"

Whether this young man would ever again experience God's love totally depended on his willingness to put himself aside and focus on a loving God. If he refused, he had no chance of knowing and feeling God's love. In his desire to redeem himself he had become a religious workaholic, addicted to the job of making himself feel good about himself. A deep hurt and lack of self-worth drove him relentlessly. The sad truth is that his unending work might not make God love him more— but he might get to see God sooner. His self-induced pressure might easily have caused a heart attack or a stroke. It certainly made him feel miserable, without hope for restoration.

Restoration cannot come from more work or greater focus on fixing your mistakes. All you'll get for your efforts is a miserable life of perfectionism where nothing is ever good enough. Such an attempt at restoration only further destroys faith and relationships.

The difficulty with turning away from such a toxic belief is that most of the world acts as if it is true. Most people operate under the belief that God is looking for a "few good men and women."

Some of my friends teach their children that if they are good, God will be good in return. That is probably the most common theology in existence. People are desperately trying to earn God's love—yet how ludicrous is the way they go about trying to earn his love! They make $100,000 a year and give $5,000 away, expecting God to be impressed. Or if they give an even more substantial amount, they place their names on a plaque for public display. Too few know that is not the way of God.

Restoration comes from worshiping God for who he is and trusting him to provide for one's needs. If, like my friend who was burdened with guilt, you need forgiveness, God has gone to a lot of trouble to provide that for you. You cannot earn God's love. His love does not depend on your behavior. Knowing that should be a very big relief.

INSTANT PEACE

Toxic Belief #2: *When tragedy strikes, true believers should have a real peace about it.*

The desire for instant peace in the midst of tragedy leads to denial, unresolved emotions, and a complete split from reality. People who have lost children, spouses, fortunes, and dreams have told me that they have this "wonderful peace about it" just moments later. What they have is shock! Shock is the natural reaction to protect ourselves, to deny the reality and depth of our pain. The stages of grief begin with denial, and this conjured peace is a form of that denial. The person who professes to have instant peace will have a troubled future, full of pain greater than the original loss and disappointment.

Even worse, this toxic faith is inflicted on others who try to deal realistically with the heart's condition. Individuals who express their anger and disappointment are often challenged to be stronger, trust more, and find peace.

The true believer will find peace, but it will be on the other side of resolving the rage that comes with almost every lost expectation. I have heard "spiritual giants" tell people in pain to have more joy. But they cannot even *spell* joy while trying to grasp the pain of divorce or the void of a lost child. People need time to resolve emotions. Instant peace only delays and prolongs the time it takes to adjust and move on to a new life.

Scripture tells us to be thankful in everything. True faith will lead a person to gratitude even in adversity, but it is not instant. Alcoholics who go through years of misery finally reach a point of gratitude if their recovery is real. They relate that if alcoholism had not developed, they would not have recovered, and they would have possibly missed the most meaningful dimensions of life. This gratitude comes after alcoholics completely accept all aspects of their condition and how it will alter their future. Acceptance precedes gratitude. Scripture does not demand that we be grateful immediately. It takes time, lots of time. Those who experience "instant peace" are not showing instant gratitude to God; they are denying how God made them as physical, spiritual, and emotional beings.

Having said all that, I must add that there are some supernatural exceptions. There are times that God intervenes in a miraculous way to provide peace to persons in the midst of extreme pain and adverse circumstances. For example, one mother had done everything to help her child and had to leave the rest to God. Her son's kidneys had failed, and physicians told her that he would die. She described an experience that was not denial, but an instant awareness that her son would not die. God had decided to intervene at that moment. She said she felt a calm overwhelm her. She remained silent, in awe of the experience. She knew he would be healed. She prayed that God's will would be done. Even though she believed he would be healed, she told God that she would accept the outcome whatever it might be. That night her son was miraculously healed. Her peace came from a supernatural intervention by God.

After I wrote the previous paragraph, I went to a dinner for authors—usually a boring time of hearing all about potential bestsellers. That night, however, was different. I met Becky Smith Greer, an author from South Carolina who had just completed her first book. It is the story of the sudden loss of both her husband and her twelve-year-old son in a plane crash. With this toxic-faith concept on my mind, I asked if she had an immediate peace about those deaths. She responded with both insight and conviction. She said there was no peace. Instead, she struggled with tremendous anger that took three years to resolve. But eventually the resolution did come, and her faith in God was restored. She simply needed more time than an instant to heal her relationship with God.

Tragedies bring various responses. God does not seem to deal with them, or the people affected by them, in a predictable manner. For some, a divine gift of peace prevents a total collapse. For others, such peace does not surface for months or even years. Whatever the reaction, those who experience peace early are no better or worse, no stronger or weaker. The experience of one should not be assumed for the unique circumstances of another. Lack of peace does not mean lack of faith. People in pain do not need sermons on peace. They need love and care and assistance through the healing process. Remember, faith in God will produce a peace that goes beyond all understanding. It probably won't be an instant peace, but it will be a *real* peace.

Guaranteed Healing

Toxic Belief #3: *If I have real faith, God will heal me or someone I am praying for.*

My brother died from AIDS. (He and I wrote the story of his struggles in *How Will I Tell My Mother?*) He died because God chose not to intervene in the natural course of events to cure the disease. Before he died, however, we had tremendous hope that this type of intervention would happen. Many churches, my parents, my brother, and I prayed for him to be healed. We were not asking for a spectacular event; utilization of modern medicine would have been fine with us. But it didn't happen. Jerry died, but not because of a lack of faith; there was plenty of that.

Jerry spent his last days on his knees, praying and reading Scripture. He would meditate on a memorized scripture and pray fervently. His faith had become rich and deep, and he had grown close to the God he was prepared to meet face to face.

My father has always had a strong faith. It grew stronger through Jerry's ordeal. Dad wanted Jerry to have hope, and he wanted hope for himself. On numerous occasions he asked me to believe with him that Jerry would be healed and survive.

Jerry didn't wait at home for the healing to come. He went looking for it. He attended many healing services in several states. Each time he went he had a strong faith that on that night God would intervene in his life and change the probable outcome. But nothing changed. Each time Jerry left a healing service, he felt worse about himself and his faith. He started to believe that if only he had more faith, he could direct the hand of God. His guilt continued to grow each day because he couldn't move God's hand through faith.

Thousands of mothers of babies with disabilities or serious illnesses pray with saintly faith for those babies to be supernaturally remade and infused with health. Each day that drags by with no change can bring on great guilt and even anger. Faith can become poisoned from the belief that "if only I were better, if only I were stronger, if only I had more faith, my baby would be healed." I empathize with those mothers. Some of them feel like second-class citizens in God's kingdom, and they often believe they are being punished for being bad and the baby is paying the price.

God doesn't work that way. That he chooses to allow a child to remain sick is his sovereign will. Faith will help us adapt to his will, understand it better, and grow from and through it. But God is God. He heals whom he chooses. We may not like that one bit. We want to be God or like God, able to change events to meet our pleasure. When we find this to be impossible, our guilt and anger come between us and God.

Just because God didn't heal my faithful brother doesn't mean that he won't heal other faithful believers. It also doesn't mean he refuses to heal unbelievers. It is quite the opposite. While preparing to write this book, I was discussing with a dear friend about how God chooses to heal some and not others. He relayed a story about his secretary that illustrates God's supernatural intervention.

His secretary had not been a believer, but she had always paid close attention whenever someone mentioned God and faith. One day as she flipped through the TV channels she stopped to see Pat Robertson on *The 700 Club*. He was praying for people to be healed of various ailments. This nonbelieving skeptic was startled to hear him say that he believed someone with a deformed bone structure in the hand would be miraculously healed. The surprise came because her hand was deformed, a bone protruding in an unsightly way. At the instant she looked at her deformed hand, a sensation overcame her, a peaceful calm she had never felt. She looked up to see something bright, like a large beam. A finger of light burst from the ceiling and ended at her hand. In an instant, the bone deformity vanished; her hand was completely and instantly healed. God's intervention profoundly changed her. She became a believer and has grown in her faith ever since.

Now, her faith was not the reason for the supernatural event. She didn't *have* any faith at that moment, yet God decided to deal with her and show his love to her. This should provide some relief for those who have tried to earn God's attention and provide hope for those who think that the reason God does not heal them or their children is that they lack faith. This secretary is not the only nonbeliever God has changed. Consider Saul (who became the apostle Paul), smitten on the road to Damascus. One's degree of faith does not bind the divine will of God. He knows the needs of every person and has a mysterious plan to meet those needs.

Second, we must remember that God does not deal with everyone in the same way. You may have the most incredible, powerful, mature faith in the world, but if God has a different plan, you will not be healed. You can't "faith it" into a divine intervention if God knows it might lead you away from him rather than toward him.

Last, one aspect of the secretary's story is more mysterious even than her healing. You see, the show she was watching was not live; it was a rebroadcast of an old show. This reminds us that a powerful God can work any way he chooses. Just because he doesn't choose to intervene in your problem in a miraculous way doesn't mean he hates you. Lack of healing does not indicate lack of faith. It simply indicates that the all-powerful God cannot be controlled or predicted. If he could be commanded at our beck and call, he would cease to be God. But he is God and does what he chooses. As frustrating as it may be, we can't control him with our prayers.

Irreproachable Clergy

Toxic Belief #4: *All ministers are men and women of God and can be trusted.*

One evening I was discussing the elements of toxic faith with a group of people. I asked if anyone had ever been negatively impacted by a minister in a way that affected his or her life. A woman in the group told how, while in high school, she won the honor of attending Girls State. (Girls State is an educational program that sends kids to the state capital for a week-long lesson in state government.) She was thrilled with the opportunity and excited to receive the honor. Then her pastor heard of her plans.

This pastor was a very controlling, manipulative individual. He told her that if she went to Girls State, it would be the beginning of many problems. He claimed that Satan would use the experience to damage her faith. He demanded that her parents not allow her to go.

As a former Boys Stater, I can tell you that nothing happens there to hurt a person's faith. It was one of the best experiences of my life. I learned more about being a responsible citizen in that week than in years of civics and political-science classes.

This pastor was terribly misinformed. His influence led to the parents' decision not to let her go. It hurt her deeply, and she never forgot it. Her chance to shine was stolen from her.

Compared to other scandals, this incident seems insignificant. But more people have been the victims of mistrust in small ways than have been hurt by major media figures. Ministers, whether in a church speaking to fifty or on television reaching out to millions, are real people with real problems. They are not superhuman, and they are not immune to all the temptations the rest of us feel. Even those ministers who remain faithful must be seen as imperfect and flawed. No matter how full of integrity, they cannot be the ultimate authority on every area of life.

Authority figures can provide tremendous relief to persons needing counsel and advice. A single person living alone may feel secure in trusting a pastor. Looking to that person for authority is okay as long as there remains a high degree of discernment about what that person demands or how he or she directs.

While living in Texas, I developed a close relationship with a pastor. Some of my problems demanded strong counsel and guidance. I met with this man for several weeks and grew to respect his judgment and counsel. As the relationship progressed, he learned that I was paid a base salary along with quarterly bonuses. I believed he was a man of integrity and was unafraid to share anything with him.

Two sessions after I told him I had been paid the bonus, he asked me for a sizable loan. Blindly believing in him and thinking his purposes were noble, I lent him the money at no interest. Eventually, I discovered he had no intention of repaying the loan. With extreme difficulty I got the money back. I felt victimized and my faith was shaken. Fortunately, I realized I had placed more faith in him than in God.

When a defective pastor crops up, those who have placed ultimate faith in him or her (rather than in God) come to believe that God is defective. They attribute all the evil of that one individual to all people of faith. While this toxic leap is irrational, it is the reason many people turn away from God. But just because a particular individual lacks pure faith doesn't mean that the object of faith also is impure.

God needs ministers who face life's problems and grow from them. He will not remove temptation from them so that more people see their perfect behavior and place their faith in them. Each time ego, greed, power, or lust turns a minister away from the faith, it should strengthen our faith in God by taking our eyes off of people. I am always saddened to hear individuals say they have turned away from God due to a disappointing experience with one person. Those pastors who molest or cheat are always the exception and show us how vulnerable we all are and how much we need to grow in faith. For every one who falters in the faith, there are thousands who remain faithful and true. We must not allow human failure to hamper the development of a godly faith and trust.

MONETARY REWARDS

Toxic Belief #5: *Material blessings are a sign of spiritual strength.*

The toxic belief that material blessings are a sign of spiritual strength is a reflection of our materialistic society that measures people by the amount of money they make. Those who have much want to believe it is a direct result of God's blessing for faithfulness. A physician stated that he believed his house and cars and booming practice were the results of God's rewarding him for his godliness. This wonderful Christian had been tainted by his own materialistic existence. Those who get puffed up over all they own should reevaluate the lives of the truly faithful who live in poverty and inconvenience so they can serve others. Wealth is not an automatic reward for faithfulness.

Before Sandy and I were married, we took a missionary trip to India. There we met the most Christlike person either of us has known. He was a physician practicing out of the Baptist Hospital in Bangalore, India. When he saw the need for emotional care of so many mentally ill people, he went back to school after his children had been raised, and he obtained a degree in psychiatry. He then started a counseling center next to a Methodist church, where he would see people for free if they had no money.

While psychiatrists around the world drove expensive sports cars or were chauffeured in stretch limousines, he drove a car that had to be pushed to start. Only the horn worked consistently. On Sundays he would go to a small church in the slums just outside of town and hold a service for faithful believers. We went with him to participate in the service.

The church met in a small lean-to shack made of scrap boards and raw lumber. As the hot sun beat down on the roof, it became a sultry oven. The open sewers outside pumped billows of odors on waves of humidity through the church walls. The faithful walked, limped, and dragged themselves to that mat-covered room to worship.

No one made more than one hundred dollars a month; most made nothing. It was poverty at its most extreme. The people listened to the sermon, sang, prayed, and had Communion. Then they did an astonishing thing. They gave their money. Having almost nothing, they gave very little, but an extraordinarily high percentage of their earnings went to God. Although they were barely able to feed their families, their donations revealed their great spiritual strength.

If God always blessed people materially for their faithfulness, that slum area would have miraculously turned into a row of mansions, or at least a subdivision of comfortable tract houses. But it did not, because faith does not work that way.

Our doctor friend did whatever he could to serve people in need. While others sit through retirement, he and his wife became a wonderful ministry team. His wisdom and insight exceed that of anyone I know. Yet he lived in a small house that lacked hot running water. Material blessings have not come his way—but I have a hard time thinking of what he could do to have more faith. Many have more money, but few are closer to God.

If you believe that the more faithful you are, the more wealth you will gain, you can look forward to great disappointment. In my experience, greater faith has often brought an end to financial wealth. For some reason, God often tempers a faithful follower in the fires of loss and financial poverty. These tested saints seem to prove that when all you have left is God, you get as much of God as you possibly can. The comforts of wealth often rob people of dependency on God. Although wealth is not bad and can be a great blessing, it is no sure indicator of spiritual strength.

INVESTMENT TITHING

Toxic Belief #6: *The more money I give to God, the more money he will give to me.*

It just isn't true that the more money you give God, the more money he will give to you. Yet you hear this all the time from fund-raisers who try to manipulate you for their gain and the establishment of their empires. If you give your money to churches and other ministries so you can get more money back, save your money; you are wasting it. God is not a financial investment opportunity. He isn't "a good bet" on which to place your money. What kind of faith would it be that guaranteed a return on money invested? That would not be faith; that would be a bank account.

Giving a portion of what you make is an act of faith going back to the days when the Jews sacrificed the very best lamb and gave one-tenth of their earnings to the temple. This form of giving has always been an act of worship and an act of faith. The ancient Hebrews sacrificed to God because they wanted to show him their love and dedication. It was not a scheme for wealth accumulation.

Today the element of sacrifice is absent. Too few understand time-honored principles of giving. Rather than sacrifice, they essentially give God a little tip (but far less than they would an efficient waiter). The key in giving is motive. Do you give to honor God, or do you give to get?

An interesting phenomenon occurs when people give with godly motives. I have heard many people say that the money they have left over after giving to God seems to go further than when they kept all of the money for themselves. They did not become wealthy, but they were much more satisfied with what they had. The worry factor greatly decreased. Once they gave the first portion of what they earned to God, they were better able to relax about how the rest would be spent. Putting their money where their faith was allowed them to believe more deeply in a God who would provide for all of their needs.

I never had strong faith in God until I trusted him with my money. Once my faith grew strong enough to let go of the money, I could grow spiritually as never before. I believe this to be a common experience with those who finally learn to write out the first check to the church. Giving to God first is a real test of motives. It is an act of faith that strengthens commitment at every other level.

Giving is often the first step in moving out of merely believing into taking action. When people do not commit their money in this way but use it as a ransom for future blessings, they might as well toss their coins in a wishing well. Giving money to get more money always ends up with getting less of God. If the motivation is for money, faithless givers have chosen a master: money. No one has ever been able to serve two masters at once. Money will master the heart and rob the greedy of any relationship with God.

Salvation by Works

Toxic Belief #7: *I can work my way to heaven.*

Just as some think they can get God's love by being good and others think they can overcome some bad past event by working hard, there are those who believe heaven can be earned. They spend their lives in a working frenzy, trying to do more and more so God will look down, observe their fine works, and decide they will be fit to enter heaven. It seems that most people working so hard have never resolved some tremendously debilitating issues from the past. If they could deal with those issues, perhaps they wouldn't need to punish themselves through all of the work they hope will be the key to eternal life.

A man in a small town had kept a secret from his wife that very few people knew. But those who did know the secret never told the man's wife; they were all willing participants in his personal cover-up. The man had been married before for a short while, then got a divorce. When he met the woman he wanted to be his second wife, he discovered she would never marry a previously married man. He loved her, so he decided not to tell her about the first marriage. After a month of dating it seemed less appropriate to tell her than it did in the first week. Months of courtship made his love grow deeper and the truth more difficult to reveal. He just never got around to telling her. Ten years into the marriage, there was no way he was going to blow the whistle on himself.

His dilemma created one of the most driven businessmen and church workers I have known. He would do anything to help someone. It went well beyond servanthood; it was an illness. His marriage could not have been worse from revealing the secret than it was from his religiosity and perfectionism. He died at forty-five. I think he discovered then that most of his work had been in vain. If only he could have revealed the secret, it would have saved him and his family a lot of misery.

Many others live like this due to some event in the past, some terrible secret they fear would spark rejection if revealed to others. In this cover-up mode, where the inside is dirty, they try to clean up the outside so it looks spotless. They look perfect, incapable of any wrong. They succeed in fooling most people because it is hard to see through the mask of perfectionism to the pain and other problems inside. Their drive to be and look good deceives many as they try to earn enough points to be accepted into heaven.

I'm glad I don't have to function under a system like this. I have messed up so many times, I know there is no way I could ever be good enough to make it to heaven. I know I could never make up for my messes by church work, service attendance, or bribes to God. I have to trust that he has forgiven me for my sins, just as he said he would. I must believe in Christ and what he did to wipe out the consequences of my sin.

You can't win by believing that good behavior gains a ticket into heaven, yet this is a much-taught theology. I was having dinner with one of my friends and his family. He and his two girls were discussing heaven. One asked him what a person needed to do to get to heaven. He told his kids that if you were a good person, you would make it. He said that God honors good work and lets those who measure up be with him forever.

I thought of how sad that must be for a young girl to hear. Every time she messes up, gets punished, or just can't seem to live up to family standards, she will believe she's not good enough for heaven. It must be very depressing for a child to believe the one thing that you have to do to get to heaven is the one thing you cannot do.

Heaven is a gift. It cannot be earned. Those who are trying to work their way to heaven possess a toxic faith that will drive them into a futile frenzy of activity, exhaustion, and depression. Those who live around these people will also find it very difficult to live comfortably as the driven workers impose their standards on the rest of the family. What a relief it must be to discover that you cannot earn a place in heaven!

SPITEFUL GOD

Toxic Belief #8: *Problems in my life result from some particular sin.*

A parent hoping and praying for a healthy child but ending up with a defective one is in pain beyond comprehension. My wife and I have some friends who have been through this devastation with two girls. Both were born with severe birth defects. One will never outgrow the defect; the other has a good chance of developing normally. The parents' great pain increased through the remarks of some Christian friends who told them that there must be some hidden sin in their lives for which God was disciplining them. Their grief was only compounded by the insensitive remarks.

It amazes me how many people believe God is too busy to help them and yet in bad times has plenty of time for destruction. He is not there to support, but he still may hurt. What a sad way to live!

All problems are not results of sin; many are simply results of reality. Life on this earth is imperfect. No matter how hard we try to change that, it will not change. Believers or not, we are going to suffer tragedy and failure as long as we live in this difficult world.

God has given us the freedom to make choices. Some choices will be better than others. The worst ones will cause us discomfort and pain, but the pain will not always be the result of God's punishment for sin. When people play with fire, often they feel the heat, and some get burned. The pain is from the fire, not the punishment of God. Sin is like that. Pain is often a result of sin, but not necessarily a punishment for it.

In the Bible is a story of Jesus and a blind man. The disciples asked him who had sinned to cause the man's blindness. Was it the father or the mother or the man? Jesus replied that none of them had sinned. He told them to forget about the sins-of-the-fathers idea because it did not apply. This toxic belief was poisoning faith thousands of years ago. Christ told them that the man's blindness was not a result of some particular sin (see John 9:1-7).

Problems can result from poor decisions, negative circumstances, and the fact that we live in an imperfect world. God does not choose to remove the imperfections, and until he does, we must deal with those problems. To inflict further difficulty on ourselves by believing that sin lurks behind every problem serves only to drive us further from true faith in God. Rather than focus on a fictional past sin, it is better to focus on how God can use the problem to build our faith and the faith of others.

We cannot rule out that some problems directly result from certain sins: intravenous drug users can get AIDS; theft can land you in jail; arrogance and greed can lead to the pain of loneliness. God does not "zap" us each time we choose to sin, but if we partake in sinful behavior, we may in effect be zapping ourselves.

SLAVERY OF THE FAITHFUL

Toxic Belief #9: *I must not stop meeting others' needs.*

An old joke, though not a very funny one, is full of insight. It seems a mother worked all of her life meeting every need of every family member. After her children were raised and out of the house, she was ready for a wonderful life. She had lived for everyone else, and just when she was ready to take time for herself, she died. On her tombstone they wrote, "Now maybe I can get some rest!"

A lot of great moms out there have worked themselves to death meeting everyone else's needs, taking no time for themselves. They see themselves more as slaves to God and family than as free persons equal to others. For them, life is one miserable sacrifice after another. I am sure God will honor such dedication, but I think he would be a lot happier if they would take some time for themselves. After all, he created them and loves them just as much as the people they so incessantly serve.

Women today live under a lot of pressure. Their children leave home later, marrying in their late twenties. Their parents live longer and often need intensive care. Just when a mother finally scoots her children out the door, she often stands there welcoming her mother or father or in-laws into the home. She spends the next ten years playing mother to elderly people, and before it is all done, she has spent 90 percent of her adult life as a caregiver. This role frequently produces anger, depression, and resentment of God and family. A late nervous breakdown is a common outcome.

It does not have to be this way, and thousands are starting to find out that there are alternatives to modern slavery. The codependency movement helped to open the eyes of many who thought they were helping out of love when they were actually helping because they knew of no other way to exist. They became so wrapped up in everyone else that they lost sight of who they were and what they wanted to accomplish. One woman described it this way: She was so codependent, so caught up in others' lives and meeting their needs, that if she had a near-death experience, someone else's life would probably flash before her eyes!

It is healthy to recognize that we all have some basic needs that must be met. Yet not every nice, loving, or serving deed is a codependent act. There must be a balance. Life is wonderful when it is spent serving others. Most religions stress putting others first. The Christian faith is one of self-sacrifice—but carried to an extreme, it can become a compulsive act rather than an act of compassion.

What good does it do to meet needs of others if that produces so much anger in you that you cannot relate to them in a loving manner? Why should a person work hard for others if the result is exhaustion and depression, disabling the person and causing a break with reality? Each helping heart must assess its own needs and determine if some have been neglected. God does not love only the rest of the world and expect you to serve those he loves. He loves *you*, too, and he knows you have needs. He wants those needs met.

An analogy helps explain the concept. You cannot feed the poor if you do not eat. Sacrificing your need to eat will kill you, and then you won't be around to feed anyone else. The same applies to the emotional and spiritual dimensions of life. When they are not met, those areas shut down. The longer they go unmet, the greater the problems that arise.

Christ came to serve people, and yet he took time to maintain his health. Balance reigned in his life. Christ took time to eat. He took time to rest. He took time to pray. He could not go on until his own needs were met. He spent time alone, getting away from the crowds.

Likewise, Christ calls those who choose to follow him to serve others as he did. I think he desires a place of rest and a time to regain perspective for all of us. If you do not have that time because you are driven to meet the needs of others, take a second look at where you are. If you are angry, exhausted, and depressed, take the time to back away and find the rest that God wants for you.

IRRATIONAL SUBMISSION

Toxic Belief #10: *I must always submit to authority.*

I grew up in Texas, where I witnessed some strange marriages and beliefs about marriage. The issue of submission always provided controversy. Some people believed the ultimate act of faith was to submit to an abusive authority. My parents helped one woman who lived with an alcoholic husband. He would get drunk and beat her, then she would hide in her home for a couple of weeks so no one would see the bruises. He was a very angry man, and alcohol brought out the worst in him. The abuse grew more intense until finally he broke her jaw. Yet she stayed with the man.

My father became involved in the situation and helped the woman talk about the abuse and why she continued to live with it. She revealed that a pastor had told her she must stay even if it meant she would be killed. He told her that she could have no greater act of faith than to die while submitting to her husband. He promised her that God would honor her decision to be loyal and faithful to authority.

In working with people in need of psychiatric care, I have seen some very depressed mothers who let their children be abused because they didn't think they could oppose the head of the house. Their children were badly hurt before they realized God didn't want such abuse. When they understood they could have done something to stop the abuse, many sank into deep depression. Their desire to submit poisoned both themselves and their families. Their faith withered because they questioned how God could allow such things to happen.

The submission issue is not for abused wives alone. It applies also to employees of unethical managers. Certain things are wrong, and God wants you to move out of those circumstances or make the dirty secrets known. The God I know would not want an accountant to write out a bribery check as an act of submission to a boss involved in wrongdoing.

I was aware of a misguided leader of an organization in Texas. This man was pursuing all sorts of illicit activities, one of which was an affair. A secretary was the only one willing to see the leader's flaws. When she risked her comfortable position to challenge the authority of the organization and her boss, no one believed her. In fact, many coworkers did not consider an affair a problem that should concern a mere secretary. They said a secretary should not question her boss's personal life and a boss should not question his secretary's personal life. But it was a Christian organization. The affair affected the man's job performance and harmed his integrity in a job where integrity matters. As a result of his actions, the integrity of the organization was in jeopardy. So the secretary did what most would not do. She placed the principle of integrity above the principle of submission. Although she lost her job, I believe she did the right thing. And eventually she was vindicated when it was discovered this leader had a part in other wrongful activities.

When authority is well placed, it respects the individuals over whom it has authority. When it is not well placed, it is our responsibility to expose the abuse and be part of the solution. Christ challenged the religious authorities who turned away from God and toward rules developed by men. Christ stood up to those people and told them they were wrong. He tried to produce change by what he said and by how he lived. If we are to follow his example, we must intervene when abuse is part of submission. We must have the courage to follow Christ's example and overturn the system, be it a marriage or an organization, if that system is wrong. Silent submission in the face of violence, dishonesty, and abuse will only allow that abuse to be passed to new generations. The abuse must end—even if it means risking financial security. Faith in God allows us to move into uncomfortable zones for the sake of honoring him and proving the reality of our faith.

Submission to authority both protects and liberates. When we submit to God, when we act according to his guidelines, we are freed, not bound. When children submit to their parents, they are protected. The experience of a husband and a wife submitting to each other is liberating, not confining. The relationship is strengthened and better defined as each person finds the areas that need and demand submission. Submission is part of God's plan, and it is biblical. Submitting to a husband, to a boss, or to a parent mirrors our relationship with God and helps us grow closer to him. Rebelling, confronting, and not submitting are appropriate only in exceptional cases. When God's work is compromised or when a person's life or limb is at stake, submission must give way to responsible confrontation.

CHRISTIAN INEQUALITY

Toxic Faith #11: *God uses only spiritual giants.*

This generation has seen the fall of many so-called spiritual giants. The myth has been shattered that if you are in the ministry, you are always a wonderful and dedicated human being.

Yet some individuals still do not believe we are all on equal footing. They believe God has called some into service—the ministers—and the rest must assume second-class status. Rather than minister to others' needs, many prefer to pass that duty on to those who have a special calling to do so. They also feel that because they are such terrible sinners, God could not use them anyway. Many fail to receive the blessings that come from ministering because they mistakenly believe that God uses only the perfect, the near perfect, or those he called into a special ministry.

A preacher in the twenty-first century can talk to millions of people via one broadcast on television. Because one person's reach can be so vast, others start to think of their own contribution as meaningless. They become lazy in their service and become unmotivated to find a way to further the kingdom of God. They neglect the gifts God has given them because they do not seem as "great" as those of others. They view themselves as inferior.

In my life (as well as in Scripture), I have seen nothing but the opposite to be true. God often uses those with major flaws or those who have been through a great deal of pain to accomplish many vital tasks for his kingdom. Look at Moses the stutterer, Paul with his thorn in the flesh, and David the adulterer. It seems that God uses the "spiritual giants" *despite* their flaws.

No one is too messed up for God to use, and no task is too unimportant to matter to God. On the sidelines and in the lower levels of ministry organizations, hundreds of faithful, invisible believers do the valuable, powerful work of prayer, the foundation for greatness in organizations as well as in people. When people pray, miracles occur, people change, countries develop new political systems, and God unleashes his power.

Everyone has some gift granted by God that can be exercised in a mighty way. Through stories about individuals who developed their talents and others who neglected theirs, Jesus expressed the need to cultivate our talents. When we do so, we will accomplish greater things than we ever imagined. When we do not develop our gifts, chances are we will never be satisfied or fulfilled.

Some could never speak in front of more than fifty people, but they have felt comfortable for years teaching a Sunday-school class of five. Year after year they teach, not knowing the long-term impact they have. Although they may belittle their contribution, God is using them to lay a foundation for years of future service.

My third grade public school teacher was a great woman of faith. She wanted her kids to know the Bible when they left her nine months later. Each day after we returned from lunch, my teacher read from a huge book of Bible stories. The stories started with Adam and Eve, and before the year was over, we had parted the Red Sea, gone with Moses through the wilderness, and moved into the Promised Land. Those stories increased my faith greatly. I believed them. And I believed that if God could watch over the Israelites for forty years in the wilderness, he could watch over me. I learned a lot from those stories. They taught me of

God's power and his forgiveness. When I messed up later in life, I remembered how his chosen people messed up, and he always found a way back for them.

There have always been people who have impacted the world in small but powerful ways. They take what God gives them and use it as effectively as they can. They don't stop to compare their gifts with those of others; they just trust God to use them.

We must not allow sins of the past or limited gifts to stand in the way of working for God and being used by God. A simple prayer, asking God to take what we have and use it as he sees fit, can open up a whole world of opportunity. God is big enough to take the simplest contribution and make it as significant as anything the greatest of the "giants" could do. He wants us to trust him to do wonderful things with our skills. Out of a pure faith we must first act; then we will be amazed at just how much God can do with so little.

PASSIVITY

Toxic Belief #12: *Having true faith means waiting for God to help me and doing nothing until he does.*

The toxic belief of passivity lays the foundation for laziness and disaster. I have seen many people hurt as they waited around for God to do something that God expected *them* to do.

Let me repeat, just so you don't miss one of the biggest problems facing dedicated believers. Sometimes we wait for God to do what God is waiting for us to do. Wives of alcoholics allow drinking to continue when intervention would reverse the course of the problem. Church leaders allow a minister to crash and burn under the influence of sex, silver, or self-obsession. They pray God will change him when they need to exercise the tough side of love and confront the person with his character defects. Parents allow a child to grow up spoiled and immature because they pray God will protect him rather than force the child to take responsibility for himself.

Too often in the name of waiting on God, people fail to take responsibility or action. They wait for God to perform a miracle while God waits for them to act. Remember, they call them miracles because they rarely happen. It is often easier to wait on a miracle than to do the difficult thing and take action. Tomorrow the pain will still be there, or the person will still be involved with the destructive behavior—unless we take action today.

God wants an active faith. As that faith develops, our relationship with God is stretched during uncomfortable times when we must act beyond our comfort zones. These painful times make us more reliant on God. We seek his comfort as we strive to accomplish those things that would be easier to delay. The risk we take in accomplishing each one brings us closer to God and builds our faith.

I met a couple who loved their son very much, even though he had disgraced them repeatedly with his drinking and drug use. There seemed to be no end to the agony they went through for him. Instead of making him face his responsibilities, they paid his way and made life "safe" for him. They prayed that God would heal him of his affliction. They felt it was their job to support him while God worked on the addiction. One night in a drunken stupor, their son walked off a balcony and was killed. Those parents had to live with the guilt of knowing they never did anything to help. They only enabled his negative behavior as they waited for God to perform a miracle. Out of a toxic faith in God, they loved their son to death.

I am aware of a wife who let her husband's unfaithfulness go unchecked. She knew he was running around, but she fervently prayed that God would change him. When she developed genital warts, she wondered how it could have happened. When she came down with herpes, she knew the cause. Her husband left her with a gift that cannot be cured. Had she taken action, she could have spared herself a lifetime disease and perhaps saved her marriage.

The Bible makes many references, especially in Psalms, to waiting on the Lord. Some people have misinterpreted waiting on the Lord as a call to roll over and play dead. Waiting on the Lord does not mean turning off the brain. Waiting on the Lord is waiting on God's timing and power. We are to do everything we can in faith, then leave what we cannot do to God. If we are unemployed, we should not use waiting on the Lord as an excuse to sit and idly wait for a job to appear magically. God wants us to look for a job and go through interviews, all the while remembering that God is still God and we must wait on him.

Waiting on God for help does not mean we are to neglect the mind he gave us or the will we have to accomplish things. We must take action and do those things within our power and trust God to do those things not in our power. The balance of this approach will accomplish much without producing a driven need to do it all alone. God gave us all many strengths. He expects us to use those strengths while we depend on his strength to assist us.

BIBLICAL EXCLUSIVITY

Toxic Belief #13: *If it's not in the Bible, it isn't relevant.*

The battle between religion and psychology has gone on for years. Many people have nothing to do with anything relating to emotions unless it is in Scripture. Their train of thought goes like this: If there is no scripture to back the idea, it must be harmful.

This belief is close to the truth but not quite on the mark. True faith means that a person should do nothing that opposes God's Word. It doesn't mean that *every* behavior or insight into life is going to be found in Scripture.

The Bible is not a manual for brain surgery. It does not tell us to avoid smoking crack cocaine. There is no scripture on what music is bad or good. How to operate a computer has been left out. We must figure out some things for ourselves; when we do, we should base our figuring on the foundations of Scripture. If that is a priority, what we think and feel about things will continue to line up with biblical truth. If we don't start with that foundation, we are victims of the crowd and the mood of current thought. When we have no foundation, we get into trouble and poison our faith with half-truths. But just because something is not in Scripture doesn't mean it is evil or a half-truth.

One woman who came into New Life Treatment Centers had been dealing with depression for years. She came to us from a psychiatrist who diagnosed her problem as a manic-depressive condition needing medication. Without medication, she would never be able to maintain a stable life, keep a job, or relate to her family. She was fine with her medication, and her life improved dramatically. For the first time in years she was happy and able to accomplish things without breaking down.

Then she made the mistake of attending a church that frowned on anything other than the Bible to help a person cope with life. When the members discovered she was on medication, they confronted her with her "lack of faith." They told her she was a new creature; old things were behind her and everything was new. That included her problem with depression. She was instructed to stop taking the medication and have faith that God would meet her needs and help her stay in control.

Our patient blindly trusted the minister and stopped the medication. For a couple of weeks it was difficult, but she managed to ride a religious high until her body could no longer respond. Then in a fit of depression she slit her wrists, called the people in the church office to tell them, and hung up. They called an ambulance as the men on staff rushed over to help. When they arrived ahead of the ambulance, they found her lying unconscious in a pool of blood. They tried to stop the bleeding as they waited for the paramedics. Fortunately, they made it in time to save the woman.

This event had a dynamic impact on the staff of that church. It changed the way they thought about medication and the need for some people to get help beyond what the church can provide. The church had a counseling ministry that, before this incident, instructed people to fast, pray, and read Scripture to handle any problem. The woman now goes to the same church, but there is no longer any problem with her need to take medication. The members realize that medication does not stand in the way of people's obtaining help or growing closer to God. It is the one thing that allows many to continue to develop a relationship with God.

Medication is a gift from God to help some individuals function in the real world. Of course it can be abused, but that does not mean it is evil when used as prescribed.

Why do some ministers believe that truth is found only in Scripture? Why do they resist assistance from counselors outside the church? Why do they reject the idea that many faithful believers who have degrees in mental health are following God's calling for their lives? I think many ministers are threatened by anything outside their field. They want to play physician, counselor, and parent to the flock. They want nothing to challenge their authority. They often will lead people down a path of misery rather than suggest that individuals get help from a specialist.

At one time few counselors could be trusted to build rather than destroy faith. Now there are thousands who integrate counseling and faith. Ministers need to feel comfortable in suggesting help beyond what the church can provide. If a minister ever needed brain surgery, I doubt he or she would swear off doctors. At that point, I think he or she would seek out someone who knew more about brain surgery than was revealed in Scripture.

The balance between real and toxic faith lies at the root of one's beliefs. Is your faith based on godly truth, or is it based on a make-it-up-as-you-go philosophy? Those who make it up lead very insecure lives. Those who base life on God's truth and place their faith in him develop a security found no other place. But to believe that every fact required for survival is contained in Scripture is naive or the result of manipulation. Once a toxic believer wakes up to this reality, he or she finds a new world that does not need to be feared.

Heavenly Matchmaking

Toxic Belief #14: *God will find me a perfect mate.*

Lisa was raised in a conservative Christian home in a small town in Texas. She came to Baylor University as a naive and beautiful young woman. The boys lined up to ask her out. (I'm afraid I wasn't eligible for the line. She was too pretty and too good.) Lisa loved to date and to get attention. She stayed true to her belief of waiting until marriage to have a sexual relationship; she was determined to marry as a virgin.

Lisa's senior year was a good one. She dated a senior from a respected fraternity, they became very serious, and following the traditional meeting of the parents, they decided to marry after graduation.

Lisa had been taught that through prayer and faith, God would provide her with the perfect mate. Her system said that someone out there was perfect for her in every way and God would deliver him to her. Her senior-year romance lived up to what she had been looking for. She loved Jim and was excited to marry him.

They were married, and shortly afterward Lisa began having terrible headaches. The doctor discovered a tumor that required brain surgery. She needed the perfect mate God had provided. Jim stood by her through the ordeal and remained supportive in every way. Lisa recovered fully after a year of bed rest and chemotherapy. At the end of that year, when she was ready to resume her life, Jim left her and eventually married another woman.

The divorce devastated Lisa, especially coming off the surgery and chemotherapy. It pushed her into a deep depression. While Jim deserted her, she focused most of her anger on God. How could he have let her down? How could he have taken away the perfect mate she had longed for and saved herself for? It was an extremely difficult time for her, and her faith was shaken. A new reality about God crashed in on her. Eventually, she accepted her new awareness about God and life, but it was not easy.

The perfect-mate belief has caused tremendous heartache for many people. They search for the one person God is supposed to provide, and when they think they have found him or her, they expect marriage to be instant bliss. When nirvana does not arrive, the naive believers move from a faith in a God who provides perfect marriage partners to a belief in an impersonal God who does not care about them. Going from one extreme to the other, they lose faith in God, and they lose hope for a wonderful future.

Sandy and I endured a very rocky first sixth months of marriage. We were convinced we had married the wrong partners and that whomever God had *really* picked for each of us was lost forever. We would argue, turn around, and quietly shake our heads and murmur, "Well, I've married the wrong person." Sandy sometimes slept in her clothes just in case she wanted to leave in the middle of the night. If we had not been totally committed to each other and to marriage, we would not have made it through the first year. The change came when we stopped focusing on the imperfections of God's "perfect mate" and started working on our relationship. We went from faith in a one-time event that would fix our problems for life to a life of work that helped us grow toward each other and a solid faith in God.

The perfect-mate belief is a nice idea, but it has some major problems. I would hate to think that there was one perfect person for me and that I could never be happy with anyone else. What if that one was killed in a plane crash before we met? Would I be stuck with number two all my life? What if the perfect mate made a mistake and married someone else? Would I be forced to live with the next best because of another person's mistake? If I marry God's perfect mate and she dies, am I destined to be married to a number seven or fifteen?

I don't like that system, and I haven't found much evidence that it is the way God works. God has a will for each of us, and that will might involve any one of several people. There is a will for marriage, work, and every other area of life. But in addition to this direction from God, he gave us free will. We are not robots programmed to make the "right" choices. God's way is bigger than that. He can work in our lives, no matter what foolish or wise decisions we make.

You could probably choose from several people and still build a happy marriage. Some choices would be better for you than others; some would be a disaster. God wants you to use your faith and your ability to reason to find a person who will be wonderful as a spouse. The more you use your mind, the more likely you are to discover aspects that could be problems later. Courtship is no time to overlook the obvious because of a belief that God has sent a person your way.

Toxic faith always has an element of quick fix and once-and-for-all thinking, and if you apply it to mate selection, one of the most important decisions in life can end in disaster. You need to make informed decisions and not rely on blind faith. Six sessions of premarital counseling go a long way in building a good start for a marriage. Opinions of friends and family can also help.

Once the marriage begins, nothing will take the place of realistic thinking and hard work. No matter how perfect the person seemed before marriage, flaws will continue to be revealed after the ceremony. If you aren't expecting them, they can be horrifying. If you realize that all marriages require effort, you are more likely to get busy, go to work, and create a great marriage. Marriages are never made in heaven; they are developed on earth by two committed partners.

POLLYANNA PERSPECTIVE

Toxic Belief #15: *Everything that happens to me is good.*

A preacher on the radio described the plight of a woman who married a man, lived with him ten years, and watched him die of cancer. A woman in her church insisted she be happy about it. "God has done a good thing. Everything he does is good." Two years later the woman was married again, and after one year of marriage her husband died. Again the lady from church demanded she claim this as a great and good victory provided by God. The woman recovered from her loss, married for a third time, and shortly afterward discovered her third husband had cancer.

Some people in the church believe everything is an immediate blessing. To them, only a real Christian is able to say, "Praise the Lord!" as the house burns down, the car is totaled, a child is hurt, or the cow dies. I believe that if you told these people they were going to be fried in oil, they would grin and say, "Praise the Lord anyway!"

Is this real? Can a person in touch with reality be grateful in times of crises? Is it a real test of faith to be able to greet each new piece of bad news with a big grin and a trite expression? I don't think so. I think it is evidence of unreal people manufacturing an unreal response. They try to rationalize that everything is good, even though it looks bad, feels bad, and is bad. They grow up believing that a positive attitude must be used to face every crisis. They deny how they really feel and delay dealing with the pain and agony they feel due to death or loss.

The woman who lost two husbands and was about to lose another was not grateful, nor did she believe the events were good. She was quite angry until she resolved her hurt over the losses. Years later she looked back and said that none of the problems were good but that God used each one for her good. He took the crisis and made it a faith-building experience.

The widow's perspective is much more accurate than the lady who demanded each new loss be viewed as a good thing. They were not good; they were terrible losses. But God takes such losses and over time makes them into something good. God will work everything together for our good if we will allow him to do so. Bad things provide God a stage to produce something good.

I have worked with many alcoholics who go from acceptance of their problem to gratitude. They mourn the loss of being able to drink, and then finally they see their lives as more meaningful because of recovery. The admission of alcoholism is a starting point for maturing and concentrating on life's deeper meaning. It is not instant and the problems caused from drinking were not good, but allowing God to work through the problems produced many good things.

People in pain have enough problems without some well-meaning folks trying to short-circuit the grief process by declaring that everything is a good event sent from God. I think God *allows* bad things; he does not *cause* them. The toxic thinking that all things are good makes people question whether God is cruel. It forces them to see God as a sadistic joker who inflicts pain and expects his followers to be happy about it. This perspective is a means of avoiding reality. It is an addictive habit, producing quick relief with poisonous faith, but blocking reality.

A loving God wants the best for us and is grieved when the best is missed. True faith in him allows these bad things to be woven together in a protective covering that grows stronger in fiber and softer to the touch.

Bulletproof Faith

Toxic Belief #16: *A strong faith will protect me from problems and pain.*

On the celebration of the one hundredth birthday of Rose Kennedy (mother of John, Bobby, and Ted Kennedy), NBC aired a tribute to the matriarch of the United States' most famous family. I was surprised to hear of the depth of her faith.

A daughter died in a plane crash, a son died in World War II, and two sons—John and Bobby—were killed by assassins' bullets. She had reason to be angry with God. Her faith had not protected her children. And yet she was not angry. She said that she often would think of how Mary felt as she watched her Son die by crucifixion. Rose expected no less or more for herself. She shared in the sufferings of others who had great faith.

For many, a belief in God and the practice of faith are just fine...until tragedy strikes. Then there comes the realization that the practice of faith does not accumulate brownie points of protection. It does not assure God's intervention. Bad things do happen to good people, and it has nothing to do with degrees of faith. We live in a world where big animals eat little animals. Decay, rot, and death are realities. Faith provides perspective, endurance, and purpose through the tough times, but it will not excuse anyone from them.

This toxic belief is not conjured up only by unknowing believers. It is preached from many pulpits across the land. It is used manipulatively to bring people to Christ. Rather than seek Christ, listeners seek relief. Then when evidence of lack of protection confronts them in the form of a death or other loss, sufferers become nonbelievers. They were never true believers to begin with, however. True believers know that those who walked with Christ were beset by pain, poverty, tragedy, poor health, beatings, and other hardships that stretched their faith, but the hardships built their faith. The difficulties drew believers closer to God because their faith was real *before* the difficulties started.

Those who believe because they want protection have picked the wrong faith; in believing, we often invite problems that otherwise would not develop. Those who preach this variety of poisonous faith have ruined many lives; the individuals turned away when they learned the hard truth about life.

If you're disillusioned because you were sold a bill of goods that didn't pan out, you're not alone. Many others share your pain. They, too, had to deal with tragedy and at the same time resolve many issues with their toxic beliefs. Their disappointments in God increased their pain, just as they may have multiplied yours. Let the Great Teacher use your pain to bring you closer to him. It does not have to be a barrier to God; it can be a bridge.

VINDICTIVE GOD

Toxic Belief #17: *God hates sinners, is angry with me, and wants to punish me.*

Many hurting individuals see God as an angry, vindictive old man ready to hurl lightning bolts at those who get out of step. In fact, some people do not accept a real God because they are afraid of him. They write him off as a myth because they are so afraid of what he might do if he *were* real.

And yet he *is* real, and he loves those he created.

Many people cannot conceive of a loving God because they were raised in a family where an angry father inflicted his wrath on every member. Because one's concept of God is frequently shaped by the relationship with one's father, having unresolved feelings about a father can poison a relationship with God. Individuals come to believe God is angry, just as their fathers were angry. They may even associate all love with anger. Until the father issues are resolved, the God issues remain to cloud faith.

Ever since God wiped out Sodom and Gomorrah, a rumor has been making the rounds that he is very angry with all of us here on earth. We envision a God not just angry with the world but angry with specific individuals, ready to send down his wrath. People live their whole lives in constant fear of a God out of control who might make them the next target. This view of God prevents a personal relationship with him and produces tremendous fear and anxiety.

The confusion arises over the just nature of God and the balance of his character. Does he get angry? Consider the people of Sodom and Gomorrah. They were living ungodly lives of self-obsession, lust, and pleasure. Their wayward lifestyle resulted in fire and brimstone from an angry God. God finally had to inflict the punishment that was deserved for such self-indulgence. He loved those people, but in the face of total disregard for him, he destroyed them. In God's economy, sin must be paid for.

Fortunately, the coming of Christ was designed to change all of that. What animal sacrifices pictured before Christ's coming, his atoning death was to accomplish forever. His life was offered in place of ours. His sacrifice enables us to flee the punishment that we earned. Christ paid the necessary price that wipes away our sin and wrongdoing so that we can enter into a relationship with a holy and perfect God.

Of course, sin may produce dire consequences, and these should not be mistaken for God's anger. An unwed teenager who gets pregnant should not look at her circumstance as punishment from God; it is the natural result of a sinful action she chose to take part in. God has created an ordered world where a direct relationship between cause and effect exists. If we do A, then the result is likely to be B. It could be God's punishment, but more likely it is the natural consequences of our negative choices. So many of the things we do bring undesirable results that, in essence, we punish ourselves. God might choose to punish us, but we are so busy punishing ourselves, he often does not have to.

When the AIDS epidemic hit the scene, many ministers said God was angry with homosexuals and was sending a plague to wipe them out. At a time when men and women of faith should have been reaching out to those who were dying, many were standing back and yelling, "I told you so!" The angry-God belief was used as an excuse to condemn, not acts of homosexuality, but the homosexuals themselves. Many dying from AIDS have sought to restore their relationship with God, but the anger of so many believers preaching the plague theory has caused them to search for God as far away from a church as possible.

The plague scenario doesn't make sense, and I think many ministers have figured that out. If God were sending plagues to wipe people out, he would have wiped out millions of unfaithful spouses. Adultery is rampant, as are greed, lying, cheating, and thousands of other sins. The AIDS epidemic is not a plague from God to wipe out homosexuals, but it does present an opportunity for many believers to reach out to a group of people who have been alienated from God.

God does not wipe us all out because he loves us. He knew us before we were born, and he knew all the trouble we would get into. Even knowing all that, he paid the price for our sins because we could not do it ourselves. If he hated us and wanted to punish us, he could easily do so. Yet his loving nature and Christ are our assurances that he will guide us back to him if we are willing to follow. If we are unwilling, the consequences are of our own doing.

One of Christ's greatest messages was that of forgiveness. When asked how often a person should forgive someone else, he said seventy times seven. His answer indicated the need to never stop forgiving (see Matthew 18:22-35). Confronted with an adulterous woman, Jesus didn't want her stoned for her sinful acts. Instead, he took the occasion to challenge her accusers to look at themselves. Because they all realized they were equally guilty, they threw nothing at her. Christ didn't take the opportunity to lecture the woman, make her feel bad, or try to convince her of the seriousness of her sin. His compassion for her was the convicting element. He encouraged her to go and sin no more, refusing to condemn her even after she invited his condemnation (see John 8:1-11).

When people talk of the wrath of God, I refer them to the story of the woman caught in adultery. The case made for a God who loves to punish wicked people is countered by this wonderful story of love. We should do no less. We should communicate love and compassion. That does not mean we have to compromise what we believe. Our standards don't have to change. All that needs changing is our attitude toward people who are hurting and confused and in need of encouragement. We must hate, not the sinner, but the sin. We must never confuse the two.

God is very clear at confronting us with his love in sending us his Son, but he is just as clear in his opinion of sin. Because he wanted a relationship with those he loved so much, he provided a way to cover the payment necessary for sin. The cross makes it obvious that while God does not hate the sinner, he does hate the sin.

One day I was visiting some patients at New Life Treatment Centers who were discussing various childhood tragedies. Many felt that God had singled them out from birth and was angry and vengeful, bringing terrible abuses into their lives. One man had never moved beyond childhood to adulthood. He had been badly abused while young and was opening up for the first time. His view of God had been distorted by his sexually abusive father. Our program stresses forgiveness and the loving nature of God. He said to me, "Coming here and finding that God loves me is the greatest experience of my life."

I wish everyone could see the love of God rather than a distorted image of his anger. Many people use this toxic belief as an excuse. They mess themselves up through irresponsible behavior and then blame a vindictive God who is supposedly showering down wrath. They behave just like those who continue to walk around with guilt for something they did years ago, and their guilt becomes an excuse to stay stuck in pain and disappointment.

An angry God is used as an excuse for too many blunders and mistakes. God loves us. He wants the best for us. He doesn't want to punish us. He wants us to be free from the past. He doesn't want us to spend the rest of our lives trying to hide the skeletons in our closets. He went to a lot of trouble so we would not have to be punished and feel guilty. His system enables us to start over. He is there for all of us, encouraging us to go and sin no more—no lightning, no plagues, no earthquakes, just love with the expectation that we will respond to that love.

At the same time, God's love, grace, and expectations are balanced with justice. He is not vindictive, but he disciplines those he loves as a father or mother would discipline a child. He does this not out of anger, but out of a love tough enough to stop the progression of irresponsibility. His discipline is always for our own good, provides opportunity for growth, and stems from his measureless love.

It is hard to differentiate between problems we cause and problems that come as God's discipline. Perhaps God most often simply uses the consequences of our own poor decisions to discipline us.

No one seems to have the authoritative word on consequences and discipline. The key to understanding both is God's love and great desire to help us grow toward him in faith. He will never give us more problems than we can handle, and he will assist us through the problems if we will trust him for help. His loving discipline comes when we veer away from his will. That's when he moves to bring us back.

MORTAL CHRIST

Toxic Faith #18: *Christ was merely a great teacher.*

Moses, Muhammad, Buddha, and Christ are often placed in the same category as great teachers and philosophers. Many people say they believe in Christ, but they really mean that they believe he existed as a historical entity. And without question plenty of evidence documents his existence. But believing that he was one of many great teachers is far different from accepting him as the Savior of the world. His own statements show that either he was the Savior or a liar or crazy.

Christ made several exclusive statements about himself. He claimed he was the way to God and to heaven. He insisted that except through him, a person had no way to come to God. Was he a liar, or do you believe there is only one way to God—through Christ? He even went so far as to call God his Father—quite a heady statement for a merely human teacher to make, no matter how wonderful! He declared he was the truth and the light. Now, either he *was* truth and light, or he was a psychotic with delusions of grandeur.

To see Christ as merely a great teacher is to dismiss what he taught. He did not tell people that if they wanted to go to heaven they had to be good. He told them that he came to save the world. No sane great teacher would make such a claim—unless he really was who he claimed to be. Christ was either who he said he was or he was a fraud, an egomaniac, a manipulator, and a deceptive leader. Those around him were following either the Savior of the world or a man who masterminded one of the all-time great hoaxes. He either came to save us, or he deceived us and falsely went down in history as the most significant person who ever lived.

Many of the disciples lay low after Christ's crucifixion, thinking their leader had come to a tragic end. They remained hurt and confused until they saw an empty tomb and met him face-to-face as the risen Christ. Scripture and history both record major changes in each disciple after the crucifixion. They became stronger in their beliefs, with more determination than ever to spread the message he left them. I doubt a mere good, *mortal* teacher could have developed this kind of loyal posthumous following.

Jesus certainly was a great teacher; but he was also the Savior he claimed to be. I know this to be true. I suffered tremendous guilt and depression until I finally accepted that Christ died for my sin. Because of his sacrifice, I didn't have to endure the punishment I deserved for the problems I caused. I had tried every other way to live. Nothing worked until I asked Christ to be who he said he was, the Savior of the world and the Savior of *my* world.

Is he the Savior of yours?

Impersonal God

Toxic Belief #19: *God is too big to care about me.*

Those who do not believe in a personal God—One who cares for individuals as well as groups of people—are missing out on a personal relationship with God that can make life bearable in the bad times and incredible in the good ones. I believe God cares for people individually and that he will reveal himself to each of us if we will allow him to do so.

Sadly, faith in a personal God has declined with the decline of the family. As divorced and working parents have spent less time with kids, the concept of a personal God has faded. Our ideas of God are often wrapped in our experiences with our parents. An absent father is almost a guarantee for a belief in an absent God who is too busy to care about individuals. If your parents were not individually devoted to spending time with you, you probably began life feeling overwhelmed from a lack of support. If you carried that experience over to God, your sense of being overwhelmed may have grown to an unmanageable point. You may have broken down because you felt there was too much difficulty in life with too little support from a distant God.

One of the first individuals to enter New Life Treatment Centers was a confirmed atheist. One night, desperate and in a suicidal rage, he went to the phone book to find the number of a psychiatrist. At 3:00 A.M. few psychiatrists are available, but ours answered her own phone. She instructed the distraught man to come into our center that night. He woke up the next morning and said that if there were a God, then he had played a terrible trick on him by landing him in a Christian treatment center. It was tough for him to stay, but he struggled and managed to make it to the fourth day.

On the evening of the fourth day, a remarkable event happened. The man, an alcoholic, attended an Alcoholics Anonymous meeting with other patients. At the end of the meeting a young boy stood up and asked for help. He told the group he was suicidal. He said that he was visualizing, in color, putting a gun to his head and pulling the trigger. The atheist could relate to him since he had been in the same frame of mind four days earlier.

When the boy sat down, the room went silent. Suddenly the back door of the room opened and a man walked in, wearing what looked like a turban and a robe. He said his wife and kids were in the car, but he felt that God wanted him to come into the room and say something. He had not heard the boy but said, "If anyone here is thinking of killing yourself, I want to encourage you to reconsider. God loves you and wants you to live. This turban on my head is a bandage from where I put a gun to my head and pulled the trigger. Fortunately, I survived so I could come here and tell you not to do it. God loves you."

At that moment our atheist patient left behind his atheism. He believed God had sent that man especially to talk to that boy. The other patients believed God had sent the boy and the man to show the atheist that he is real. I believe God interrupted the natural course of events to build the faith of all those in that room and potentially all who read this story.

This is one of millions of stories about people who have met a personal God who is not too big to care about each individual. When we understand how powerful God is, it is not too hard to believe he knows even the number of hairs on our heads. I can point to many times over the years when God has moved to intervene personally. In a thousand ways, through good times and bad, God tries to make himself known through meeting personal needs. I believe everyone can point to instances where God's divine intervention makes more sense than mere coincidence. We search the universe for God, but all the time he is with us. I believe he is in love with each of us and cares for us individually.

DIVINELY ORDAINED HAPPINESS

Toxic Belief #20: *More than anything else, God wants me to be happy.*

Every day a career is ruined, a marriage is destroyed, and a sexual relationship is started in pursuit of happiness. People want to be happy. In our society, everything is acceptable as long as it makes a person happy. Entire belief systems are based on the search for happiness, and someone is always around to utter the modern bromide, "Well, as long as you're happy!" When people are asked why they do certain questionable things, they reply:

> "I was never really happy in my marriage. I have found it in my new eighteen-year-old wife of three weeks."

> "I don't think God would object to my finding what makes me the most happy. I moved in with him, and I've never been happier."

"We divorced because of the kids. If we didn't do what would make us the happiest, we knew our kids would never be happy."

Wrong!
Wrong!
Wrong!

God's primary goal is *not* for us to be happy. Although he grieves with us when we are in pain and would prefer that no one suffer problems, he sees the bigger picture and knows that the pain is only temporary. He wants more than mere happiness for us. Trusting in God will allow the pain to be transformed into joy, which is a deeper, richer experience than happiness.

You cannot justify rejecting God's teachings for the sake of happiness. A female who is abused may need to leave a marriage for the sake of survival, but to leave just to be happy would be wrong. The search for happiness apart from God always ends in ruin. The truth is, when you search for something more meaningful, happiness develops as a by-product.

If God wanted us all happy, the world would be one big Disneyland with no lines, no admission fee, and continuous rides. But that is not the world I live in. That might be a modern-day description of what God intended for us when he created mankind in the Garden of Eden, but because of Adam and Eve's sin and the fallen nature they bequeathed to us, we live in a fallen world. Physical laws govern our created world: For example, a knife always cuts, whether in slicing a piece of bread or in committing murder. God does not magically make it blunt because it is used in an evil deed. And so there is pain—not because God prefers it, but because we live in a fallen world.

Pain can be a great motivator to draw us closer to God. I have been closest to God when I allowed him to produce a deep satisfaction and joy, even in the midst of the worst sacrifices or pain or hardships. Exhausting all my resources to find joy, I finally turned to God and drew closer to him.

God's primary goal for us is not happiness. Happiness is a temporary good feeling based on our circumstances. It is a meaningless pursuit. It is the counterfeit of what God wants for each of us. The heroin addict who shoots up is instantly happy, yet the word *joy* cannot be associated with a quick fix. Joy is a deeper satisfaction, regardless of circumstances. It comes only from faith in God and his involvement with an individual who trusts him totally. Happiness can be obtained alone; joy requires teamwork with God. Happiness is always fleeting; joy can grow over time.

Joy and satisfaction are results of faith in God and living out that faith. With God, circumstances are much less important than perspective. Perspective allows you to accept that each painful moment matures you to handle greater pain and to develop wisdom from the experience. Growing closer to God through adverse circumstances produces joy. Rejecting his teachings may result in a quick thrill and a fleeting bit of happiness, but it will squash joy and satisfaction.

God wants us to be mature, wise, and full of satisfaction. He paid a big price for those things to occur. Once we begin to mature and develop wisdom, we want more of it. As we grow in wisdom that produces a lasting joy, we are less satisfied to return to those childlike behaviors that provided cheap thrills and instant relief. We can no longer act out the opposite of God's standards and rationalize that we are doing what God would have us do to find happiness. God wants us to find lasting joy, and the cheap counterfeit of lasting joy is fleeting happiness. The search for happiness has destroyed our joy and left us empty, looking for another fix. But when we stop seeking happiness and start seeking God, joy—lasting joy—comforts and sustains us.

POSSIBILITY OF GAINING THE DIVINE

Toxic Belief #21: *I can become God.*

The idea that we can become God is perhaps the most depressing of all the toxic beliefs. Many ungodly people believe they can become God. They say if you just focus on all that you are, you will discover that you are God and in control of your fate. But such an idea inevitably becomes overwhelming and confusing.

I was listening to a lecture by a woman who said that each individual knows everything. She said that inside everyone is an unconscious knowledge. According to her, you know it all, but you don't *know* that you know it. Now it seems to me that if you knew everything, you would know that you know it. If you didn't know you know something, you wouldn't know everything. The process of trying to become God when you have absolutely no ability to do so will drive you crazy. When you know you are not God, it is necessary to engage in many rationalizations and mental games to convince yourself that you actually possess a divine nature.

Many men and women devote their lives trying to achieve the power that God alone has. They pick up trinkets along the way and attribute special powers to those trinkets. A recent power-trinket fad involved crystals. For many, crystals became the source of healing and power, the cure-all to life's frustrations. Playing God becomes easier if you have the right crystals with the right powers! So the message came through: "There is nothing you can't do."

I have been amazed that those who reject the traditional values and teachings of the Jewish faith or those who refuse to believe that Christ is God's Son find it easier to believe that each of us can become God. I find it much easier to believe in a powerful Creator than that *I* am the Creator. I know my limitations, and I fall short of being all-knowing or all-powerful. A quick assessment of my life reassures me that I am not perfect and have no way of being perfect! The "you are perfect" saying is part of the "you are God" mentality. Both concepts keep one from developing a relationship with the Creator.

My wife and I visited a town in northern California where one person spends his days playing God. To everyone he meets, he says, "You are perfect." He believes that each person is perfect, but the problem is that no one recognizes the perfection. This is like the "I know it all, I just don't know I know it all" dilemma. His proclamation of perfection is supposed to free persons to discover their godliness, release them from their mere human limitations, and help them move to their heavenly state of existence. It is incredible how many people buy into the silly concept.

"Buy into it" is a good description, too. Few are satisfied with the man's free proclamation. They pay hundreds of dollars to attend seminars where they are told they are perfect, they are powerful, and they are God.

But you can't turn mortal man into God. You can't take a sinful person and make him or her perfect just through thoughts of perfection. A limited mind cannot know all or comprehend the eternal truths of the universe.

This is not bad news; it is a relief. We can end our frustration of trying to become perfect or powerful. God took care of that problem when he sent Christ to form the bridge between finite man and infinite God. It is easier to accept Christ's sacrifice for all than it is to accept the idea that all are free from the need for sacrifice. Each day our mistakes and difficulties reinforce the knowledge of our limitations. We cannot become God, but we can accept the means by which God has made a way to him. His Son alleviates all need for perfection and power. Accepting his perfect sacrifice and the power through his Spirit into our lives, we no longer need to fake it or convince ourselves we can be who only God is.

The Bible: God's Cleansing Agent

Toxic beliefs are the bases of toxic faith. Possessing just one toxic belief can poison an entire relationship with God. Until each person has eradicated all of the toxic beliefs in his or her relationship with God, faith in God will not be what it could be.

Pure faith is a rare thing in our world of many religions, cults, and mind benders. To possess pure faith, a person must come to believe in a source of knowledge, a point of reference held up as an authority. That authority for me and millions of others is the Bible.

Men and women distort what Scripture says; they add to it, subtract from it, and make it say something it never intended. In its untainted form, it is the means by which faith in God is developed.

All of the spiritual truth we need is within the Bible's covers. It is the Word of God. Faith in God cannot be developed without knowing God's Word. It may seem easier to make up our beliefs as we go, but relying on the source of faith that has been used for thousands of years has never failed. To detoxify the mind and purify faith, God's Word is the cleansing agent.

Twenty-One Toxic Beliefs of a Toxic Faith

1. God's love and favor depend on my behavior.
2. When tragedy strikes, true believers should have a real peace about it.
3. If I have real faith, God will heal me or someone I am praying for.
4. All ministers are men and women of God and can be trusted.
5. Material blessings are a sign of spiritual strength.
6. The more money I give to God, the more money he will give to me.
7. I can work my way to heaven.
8. Problems in my life result from some particular sin.
9. I must not stop meeting others' needs.
10. I must always submit to authority.
11. God uses only spiritual giants.
12. Having true faith means waiting for God to help me and doing nothing until he does.
13. If it's not in the Bible, it isn't relevant.
14. God will find me a perfect mate.
15. Everything that happens to me is good.
16. A strong faith will protect me from problems and pain.
17. God hates sinners, is angry with me, and wants to punish me.
18. Christ was merely a great teacher.
19. God is too big to care about me.
20. More than anything else, God wants me to be happy.
21. I can become God.

CHAPTER 4

When Religion Becomes an Addiction

Religious addiction is often used as a means to avoid reality. One example is Rick, who entered our sexual-addiction program. Because of a religious experience that had "delivered" him from his sexual compulsivity, however, Rick left before the staff thought he was ready. His pastor had enabled Rick's toxic faith by repeatedly negating the need for psychological or medical treatment.

Rick was an exhibitionist who every week acted out his compulsion. While in prayer on the unit, he experienced "deliverance" from his sinful behavior. What Rick really experienced—as do most addicts diagnosed with religious addiction—was relief from feeling guilty or responsible for his sexually compulsive behavior.

Rick's religious addiction allowed him to avoid taking responsibility for working through his exhibitionism. It enabled him to dismiss the truth that his problem was primarily an act of passive aggression. With a means of mood alteration provided by toxic faith and prayer, he distanced himself from the undesirable emotions of anger toward women. Rick used his religious addiction to avoid the reality that exhibitionism is a symbolic act of aggression toward women, a maladaptive way of expressing repressed anger.

Rick's addiction relieved him from dealing with the brokenness that led to his exhibitionism. Many exhibitionists have repressed anger toward their mothers or female caregivers; their exhibitionism accomplishes two goals: to be seen and to express anger toward females. These are complex, and often painful, issues for the addict to deal with. Compulsive behavior circumvents angry, sad feelings. Rick's compulsive exhibitionism allowed him to skirt the real issue of his feelings of low self-worth.

For Rick, some very real issues went unaddressed. Most likely he will return to his previous well-established behavior—sexual acting out alternated with religious compulsivity. Like most religious addicts, however, Rick will put the responsibility for his change on God. Rick believes that God delivered him. If he acts out again, he would feel that the reason was sin, not addiction, and that God can and will forgive and deliver him from sin. Once delivered from his "sin," Rick can continue with his denial intact. When he acts out again, the process repeats itself.

Rick's behavior is not reality based. The reality is that his "sinful" behavior is rooted in addiction and is something for which he must take personal responsibility.

ADDICTION BEYOND CHEMICALS

Individuals become addicted to alcohol and drugs for understandable reasons. The substances contain potent chemicals that lock a person's psychological desires into a physiological need that must be fulfilled. These days the term *addiction* has been used to characterize behaviors that go beyond chemicals. Some have criticized a growing trend to label every problem as an addiction. They complain that, rather than accept responsibility for their behaviors, people continue in those behaviors, justified in doing so because they are "helplessly" addicted. Others argue that persons focused on recovering from an addiction are less likely to investigate the issues surrounding the development of the problem and more likely to concentrate on extinguishing the behavior. Instead of fixing a deep inner conflict or admitting a serious spiritual deficiency, they simply try to stop a behavior and miss out on God's power to completely change them physically, mentally, and emotionally.

But addiction and responsibility never have been mutually exclusive characteristics of a condition. Few people addicted to alcohol would say,

"Of course I drink. I'm an alcoholic." The person is much more likely not to use the label of alcoholic, because once it is admitted, the person must choose whether to accept responsibility to address the addiction. For this reason, alcoholics, drug addicts, and other types of addicts do all kinds of things to get around the label of addict. Their denial becomes complicated and well developed.

To use the term *addiction,* therefore, is an invitation to accept responsibility for the problem and to determine to do something about it. The challenge is to break through denial and be willing to do whatever it takes to be free.

Sin and addiction are not mutually exclusive in a condition either. All of us, as much as we hate to admit it, sin. Whether we are alcoholic or not, our drinking anything is sinful if it does not honor God or if it leads another person into sinful behavior. A three-hundred-pound man who has never had a drop of alcohol sins when he drives up to a convenience store and orders a "Big Swallow," which is full of sugar, caffeine, chemicals, and more calories than most people consume in one meal. That is no less sinful than the man who downs pure vodka until he passes out. Whether either fellow is addicted to the substance is irrelevant. Neither behavior honors God, and both negatively influence society and younger, impressionable men and women.

Sin and addiction exist simultaneously. But because of the demeaning manner in which the church has treated addicts, many people have overreacted and attempted to remove the issue of morality and sin entirely from addiction. Talk to recovering people about how they behaved in the midst of their addiction, and most will not deny they were involved in a multitude of sinful acts. The original addiction destroys the relationship with God, and then other areas fall prey to sin and cause further separation from God.

Many individuals feel so guilty about these sins that they don't do well in treatment. Fleeing the sins of the past had nothing to do with their use of the term *addiction.* Their recovery isn't based on the ability to deny their sins. Instead, their recovery begins when they accept that they have been involved in many sins and can feel forgiveness for those wrongs. Without a renewed relationship with the Creator, the feeling of being fully forgiven cannot be achieved and the recovery becomes an act of compensation rather than a process of change. In that case the term *addiction* is used to avoid responsibility, not to avoid the issue of sin.

Why, then, is it such a desirable term for many current maladies, and what advantage is there in calling something an addiction? First, it is used so frequently today because many people who are doing a great deal with their lives have had addiction problems. Recovered addicts are leading the way toward personal change and growth. While the rest of the world seems satisfied to deny and continue to compensate for their losses and ill feelings, addicts are busy doing an inside job on themselves to "devictimize" themselves from the addiction.

If something can be labeled an addiction, our culture feels more hope for overcoming it; we know how to fight addiction. There are steps to take. God is part of addiction recovery. Families are expected to receive help when a family member is addicted. Groups of addicts band together to help one another with similar addictions. In our society, it seems that addiction problems are the ones to have because help and support are available, there is hope for change, and many other people have had a similar problem. The label of addiction invites others to the point of recovery.

Another advantage of the addiction label is that it identifies a specific condition with a specific set of symptoms. Often people are miserable without knowing the source of the problem. They feel hopeless because no one seems to understand. Others who haven't been through the same feelings and circumstances don't have the credibility to help. But when a person can relate to an addiction, that person discovers that others have had the same problem, the problem has many similar characteristics, and others have found relief for their misery. When overeaters find that they don't just overeat, but they eat addictively like thousands of other food addicts, they have a greater sense of hope. If a driven businessperson discovers that his work habits parallel workaholism, the isolation is over, and a greater tendency to find help motivates the person to find others who have overcome their addiction to work.

Addiction's biggest benefit is its invitation to stop the denial, accept the full dimension of the problem, and join others in the recovery process. This happens when the person locks in and identifies with the common elements of addiction.

If people could identify their toxic-faith behaviors as an addiction, they would be in a better position to admit that there is a problem rather than to justify what they are doing. Some individuals have spent their whole lives in a world of religious fanaticism and fantasy, hiding in their compulsive behaviors and delusions. They believe they are honoring God, but they are only circumventing reality, easing their pain, and attempting to work their way to heaven.

Some are in dangerous cults, some are in denominational churches, some are attending a local church on the corner in your neighborhood, and others are seeking God in isolation. Some learned their toxic faith from their parents, while others developed theirs on their own. But because there exist so many others like them, they do not believe there is a problem. They are unaware they have completely missed God in their search for him.

Until they look at their lives and see the parallels to a condition common to others, they may have little hope for change. If they can see that their practice of faith is off-center, there may be great hope for change. If they perceive that what they have done with their lives is an addictive process, they may break through their denial and band with others to pursue a pure relationship with God. With the power of God and the support of fellow strugglers, there is great hope for recovery.

A DEFINITION OF ADDICTION

When an individual is excessively devoted to something or surrenders compulsively and habitually to something, that pathological devotion becomes an addiction. The presence of psychological and physiological dependency on a substance, relationship, or behavior results in addiction. When a person sacrifices family, job, economic security, and sanity for the sake of a substance, relationship, or behavior, addiction exists. When a destructive relationship to something becomes the central part of a person's life, when all else is sacrificed for the sake of that sick relationship, the person is said to be addicted.

Addictions develop when individuals seek relief from pain, a quick fix, or an immediate altered mood. When a person develops a pathological relationship to this mood-altering experience or substance, addiction exists. The addict becomes devoted to the source of mood alteration and, by giving up everything for that change in feelings, comes to worship the addictive act with body, mind, and spirit.

Most discussion of addiction focuses on drugs and alcohol. These substances are the most widely known producers of instant mood alteration. More is known about those who enter into a pathological relationship to alcohol and drugs than any other addiction. The life-damaging consequences are easiest to see with these chemical forms of addiction. Even though chemical addictions are common, however, there is great confusion over them, especially when it comes to mood alteration.

Drugs and alcohol are both mood and mind altering, even in small amounts. Many people think of addictions only when connected to a condition of inebriation resulting from extreme overindulgence. This is a gross misconception.

Drugs and alcohol alter the way the mind interprets the perceptions provided by the senses; they alter the mood or one's feelings and emotions. Even small amounts of a mood-altering chemical allow the user to flee the depths of feelings and pain. The addiction is allowed to flourish because of its ability to alter reality in small or large doses.

The addict, possessing little self-worth, forms faulty perceptions of God and the world in general. The mood- and mind-altering chemicals allow these false perceptions somehow to make sense and feel less burdensome. The more the reward from the chemical, the more likely the person will continue to rely on the chemical as a translator of reality or an insulator from it. If a small dose can provide this insulation, that small dose can become just as psychologically addicting as a large amount is physiologically addicting.

Addiction is not confined to chemicals, whether in large or small quantities. Addiction goes beyond drugs and alcohol and branches into emotional and process addictions. All addictions serve the same purpose: to change reality into a more tolerable form. They all eliminate God or at least distort the relationship with God. Every form is just as destructive as another; all result in disillusionment and isolation.

EMOTIONAL ADDICTIONS

Some people become addicted to negative emotions. It may seem strange to think a person could become addicted to something painful rather than something that brings instant pleasure, like alcohol or sex. As negative as the emotion might be, however, it becomes addictive because it is easier to manage than another more painful or difficult emotion. If sadness and depression become more tolerable than anger and rage, retreating into depression can become just as addicting as retreating into a drunken stupor.

I know this to be true from my own experience. I had a relationship with a wonderful girl whom I wanted to marry. When I broke off the relationship, I should have grieved and expressed my anger and rage at myself until I rid myself of every ounce of venomous emotion. Instead I lived with self-anger and self-hatred, masking them with depression and long bouts of profound sadness.

People like myself live with their negative feelings rather than express them. They retreat to less negative feelings in an attempt to cope. In our society, men and women differ in what they have been allowed to express and what they have been asked to suppress. For example, it's not considered ladylike to be angry. Many women were never allowed to show anger as little girls. Getting angry would mean risking the wrath or perceived loss of love and attention of their parents.

To be pleasing to a power greater than themselves (their parents), the women-to-be sacrificed their anger. But without their anger, they could not set boundaries and protect themselves from the violations of life. Without their anger, they become victims to be violated, beaten, battered, and bruised. Without their anger, they cannot muster the courage to address their God. No matter how intense their rage at their plight, they cannot protect themselves or get the victimizers out of their lives. Their role is to be pleasing, and angry people are not pleasing.

These victims' anger did not just go away; it remained deep and hidden. To compensate for its suppressed presence, some resort to depression, as I did. They exhibit the miserable personality syndrome: Nothing is right, and everything becomes a source of misery and irritation. Instead of expressing deep hurt, the wounded female lives a miserable existence and gripes and complains about everything. She becomes addicted to her misery because it allows her to forget about her anger, or at least postpone dealing with it. Her dependency on misery is just as difficult to break as someone else's dependency on crack cocaine. Both are means to a different reality that allows for pain to be deferred.

In some expressions of the Christian faith, anger is a no-no for both men and women. Some believe that everyone must be completely loving and forgiving at *all* times and that anyone showing anger is not a good Christian and should work on the sinful attitude at the heart of the anger. But that belief is a distortion of how Christianity and reality are to be joined. Everyone, Christian or not, is going to get angry. The sooner this anger is expressed and resolved, the better. Yet many angry Christians don't acknowledge that they are angry, even while they seethe with bitterness and resentment. And their denial of their feelings is ineffective and unnecessary.

Christ became angry, expressed it, and did something about it. His anger led him to cleanse the temple of moneychangers. These were toxic believers who exchanged animals for money. Their interest was not in God but in the money that could be made from buying livestock low and selling it high. Christ knew their hearts and was hurt and angry over their toxic-faith activities. Without his anger, he never would have removed those violators of the temple's sanctity.

Mrs. Jones is addicted to her depression. She uses religion to medicate her misery, much like the alcoholic or compulsive overeater uses compulsive behavior to medicate and reinforce depression to avoid having to acknowledge repressed rage.

Mrs. Jones sent a good portion of her retirement money to the church, which used it to buy a fancy sound system. She had given the money at her pastor's urging to help pay the church's rent. When she realized that she had been used, she was unable to express her anger. She saw the situation as just another bad decision. *God will judge him,* she reasoned, as if the fact that God will judge means she ought to let herself be used time and time again.

Unable to show anger at those who used her, Mrs. Jones became more depressed, bitter, and resentful. To get angry with those in authority was a no-no, a lesson she learned early in life. She never learned that it is human to be angry with those who misuse and abuse authority and who take advantage of others.

Whether it was her church, children, friends, or family members who used or abused her, she would "put it in God's hands" rather than confront the abuser or set some boundaries. What she was really doing was making God responsible for her inability to use her anger in a healthy way, to be assertive, to set boundaries, and to say no.

Mrs. Jones's use of Scripture to justify her position helped her to avoid having to set and maintain boundaries. She operated under the principle that if all persecution is ordained by God, there is no need to say no. Without a healthy sense of anger, she wasn't able to be assertive and protect herself from being violated. Without her anger, she didn't have the capacity to defend herself in a world that is often quite unsafe.

If Mrs. Jones became angry, she would have to take responsibility for the toxic shame connected with an angry child of God. Her shame is toxically bound with her anger. She learned early in life that if she were angry she would experience the shame of being unacceptable. This connection, which is not reality based, causes problems in her relationship with God, herself, and others.

Mrs. Jones's toxic faith has nothing to do with God. Her religious addiction provides her only with an illusory relationship to God. Her god of religion provides her with a false sense of acceptance for playing the role of the miserable martyr. Mrs. Jones needs to take responsibility for her own life.

Without our anger, we are unable to cleanse the temple of God and maintain its sanctity. Without our anger, we cannot get those people who violate the sanctity of our beings out of our lives. Without our anger, we are relegated to playing the role of enabler and victim.

Without anger, people must allow themselves to be defiled and victimized without objection. Anger can be a mechanism for self-defense; those who deny its presence are vulnerable to manipulation and all forms of exploitation. People who don't have the right to be angry become powerless, unable to stand for what is right.

Men are supposed to deny a different set of emotions. In our society, big boys don't cry. But without our grief and sadness, we can't release our sense of violation. The pain and shame that come from abuse have no way of being processed. It is well said, "That which cannot be processed is repressed." We stumble through life without understanding our feelings, completely out of touch with our emotions. We are deeply grieved by our lost expectations and sense of inadequacy, but we don't feel safe acknowledging our sadness.

We show our anger, but never the deep hurt and sadness beneath it. When we feel sad, anger becomes a safe retreat. It causes the adrenaline to rush through us so the payoff is not just that we avoid looking weak, but we also feel differently because of the chemicals coursing through our bodies. The more adrenaline we pump through anger, the less sadness we are forced to feel.

This lack of grieving is a poison to our existence. There is no biblical precedent for men not expressing openly their deepest hurts and sorrows. The Old Testament depicts many real men showing their real emotions. The men of the nation of Israel would rip their clothes, sprinkle themselves with ashes, wear black armbands, and spend time in public mourning and grief. They would wail before the Lord to process their sense of shame and pain. That extremely freeing experience allowed them to express their emotions to the full degree and then move on without the needless baggage of building negative emotions. Without the ability to "wail before the Lord," we are forced to repress our disappointments and sadness and find ways to compensate for these emotions by replacing them with others less threatening to express.

The aggressively virile American male is the unfortunate result of a man's unwillingness to grieve. The macho image is a defense against life and the possible situations of vulnerability that would leave him open to be controlled or ridiculed by others. Macho men, without their grief, must find a way to gain power and control over their environment. They have a unique way of rationalizing and justifying their behavior and violations of others, and they are driven to perform to gain the prestige needed to command the respect of others. Many times what is seen from the outside as giftedness or "anointing" is simply an overcompensation to defend against a position of vulnerability. Many men, driven to power by their anger, are full of grief and sadness that remain unfelt until a crisis or breakdown brings all of these emotions to the surface.

It is incredible that so many men in our churches today are out of touch with their emotions, when the Christ they say they follow was so in touch with his. From Scripture we can see that Christ did not deny the depths of what he felt. In the Garden of Gethsemane, with his soul "exceedingly sorrowful, even to death," as "His sweat became like great drops of blood" (Matthew 26:38; Luke 22:44), Christ was able to grieve the unfairness of his impending persecution. He did not withhold the expression of those emotions out of fear that others would no longer follow him. He honestly expressed the full degree of what he felt as he was feeling it. Many emotionless followers are not using Christ as a model.

If Christ walked the earth today, some people in our churches would be uncomfortable with his open display of emotion. There is a good chance they would shame him for that conduct. "Where is your faith?" they would say. "Rejoice always,...in everything give thanks; for this is the will of God," they would admonish (see Luke 8:25; 1 Thessalonians 5:16,18). I can just hear some religious addict saying, "Come on, Jesus. You need to have real peace about this." They would shame his feelings because such raw emotions don't live up to their image of a man of God or how easy faith in God is supposed to make life.

Church people are not the only ones who would struggle with Christ's honest and open display of emotion. Many in the mental health profession would be just as likely to respond poorly to his grief. They would perhaps say he was having a nervous breakdown or an anxiety attack. They would perhaps suggest he be involuntarily restrained until the crisis passed. His open and honest display of emotion would be too much for them, too threatening to their inner worlds of hidden feelings.

When Christ walked the earth, he set a great example for us to follow. He didn't leave out the emotional side of life. It's too bad so few choose to live after his example and instead deny their emotions and the need to express them.

Rather than accept their negative feelings and resolve them, emotional addicts become addicted to the emotions that make life bearable, the familiar emotions that seem easier—the emotions the toxic family tolerated. To be accepted, the addicts were forced to find or create a delusional world that allowed them to avoid what they never learned to handle. That way, they could hide or kill the feelings of shame of being unacceptable. They became addicted to the pretense and the emotions they relied on to survive.

We have become an emotionally addicted society. We are walking paradoxes of what we are willing to show and what we are actually feeling. We are in a constant state of denial when it comes to our emotions. Women, though angry on the inside, feel safe only if they show their misery and depression. Men, feeling sad and depressed, will not risk being labeled weak by expressing their sadness. They push people around through their anger, thus masking their depression. An angry female without her depression could not exist. A depressed man without his anger could not cope. Both become addicted to the emotion that appears to be more tolerable and acceptable. Fortunately, many are breaking through the denial and beginning to live comfortably and honestly with their emotions.

Process Addictions

In addition to chemical addictions and emotional addictions, there exist process addictions. Process addictions, such as work and religion, are more pervasive in our society than the more commonly recognized chemical addictions. Work becomes the means by which individuals establish a sense of self and acceptability. Process addicts focused on work believe that they are valued only for what they can accomplish rather than for who they are.

Behind every workaholic is a person who feels inadequate and is driven to compensate for a lack of self-worth. Compulsive achievers defend against the day when they might be forced to admit inadequacy or inferiority. Workaholics are actually quite spiritually focused persons. They attempt to find God through work. If god is money, the work is intended to bring them closer to that god. If they have a relationship with God the Creator, they work to gain favor and be pronounced good.

Workaholics follow after a fabrication of the true God. They become addicted to the sense of power attained from the work and the striving to excel. People addicted to a process such as work become addicted to pursuit of a god of their own making. They lose the real God and worship the fruit of their labor, be it money, fame, or whatever earthly pursuit they most value.

Addiction As Idolatry

All addictions have at least one element in common: worship of the process and worship of the outcome. The worship aspect of addiction is easily seen in the lives of most addicts. An extremely overweight friend of mine would not stop eating excessively, even for the sake of his family. He loved food and had some with him most of the time. He could go hours during the day without touching food, but when he was home in the evenings, he spent most of his time eating—a reward for his hard work. It compensated for his deprivation as a child. He lived to eat.

It didn't matter that he embarrassed his children. It was insignificant that his cholesterol level shot up into dangerous levels. He didn't react when his wife threatened to leave if he refused to lose weight. Food was too much a portion of his life to do without. He was always thinking about what to eat next. While he was eating, nothing mattered but how good he felt. No follower of any religion had a more devoted member than this man who served the god of food.

Worship is built into addiction. The addict serves the act of addiction with every element of his or her being. Initially, a drink alters the person's mind, bringing a brief, temporary change. As the problem progresses, however, the person becomes a slave to drink and gives up everything for it. Family, friends, work, and self-respect are all placed upon the altar of alcohol. Everything is offered up as sacrifice for what was once a drink but has now become an idol of worship. In the end, all addictions become a form of idolatry—that is, the worship of a relationship, substance, or behavior instead of God. The object of idolatry stands in place of and in the way of God.

It may be drink, sexual encounters, or work, but all addicts find a means to make life tolerable. These objects of addiction allow the addict to avoid pain and manage his or her internal conflict. It may kill the person in the long run or destroy all relationships, but the object of addiction must be maintained for survival. The addict will live for the addiction and die for it in the ultimate act of worship and devotion.

RELIGION AS ADDICTION

A person with toxic faith can worship a false god just as easily as an alcoholic can worship a bottle of booze. The person with toxic faith is just as likely to be willing to die out of devotion to that false god as a drug addict is willing to die out of devotion to drugs.

The toxic faithful adhere to a toxic religion in order to dodge the emotional turmoil that comes with facing the reality of their circumstances. Their lives focus on the religion and not on God. The religion engulfs them, and they lose themselves to its practice.

Van grew up in an abusive home. His father was an alcoholic who became belligerent when he drank. Van remembers vividly the fighting between his mom and dad. And he remembers his older sister secreting him and his two brothers in the closet until all was clear. It was not unusual for Van's mother to wake the children in the middle of the night and go into a tirade about his father. Other times the children would be wakened by their dad coming home drunk, yelling, screaming, breaking things, and beating his mom. Van and his brothers and sister would go to bed each night in fear of what might happen.

If Van's father wasn't venting his anger on his mother, he was venting it on the children. When the father came home, the mother often greeted him by relating how rotten the kids—especially Van—had been that day. Van's father would stop the kids in the middle of what they were doing, or drag all the children out of bed, and beat them. Many times, at his mom's insistence, he would line up the kids, tell them to drop their drawers, and spank and humiliate them. Van remembers the pain and the shame inflicted on him and his brothers and sister. The siblings reported the fear and terror they felt being forced to watch the beatings. The threat, "This is what is going to happen to you if you kids don't straighten up," has an all-too-familiar ring for Van and his siblings.

All Van knew was that he wanted to escape the pain and shame of his family. He wanted someone to care for him and not hurt him. He needed someone to be nice and protect him. He needed someone or something to make his life safe and worth living. One of Van's friends introduced him to a church where he heard how God loves him, how the fruit of the Spirit could be his, and how, upon his acceptance of Jesus Christ, God would fill him with the Holy Spirit.

Van became a Christian. He spent all his time in Bible studies, worship services, ministry outreaches, home fellowships, and other work of the Lord. Van found his escape from the pain of the past. Van became more dependent on religion than on his God.

Van found the affirmation he always wanted in church, unaware that his teaching the Word of God had more to do with his need to be affirmed and accepted than with his love of God. Van relished the mood alteration he experienced when those around him esteemed his ability to teach. But Van was unable to generate self-esteem for himself or to feel worthy of God. He valued and was valued for what he could do rather than for who he was. All Van knew was that he had found a way to experience the joy of being valued. He was hooked.

Van began to find himself at odds with the sister who once protected him and the brothers who had shared his pain and shame. He began to berate his siblings for their rebelliousness toward God. He preached and "Bible-bullied" and shamed them. They just didn't measure up to Van's expectations. Just as his father had berated them because of his alcohol, Van began to berate and shame those around him because of his religion.

It became clear to Van that he had the answer and that he needed to abandon those who loved him the most; they just didn't measure up. Van dove into the only thing that seemed to bring him a sense of relief and comfort: religion. Religion made him feel like he was somebody. He had found a way to hide those feelings he desperately needed to rid himself of.

Van got married and things went well—at first. After a while, however, he began to notice his wife's shortcomings. He would constantly condemn and demean her for her lack of commitment. Altering his mood with his sense of righteousness, he would constantly throw the scriptures on submission in her face anytime she complained about his insensitivity and her need for a caring husband. His father's abuse to his mom lay in the abuse of alcohol; Van's constant belittling and badgering of his wife lay in the abuse of religion.

His wife finally had enough. No longer able to endure his sense of self-righteousness and his religious abuse, she filed for divorce.

Forced to endure the loss of marriage, Van dove further into his toxic faith for relief. He would do anything to be involved with religion if it allowed him to keep his focus off his own problems. He would stay up all night with street people and not be able to show up for work the next day. His employers became more and more irate with his tardiness and absenteeism and gave him an ultimatum: If he continued to be late or absent, then he would have to find employment elsewhere. Van responded indignantly and continued to preach the "godly" lifestyle to his fellow workers and to show up late, if at all. Fed up with his behavior, his employers fired him. Nevertheless, Van deluded himself into believing that there wasn't anything wrong with his behavior and that his employers were persecuting him for his faith.

Divorced, unemployed, and feeling abandoned by the "god" he tried so hard to please, Van came to us depressed, lonely, and suicidal. We talked about how many times the children of alcoholics become obsessive-compulsive, and we looked at the characteristics of toxic faith. Van began to realize how he had used religion like a drug to alter his mood and justify his behavior. He identified how much of his behavior was like his dad's. He was as insensitive, demeaning, abusive, and irresponsible as his father had been, except Van had used religion instead of alcohol.

Van was able to talk about his abuse as well as his abusive behavior with a group of caring people who understood what he had gone through. He is now in the process of healing his own wounds, making amends, and working with a twelve-step program that allows him to adopt a healthier faith.

Like any other addiction, the practice of religion becomes central to every other aspect of life. All relationships evolve from the religion. Like an alcoholic entering a favorite bar, the religious addict feels total acceptance in the company of other like-minded believers. They offer support and encouragement. They permit a diversion from responsibilities and growth. Any sign of pain or conflict becomes an excuse to retreat into the assembly of other deluded followers who reassure the addict that everything will work out.

The religious addiction becomes tied to these people who support the addiction. The addict depends on the rituals and the others who go through those rituals. Dependency on the religious practice and its members removes the need for dependency on God. The believer becomes hooked on a substitute with others who will not let go. The religion and those who practice it become the central power for the addict who no longer is in touch with God.

While I attended seminary, I worked in a counseling center on campus that allowed all of the rookie counselors to practice counseling skills.

One evening I met a couple who had been having difficulty with their daughter. She had gotten pregnant at age sixteen and moved in with the baby's father. The parents were respectable members of the local church, and the experience had humiliated them. The incident radically changed their relationship. They grew apart and existed without intimacy. They rarely talked when they were together, and the times they were together became less frequent. They came to counseling because the wife wanted the relationship to change.

The woman had fled to a new church when she became too embarrassed to attend her old one. The pastor incited the congregation to screams and howls every time he preached—quite a change from her staid pastor of twenty years. Everyone welcomed her, and she felt as if she had found a new home. That her husband was not with her made it even better for her; at least for a little while she could forget about her responsibilities and struggles at home. Everyone threw her a lot of attention because they wanted her to become a member of the church.

The wife's dedication grew more and more intense. She attended on Sunday mornings, Sunday nights, and Wednesday evenings. On Tuesday mornings she baby-sat for the young mothers' class, and on Thursday afternoons she attended a women's Bible study. Almost every day she showed up at the church. She started doing volunteer work around the church office, and that was when the pastor noticed her and began to develop a relationship with her. When he suggested that each Friday afternoon they have a counseling session, she was thrilled to be able to spend the time with him. She thought of it as a totally innocent involvement.

Her first uneasy feelings occurred when he suggested that she leave her husband. She was angry with her husband, but she had no intention of leaving him. A bolt of reality struck her, and in a moment she realized that the minister was unhealthy, the church was unhealthy, and her involvement was unhealthy. She had become fanatical in her church activity. God had nothing to do with it. It was all out of a motivation to relieve the pain from the situation with her daughter. She was able to admit in our session that her involvement had become an addiction.

Many others have become trapped in an unhealthy involvement with a church. Conviction turns to addiction, and excess activity eases the pain. Most are not able to see for themselves the unhealthiness of the involvement. If someone is not able to point out what they are doing, they continue in their compulsive actions, believing God is honored. Like this woman, they allow intimacy to fall from their relationships, and they become vulnerable to other unhealthy relationships. The warmth of the other followers melts away the individual's ability to evaluate the experience objectively. Before the experience is over, the addict is lost inside the organization—an organization that looks good to most but actually erects a wall between the follower and God.

Compulsive Churchaholism

In the case of the bereaved woman who lost her unwed daughter to pregnancy and an undesirable boyfriend, religious addiction took the form of activity, much like workaholism. A compulsive churchaholic accurately describes a person obsessed with the need to do more and more through church work. Like the workaholic who invests everything in work, avoiding the responsibilities that come with relationships, the religious addict creates an atmosphere that revolves around church work. Any interpersonal relationships are developed as a result of or a part of service to the organization. At any sign of conflict, the churchaholic retreats into more church work. All intimacy can be avoided by spending increasing amounts of time doing what appears to be dedicated service. In times of great pain and disappointment, the religious addict has church work for protection from the rejections and abandonments of life. The addict does not depend on God, but on the work and comfort that comes from being too involved to cope with problems.

A certain kind of peace is found in activity. Just as alcoholics drink to find relief, religious addicts find relief in work. What is labeled as peace, however, is actually avoidance. Hard work is the enabler for avoidance. Essentially, they work hard in an attempt to outrun the pain. Real people are lost and replaced with those who will assist in the charade. Busyness becomes the goal, and religious compulsivity provides a false presence of God. The compulsive working out of their religion gives the mood alteration necessary for the illusion of being okay. Though those feelings of being okay may be fleeting, it is still better than living without a moment of rest or relief from the conflicts of life.

Churchaholics have embraced a counterfeit religion. God is not honored, and the relationship with him is not furthered. Work is the focus of everything. It—and not God—allows the individuals to feel safe. Rather than retreat to the loving arms of God, they literally bury themselves in their compulsive acts. The harder they work, the better they feel because they convince one another that God applauds their efforts. They have grown so entangled in the world of the church that they no longer have time for the family. They are trying to work their way to heaven or pay the price for their guilt. Without intervention, they lose all sense of reality and rarely come to understand God as he really is.

ADDICTIVE COMPONENTS OF RELIGION

Anyone can become addicted to just about anything. Whatever hides or kills the pain of being unable to process the conflicts of life will serve well as an addiction. The practice of faith and involvement in religion offer many potentially addictive components. One can become addicted to feelings of righteousness or feelings that come with finally being right about something; one can become obsessed with prayer; one can become addicted to the emotional highs resulting from worship and praise; one can become addicted to feelings of being a part of something exciting; one can become addicted to feelings of belonging to something big. Being a part of a group of other believers produces wonderful feelings. Those feelings of relationship should be enjoyed. They are addictive only when they become the *purpose* of the endeavor rather than a wonderful *by-product* of worshiping God.

Worship provides an example of how an unbalanced practice of faith can cause problems. Many people who worship God in song and praise achieve emotional highs. In God's presence they feel better about themselves and their future as they focus on the wonder of God. If they lose focus—if the feelings, rather than God, become the central part of the worship experience—the worship is toxic and addictive.

Many retreat into a religious group in times of stress or disappointment. They seek the safety of God's church when their powers are exhausted and they continue to feel lonely, abandoned, and scared. Security is found with other believers focused on God. Often the individuals feel so welcomed and safe that they desire to continue in the faith, yet God is not the primary factor. Feelings of acceptance and warmth become addictive. Toxic believers think they are growing in faith, but they closely resemble the businessmen who go to church just to make contacts. Sometimes, though, the involvement will continue until reliance is placed on God and not on feelings of belonging.

ADDICTION REPLACES GOD

True addiction always results in separation from God. It starts as a substitution for God and eventually becomes a wedge between the person and God. The alcoholic feels unloved and rejected by God. The booze efficiently destroys the presence of God and blocks a person's knowledge of God, and the person becomes overwhelmed without tapping into the power and strength of the Creator. Where God could be found becomes off-limits for the alcoholic. A religious addict replaces God with a caricature of God. The addict sees God with a scorecard, writing down every wrong thing that has happened. To the addict, the only way to erase sins from the scorecard is hard work. Hard work and the feelings derived from it replace God completely.

Some addicts replace God with a caricature through their use of Scripture. This comment seems strange because most people use the Word of God to grow closer to him; meditation on God's Word and memorization of God's Word normally align believers with God. But for some people the Word can become a god unto itself. Memorization can become an addiction rather than an act of devotion. Individuals become obsessed with verses and, in the process, forget that the verses are about a God who communicated his love to his people.

The churchaholic obsessed with Scripture stops communicating because he or she fills every conversation with verses and sermonettes. No one wants to listen to or even be around the person. Such pseudo-speech becomes a form of religious intellectualism; someone becomes so immersed in an aspect of faith that real faith gets lost. The comfort of God is pushed aside by the self-induced comfort of superiority that comes from being able to rattle off a verse rather than connect with another human being as Christ did.

A family member abuses Scripture in this way. Every relationship turns into a student-teacher dynamic. She holds herself above the others, ready to set them on course with a helpful scripture. She has alienated everyone in the process. If her faith were pure, it would attract others. Instead it repulses them and drives people from her and from wanting to pursue a relationship with God. As she builds up her image with this "admirable" form of communication, she puts God down in the eyes of those who see her faith. Her position as "teacher" brings her a sense of power, prestige, and control, while it alienates all others. She uses her sermons of superiority to gratify her need for security. She feels safe because people don't dare come too close, lest they be chewed up by her Scripture-quoting tongue. The Word of God has become her god.

RELIGION WITHOUT ITS TRUE OBJECT

Adrian Van Kaam states that "addiction is a perverted religious presence that has lost its true object."[1] All addicts in all forms of addiction seek something spiritual when they first begin to tangle with the addiction. They seek relief or, to use a more spiritual term, *peace.* The interaction with the addiction actually becomes a religious experience with its own rituals and rules. The less relief the addiction provides over time, the more intricate the rituals become. As the rituals and rules increase, God is left further behind, and the true object is lost.

Van Kaam further describes addiction:

The object…of my striving will be a situation, object, or experience which promises me the deepest and most lasting experience of wholeness and fulfillment with the least possible responsibility, mastery, decision, or commitment.… I am addicted only when one or the other type of addiction becomes a central mode of life for me around which my personality organizes itself and when every other mode of life becomes subservient to this addiction.[2]

Alcoholics and drug addicts are not the only ones who reach a point where the personality organizes itself around the addiction and every other mode of life becomes subservient to it. Religious addicts do exactly the same thing. Rather than become more filled with the Spirit of God, they become filled with the activities of the church. Rather than become more like Christ, the individuals become more like the church wants them to be or more like they want to be perceived. The personality changes as it revolves around the compulsive behaviors of religiosity. Nothing is more important than the distorted practice of faith, and nothing must deter the addicts from practicing faith in this driven manner. It becomes everything; God and others come in second.

All addicts crave something that will grant them the experience of wholeness; the experience of being significant, of having meaning and purpose; the experience that offers fulfillment for an ever-more-fleeting moment. Those who refuse to risk throwing themselves wholly in the arms of God find it safer to pursue religious activity. The activity of religion becomes a drug, the quick fix of choice. It appears to be so admirable that it makes the addiction more deceptive than most. The ones who rise to the top of the organization are provided with meaning and purpose, or at least the feelings of meaning and purpose for which they long. The ones who cannot find fulfillment at home with their families attain it at the church every time the doors are open.

The true presence of God in one's life doesn't provide an escape from reality and personal responsibility. The presence of God provides a firmer grip on reality and a hope that reality can be faced with all of its pain and sorrow. A caring God provides comfort and offers an interlude for refreshment, restoration, and recreation. These interludes never replace God or others, but are intimately involved with God and his creation.

True faith enriches the believer and those who know that believer; it doesn't form a wall between the believer and God and others. Faith is never an excuse to escape, pack the bags, and head for the hills. Faith without addiction is an invitation to develop a relationship with God and enrich the lives of others through that relationship. But when the practice of faith becomes an addiction, all of this is quickly destroyed.

CHAPTER 5

Religious Addiction: The Progression

In the early stages, it is difficult to identify when religion becomes addiction. It looks so good. As the addicts serve themselves, they appear to serve God. No one guesses that they are playing out dangerous roles that will deprive them of faith and hope. As the addiction progresses, it does so along a predictable course. Like other addictions, it grows in its destruction. The addiction intensifies as the abusive behaviors and toxic beliefs provide less and less relief. Addicts get hooked on the false hopes, mood alteration, and ability to distort reality. Those who fall deepest into the addiction deny reality altogether.

Addiction comes from the desire to escape. Addicts will destroy everything else to be able to escape into the addiction of choice. Nothing else matters. But as relief becomes more difficult to achieve and escape is no longer possible, addicts will turn to other addictions. They will eat, drink, steal, lie, have illicit sexual encounters, or engage in many other compulsive behaviors that also will eventually control them. Everything that can become a form of escape is used to run from feelings and brutal reality.

Toxic-faith systems are all too willing to have religious addicts join, because they are created to take advantage of those who seek escape. So the addicts escape into the accepting arms of those who seek more and more new recruits. They escape into an unreal world where people, ideas, and rules replace a relationship with God. The farther they drift from

God, the more desperate the addicts become, until they are willing to lie, cheat, steal, or kill for the toxic-faith organization or its leader. They become so hooked that they are almost unreachable or unapproachable. Finally they hit bottom and change, go crazy, or kill themselves. Those are the only three options for religious addicts who have progressed through all of the addictive stages.

Religious addiction doesn't occur overnight. It is a long progression that subtly captures every aspect of the addict's life. It rarely begins in adulthood. Most of the time the roots of addiction can be traced back to a difficult childhood. In the early years, seeds of toxic faith are planted that eventually grow into addiction. Those seeds can be anything from rigid parenting to ritual abuse involving children in the occult. Whatever the source of the toxic-faith seeds, the future addict is in search of a god that does not exist, a god created by man, like any other idol created in our own image.

But just as a foundation is laid, it can be ripped up. No one is doomed to a life of religious addiction and toxic faith. If a person is willing to go through the painful process of breaking through the denial and seeing the addictive progression, there is hope for change. The following section traces one woman's addiction from the foundation through the late stages.

THE FOUNDATION

Faye Stanley was an only child born into a dysfunctional family. Although she survived emotionally, her family's problems affected her entire life. She never escaped the destruction caused by her father and the family he created.

Faye's father, a rugged man, worked in a machine shop. He normally came home from his dirty job with grease on his work pants and black grease under his nails. He would enter the house after work, grab a beer, head for the shower, and then spend the rest of the evening walking around the house in his pants and a sleeveless undershirt. Rarely did he shave except on Wednesday nights and Sunday mornings when he would take the family to church. He was mean, uncaring, and miserable to be around. He did not allow his family to display any feelings.

Faye's mother never graduated from high school. An unskilled woman, she would have left her husband long ago, but she had no way of making a living; she feared that she and Faye would starve on the streets. So she stuck by her husband and tolerated his abuse, partly because of her feelings of dependency and partly because of her belief that a woman should not leave her husband. While Faye's mother prayed for her husband to change, Faye and her mother suffered his abuse. He hit his wife and abused his daughter verbally. He projected his feelings of inadequacy onto the two females by demeaning them in all sorts of ways. By the time Faye was ten, she felt totally inadequate and inferior to her friends; she felt especially inferior to men.

Faye developed physically quite early. Her father was the first to notice the shapeliness of her hips and the budding of her breasts. Her menstrual cycle started when she was eleven—and so did her father's sexual abuse. One night a week Faye's mom met with the other women at church. It became a time of terror for Faye as "Daddy's special time" came around each week.

Faye stopped facing life as other little girls did. She crawled into a complex world of fantasy to survive the abuse. She felt as dirty as her father smelled when he came home from work and labored under extreme guilt. For two years the sexual abuse continued until Faye's mother came home early one night to find the two of them in bed. None of them talked about it again, but Faye's mother never left her alone. They lived with the nasty little secret, each one rationalizing it away.

The verbal abuse continued throughout adolescence. Faye was always ridiculed for less than perfect behavior. Her parents expected her to excel above them, which drove her to work hard and make something of herself. She did well, but that was never good enough. Her parents merely affirmed her efforts. They commented about how something could have been better or how someone else appeared to be working harder and doing more. Faye felt driven to meet their needs but never saw how incongruous it was to have two underachieving parents demanding more than she could possibly deliver. The pressure became so intense that

---

Foundations for Religious Addiction

- Abusive parent, often the father. Abuse is physical, emotional, or sexual.
- Child deprived of nurturing. Neither parent meets the basic emotional needs of the child.
- Feelings of alienation. Child feels detached from the family and what is perceived as a perfect world for others.
- Attitudes of perfectionism from imperfect parents. Demanding parents inflict the child with an irrational desire to be perfect and make no mistakes.
- High expectations. The parents are relentless in demanding the child be what they were not and attain what they did not.
- Low affirmation. Although the child exerts tremendous effort, the parents are never satisfied and rarely provide positive feedback.
- Parents' addiction problems. Frequently, one or both parents will be alcoholics or sex addicts, or they will exhibit some other obvious compulsive behavior.
- Absent father. A child of divorce may have little male influence.
- Feelings of being dirty. Abuse and negative attention leave a child feeling guilty and dirty.
- Poor peer relationships. Afraid to share personal reality with others, the child feels cut off emotionally from friends and often seeks destructive relationships.
- Vivid fantasy world. Reality becomes so difficult that the child creates a fantasy world and retreats to it frequently.
- Feelings not shared. The home has provided little freedom to express emotions, and the child never learns how this is done or why it is helpful.

---

shortly after graduation from high school, Faye married and moved out. Within a month she was pregnant.

At the age of twenty-four, Faye Stanley grew fed up with the way her life was going. Her husband left her three years before, and she felt miserable raising her daughter alone. Between her job at the phone company, her housework, and the care of her daughter, she had little time for herself or a social life. She became deeply depressed and wondered if life could ever be any better. At times she thought of suicide—and probably would have done it if not for her daughter.

Faye had few opportunities to fix herself up and feel good about the way she looked. She dressed up only when she went to church, which she rarely did because she felt so alienated. When she married, church people were her best friends; when she divorced, they treated her like she threatened their marriages and images. In her loneliness she became a seething caldron of unresolved emotions. Every area of her life seemed to be drifting out of control.

THE EARLY STAGE

The First Experience

In Faye's darkest moments she cried out for God. She felt a deep emptiness that she knew reflected a lack of spiritual growth. It was hard for her to completely trust her life to God since she had never resolved some of her childhood faith problems. She felt distraught over how a loving God could have allowed her to be abused. It made no sense to her that her father could be so evil and yet continue to be part of the church. Many doubts hampered her spiritual journey. She longed for a relationship with God and with a man. Any attention would be better than the loneliness crippling her.

One day at work a fellow worker saw Faye's depression and provided her with a listening ear. In the middle of expressing her pain and explaining her extreme stress, he asked her to attend a meeting with him. She was more than happy to go. She arranged for a coworker to keep her daughter, and off she went on the closest thing she had had to a date in three years. She felt like a little girl in the presence of the man. She giggled and talked nervously while he silently drove the car to the meeting. She admired a strength and calm about him. She was pleased that they were going to a religious meeting their first time out.

They arrived at a church building with no name on it. As they entered the rear of the building, the people were silently praying. At the front of the church a woman dressed in a colorful robe chanted. As she chanted, she motioned with her hands in small circles, her middle fingers touching her thumbs. No crosses or Bibles could be seen in the church; it looked very stark and plain, unlike any church Faye had attended. The minister asked the followers to raise their heads and slowly open their eyes. The flutist who had been playing during the prayer stopped, and the minister began to speak.

The minister's voice mesmerized Faye. She felt warm listening to the words and sitting next to her friend and the others in the room. The minister instructed the people to hug one another and express something positive about the person being hugged. Faye hugged her friend and told him she admired his calm strength. He then told her that she was very beautiful and obviously a very smart lady whom he was proud to be with. She almost melted at his words. Later she would remember that during the hugging time she began to feel wanted. She felt good, and a wonderful sense of relief came over her. She felt like she belonged, like she had found a home.

When the hugging was over, the minister began to speak about a life free of pain and disappointment. She talked about the incredible faith that must be developed to find the level of living where even the death of a friend is seen as something good. She said that the suffering of the most sincere believer is accompanied by gratification in the midst of the crisis.

Faye saw the evil in her life and how she had been so negative. The woman was speaking right to her, it seemed. It was the first time a minister had communicated so directly to her need. She told her friend she wanted to join the group. He told her it was too early. He encouraged her to return a couple of times before she made a decision. She agreed that she would come back.

Faye was astonished that they didn't ask for money. They encouraged people to come for a month before deciding to give anything. That made a great impression on her. She was tired of the money-hungry ministers always begging her to give more than she had. She felt it was a true sign of their integrity and sincerity that they would not immediately solicit financial contributions. Before she left, there was another hugging session, and the minister gave her a special blessing. She felt great and looked forward to returning.

On the way home, her friend told Faye that she fit in well with the group, that she seemed to be one of them. He said that the minister had spoken to him on the way out and described her desire for Faye to be part of the group. Faye was overwhelmed with his comments and the evening. Before he had spoken to her that day, she was depressed and lonely. Within a short eight hours she felt loved, accepted, and part of something very good. In her glorious feelings of euphoria and belonging, she never stopped to realize that no one had ever mentioned God.

Intoxication of Belonging

The first experience with a toxic-faith system can be intoxicating. One feels a rush in breaking away from isolation and into the arms of several others who appear to care deeply. The leader's attention only enhances the intoxicating effects of finding a place to belong. The hurting person reaches out and needs are met, attention is paid, and the potential addict becomes hooked on the warm fuzzies of the worshipers.

It seems amazing that a person feeling so left out could feel so wanted so quickly. The victim equates sincerity with attention and wants to belong to something that provides such a sense of belonging. If the victim was depressed before hooking up with the toxic-faith believers, relief from the depression is so dramatic that he or she often feels emotionally healed just from being with others who care so much. The person discards rational thought and objective evaluation in order to enjoy the emotional rush that comes from breaking out of isolation and joining others in spiritual pursuit. It feels so good that the victim is convinced it must be right and it must be of God.

As in any addiction, the initial experience alters the mood. A person tries something and feels better. God doesn't have to change or heal the person's emotions; the group's affirmation is the only thing necessary. Although some individuals feel uncomfortable in the presence of other followers, a susceptible victim, full of pain and disappointment, doesn't evaluate the experience or feel threatened. He or she simply feels the warmth, and it feels wonderful. The religious experience, intensified by contact with the religious leader, is just as powerful as a shot of tequila or a hit of cocaine. It radically changes how the person feels, and that person will come back for more.

The susceptible religious addict doesn't realize that every aspect of the first exposure to a toxic-faith system has been premeditated. None of what happens and what is said to that potential follower is accidental. Everything works together so the person is easily manipulated into liking the group and wanting to return. Having physical contact, hearing a special word from the leader, statements that make the victim feel exceptional, no plea for money, and delaying a decision to join—all are tools calculated to win the person into the group. The leader wants control of the victim's life and provides a very addictive initial experience to lock the person into the toxic-faith system.

The initial experience does not have to be in a worship setting; it may occur over the telephone. My wife and I were watching television one day when we flipped the dial to a program featuring a man who was trying to build his following on the air. I wondered aloud to my wife what would happen if I offered to give money to the organization. I called the number and acted as if I were a susceptible victim. I told the woman that I wanted to give money. She astounded me by saying that she did not want a first-time caller giving money. She was there to help and suggested I listen further before giving money.

If I believed the fellow was a wonderful man of God, I would have thought that such a response indicated a sincere heart for ministry. I suspected the man was a fraud, however, because I recognized the organization's strategy as a very clever scheme to hook a person into the toxic-faith system. Every day, susceptible victims enter the early stages of addiction by naively aligning themselves with a toxic-faith system. A remarkable initial experience is the hook.

Growing Attraction

Faye soon received a visit from the group leader. Their time together bonded Faye to the group. Faye thought the leader seemed very spiritual. Faye was told that she, too, possessed many spiritual powers that would be developed as she participated in the group. The leader assured Faye that they were there to meet her needs and she should call on anyone in the group at any time. That this person came to her house made Faye feel very significant. She loved the sense of belonging and the special attention.

Before leaving, the woman spent a few moments with Faye's daughter. She told Faye that she sensed some very deep spiritual rumblings within the center of the child. These needed to be calmed, she said, so she asked Faye to bring the girl to their next gathering for a special time of spiritual cleansing. Faye had worried about her daughter, so she was relieved to discover there would be a cure for her withdrawn and listless behavior.

At the next gathering Faye became hooked. Her daughter was prayed over, hummed with, touched by everyone in the group, and hugged until her clothes wrinkled. Also the group prayed that Faye would find a special man and that her spiritual guide would lead her out of despair and into the life she wanted. By evening's end, she realized she was feeling something she had not felt for some time—namely, hope.

It became obvious that the people weren't worshiping God as she had worshiped him in church while growing up. They rarely mentioned God and they never brought up the name of Christ unless they were referring to a teaching compatible with their beliefs. Because Faye was caught up in the ecstasy of acceptance, their beliefs didn't seem to matter. She had found a home and people who seemed to love her. Those incredible feelings of belonging seemed to matter most. She felt so much affection and love that she really didn't care what they believed. To her, being with the people and sharing in their worship were direct gifts from God. She wanted what they had, and she wanted to be a part of what they did. That they cared equally for her daughter made them all the more attractive.

Faye is like many other addicts from dysfunctional homes. Instead of growing from the dysfunction, she fell back into it. The early experiences left her (and other addicts like her) hurting and distrustful, searching for a way out of the pain. Whatever is convenient and available, anything that will provide hope or just a change in the drudgery of everyday responsibility, can become a source of dependency.

Whenever people with lingering pain and a growing sense of emptiness are not focused completely on God, they are likely to fall for a counterfeit or become dependent on a compulsive behavior for relief. They can be attracted to the most unattractive things, such as prostitutes, anonymous sex shops, smelly bars, and repulsive behaviors. *Anything* becomes attractive as desperation grows.

In the case of religious addiction, the attraction is not so difficult to see. The addict's desperation does not have to reach the same depths. The people look good and smell nice, and all the activity is supposed to be for a glorious purpose. It's no wonder so many individuals can become attracted and then addicted to a toxic-faith system.

Perversion

Religious addicts don't worship God. They use spiritual highs to satiate the need to experience something other than the boredom and pain of their existence. They use activity to distract themselves from their tough reality. They pervert what God intended for good. Seeking faith in God, they become so diverted by the experience and activity that they miss God.

Just as sex is good and draws marriage partners together in a richer relationship, religion can be good and draw people closer to God. But anything that is ordained by God can be perverted into an experience of ecstasy used only for relief. Both the act of sex and the worship of God can be perverted into the worship of self. Relief of the painful self becomes the entire focus of the endeavor.

The addict's neediness and brokenness in coming from a dysfunctional family makes perversion possible in the worship of God and the practice of religion. The foundation of dysfunction allows for the distortion of something good into something negative, self-centered, and exploitative. The severe dependency needs of the addict turn faith into a practice of rituals, beliefs, and doctrine as a way to make life tolerable. The intended focus of real faith is distorted and perverted, lost in the delusional reality that the religion drug can provide. The victim continues to practice the rituals of the religion and falls out of love with God and in love with the compulsion. The perverted faith looks good and feels good, but it is a counterfeit of a true love for and faith in God.

Transition from God

The religious addict begins a gradual transition away from God. Church attendance is no longer based on the need to know God; the addict attends church to feel significant and secure. Prayers are no longer ways of communicating with God; the addict prays to have an experience as a person of God and takes pride in being able to talk of the hours spent in prayer. He or she uses the church to avoid life rather than to find the strength and guidance to encounter all that life has to offer, good or bad. What could have been a place to find shelter from the storms of life becomes a place where the religious addict "sets up camp" to hide from life. Hiding there takes priority over worshiping God.

The addict sacrifices the family and family relationships for church work completed in the name of God. Attendance at church becomes excessive to the point of obsession. Every spare moment is devoted to a church-related activity. Other family members become concerned because when they are together, the addict is at church; the noble cause of serving on committees is not to be questioned. As the intimacy needed to maintain significant family relationships is sacrificed, faith grows ever more toxic. Each family member starts to take a separate path away from the religious addict. Unfortunately, those paths often lead away from God.

Eventually, the addict focuses back on self and away from God and others. While the addict initially judges himself harshly and wishes he could be as good as the rest of the world, as his compulsive nature develops, he starts to judge others and defend himself. Rather than recognize the personal areas that need work, the addict refuses to change and becomes increasingly locked into the behaviors that maintain the religious addiction. The addict loses all humility; he or she no longer embraces the imperfections of humanity or acknowledges any personal shortcomings. Living in denial and self-justification makes life without God easy, and the addict's rapid downward slide accelerates.

False faith becomes an excuse to hurt others. Scripture is used as a weapon. The addict quotes it to justify and rationalize her problems while she contorts it to shame, dismiss, and disqualify others. The "us versus them" mentality of the toxic-faith leader becomes a part of the addict's mentality. As the dependency on the toxic faith grows, the addict becomes more hostile and isolated. A new family replaces the old one. The new family of believers does not confront and allows the addict to live according to her delusions. The old one becomes too reality-based to tolerate.

The addict's entire perspective on life changes. Simplistic answers replace explorations of the many dimensions of a problem. The difficulty of a true walk of faith is replaced with the magical belief that all is well for the faithful. Pleasing the other faithful takes priority over pleasing God. The addict is forced to conform to the other toxic-faith believers; pressure mounts to not disappoint those who are the new source of love and encouragement. True faith is destroyed as a toxic faith grows.

The initial stage of religious addiction is difficult to spot. Many who are involved in the same activities as religious addicts are involved in a real faith, but their motives and foundations are different. Many faithful followers would be wrongly labeled first-stage religious addicts; many addicts would be considered faithful followers of God. Only in the second stage does the differentiation become marked.

Characteristics of the Early Stage of Religious Addiction

- Extreme stress. Increased stress impairs judgment and obscures warning signs of toxic faith.
- Repeated disappointments. Feelings that nothing works out right lead a potential addict to seek quick-fix solutions to lost expectations.
- Miserable existence. The addict has turned in many directions for hope and found none.
- Feelings of insignificance. The addict starts to believe life does not matter and there is no productive part to be played in it.
- Spiritual search initiated. Out of despair the addict seeks spiritual answers as a last resort.
- Loneliness. Any attention from any source would be welcomed.
- Hoping for someone to solve misery. Solving the problems seems too difficult; there is a need to be rescued.
- Increasing doubts about God. Wondering if God cares or if God is real, he or she is more vulnerable to variations of traditional faith.
- Increasing dependency on others. Association with others allows for delusional thoughts and existence in an unreal world.
- Feelings of guilt. Nothing can be done to overcome powerful guilt feelings.
- Feelings of insecurity. A terrible disaster seems to be lurking, and everything seems to be a potential sign of doom.
- Geographic cures. In an attempt to solve problems, the addict believes a fresh start will make life better—but discovers it has further complicated the problems.
- Loss of other interests. Family, friends, and other activities are replaced with the compulsive activities surrounding the practice of toxic faith.
- Abandonment by friends and family. Associates become so irritated by obnoxious behavior that they no longer spend time with the religious addict.
- Unwillingness to discuss problems. The individual becomes unapproachable about increasingly out-of-control behavior.

- One-sided sermons. Edicts, scriptures, and judgments so fill the dialogue with the person that all conversations cease.
- Faith attached to a person. A comforting person becomes the link to toxic faith.
- Intoxicating affiliation. First experiences in the new toxic-faith group produce immediate mood alteration.
- Growing attraction. Every new meeting, person, and experience increases the attraction to the toxic-faith group.
- Heavy church attendance. Attendance becomes a means of avoidance and a way to be part of the group with little relationship with God.
- Conformity with other addicts. The person starts to look, dress, and talk like others in the group.
- Lack of intimate relationships. Intimacy with friends and family is sacrificed for the sake of religion.
- Growing denial and self-justification. The person becomes blind to problems and justifies behavior.
- Scripture as a weapon. Verses are quoted to judge others and justify self.

THE MIDDLE STAGE

Complete Attachment

It wasn't long until Faye's growing attraction turned to complete attachment. She deeply immersed herself in the group. Their identity was her identity. She belonged and felt valuable and significant. She wanted to be the strongest member possible, so she talked about her religious experience at every opportunity, gathered faithfully with the others, and read books that explained how to develop spiritual powers.

She would do anything for the group. That included giving about 30 percent of her salary to the leader. Upon receiving every paycheck, she first wrote out a check to the group. Sometimes her daughter had no milk for her cereal. Sometimes they had to eat beans every possible way beans could be eaten. She didn't think it was too much to give, even though the leader drove an expensive foreign car. Some months, if the group needed more money, Faye went beyond the usual 30 percent. She was so attached to the group that she almost felt it was a commune where everyone should share everything. Her attachment to the group was complete.

Faye stopped all relationships with anyone outside the group. She didn't trust people who didn't hold her views and cut herself off from them. The only outsiders she spent time with were the ones she tried to recruit into the group. She so adopted the philosophies she learned and the practice of faith with the group that she burned with desire to bring others into the group. She saw every person she met as a potential member. She would listen to an individual, searching for a point of need she could address. Once she found it, she promised her group would meet it. Many were turned off by her pushiness, but others were attracted to the group because Faye was so strong in her beliefs and association with the other members.

Religious Self-Medication

Addiction usually begins from a desire to self-medicate pain and suffering and to remove the weight of being a responsible person. Where meaning, purpose, and spiritual strength are lacking, the developing addict will find some means to drug the pain and emptiness. Religious experience becomes the source of medication. The repeated search for an ecstatic experience becomes a quest, much like the heroin addict looking to score a new supply of drugs. Sometimes it is successful, sometimes not. When it isn't successful, the hunt for ecstasy continues.

Religious addicts work themselves up into a frenzy to experience a religious catharsis. They swoon, fall over, scream, yell, faint, jump up and down, and do anything that will pump adrenaline through the blood. They learn how to induce the euphoric rush. What looks to be a supernatural encounter with God is nothing but a chemical reaction; it's not as powerful as heroin, but it's just as destructive. Addicts search for the high—not for God. They feel inadequate and incomplete whenever they walk away from a gathering or service in which they did not have an incredible rush.

All of the pent-up hurt and depression must find a source of release. Anyone could sex it out, drink it out, or gamble it out on a temporary basis. Religious addicts choose to ritual it out. Each session of worship repeats the behaviors that led to the previous emotional catharsis. If no catharsis occurs, the emotions remain imprisoned and the addict continues to seek a source of release. Anger and rage may result from the unexpressed emotions. The deluded addicts function at such an unemotional level that they are unable to see they are out of control and their emotions are about to self-destruct. If the service or worship experience does not manufacture the fix, religious addicts may look elsewhere to find it. This leads to the development of other addictions alongside the religious one.

Dual Addictions

Religious addicts cannot find relief from a religious source every time. Because they become frustrated that they are not experiencing the same intensity as they did in the early days of their faith, they turn to other sources to supplement the addiction of choice. Some drink and become dependent on secret times of drunkenness; these binges usually follow some of the most intense worship times. Most commonly, however, religious addicts become food junkies. They love sugar rushes and they adore the hours they take up eating everything they can find. The leader of the group, who is often overweight, never speaks against overeating. Too many people would feel abandoned and potentially not return to the church. The leader will yell and scream against alcoholics, but he or she will never insinuate that someone is committing the sin of gluttony.

Sexual sins and sexual addictions also can surface as the intensity of the religious experience weakens. Secret and shameful sexual experiences produce a high similar to religious ecstasy. The tightly wrapped addict, afraid to break any of the organization's rules, is afraid to admit frailties and desires that would be labeled unholy. Unexpressed lust is coupled with the intense need for relief. The need for relief lands the addict in the arms of the first person willing to participate in meeting his or her needs. The forbidden sins of faith saturate the body with mood-altering substances as the adulterer is lost to a fantasy world of secret sex and irresponsibility. Many are hurt by it and no one understands how such a dedicated person could commit such an offensive act.

Recruiting Others to the Faith

In the middle stage, the religious addict is destined to recruit as many individuals to the group as possible. A day without an attempt to attract someone into the group is a wasted day.

Now, the true Christian also shares his or her faith in God with others. A person with the gift of evangelism loves to talk with others about faith. But the religious addict is more interested in sharing the *experience.* Each new person who is willing to share the experience becomes a reassurance that the addict is doing the right thing. Each new recruit affirms the decision to affiliate with the group and becomes a motivation to work even harder. The addict is compelled to tell others of the pleasure that comes from the group, its leader, and the practice of the faith.

Anyone refusing to participate is shamed, ridiculed, and labeled as ungodly. The addict's beliefs must be reinforced; anyone rejecting those beliefs must be discounted. The more entrenched the person becomes in the system, the bigger the threat when he or she is rebuffed. Anyone who declares why the group is not practicing true faith must be swiftly rejected. Each rejection, interpreted as rejection by God, produces tremendous pain and insecurity. It motivates the addict to try harder, talk to more people, and grow spiritually so people will be attracted to the group.

All-Encompassing Toxic Faith

During the middle stage of religious addiction, dependency on religion encompasses every aspect of the toxic believer's life. Like a junkie whose life is consumed with his next score, the religious addict is obsessed with the next crusade, worship service, street-witnessing extravaganza, or whatever the ritual that sets up the addict's next religious high.

Addicts band together and get high by acting righteous and above all others. They inflate their feelings by imagining that they merit God's acceptance. They continue their high by endeavoring to please others so that they look superior to anyone who observes their acts of sacrifice.

Everything must involve the practice of faith. Every trip to the grocery store is an act of faith and an opportunity to recruit others. A walk down the street can result in a scriptural shouting match that the addict believes will win others to God. Friends are in the group, or they are not friends. Family members are supportive, or they are avoided. Social events must involve people of the faith.

Anyone outside the group of believers is viewed as contaminated by the world and unfit for interaction. Nothing exists outside the realm of other faithful followers who have forsaken all earthly ties in their attempts to please God. They have become so focused on their concept of heavenly good, their world is so saturated with their toxic faith that they are of no use to anyone outside their group.

The toxic faith becomes a ritual of sacrifice that reaches into the pockets and the relationships of toxic believers. Religious addicts give sacrificially to merit the "blessings of God." They sacrifice their time, their finances, and their intimate or significant relationships to please their God. They make whatever sacrifice is necessary to obtain their fix, like a cocaine addict who once used the drug out of desire but now is forced to spend money earmarked to meet the family's basic needs. Religious addicts will spend vacation savings, retirement savings, Social Security checks, grocery money, or anything available to gain favor from the leader of the group. Nothing is so sacred that it cannot be devoured by the all-encompassing practice of toxic faith.

Special Gifts

The emergence of special gifts may become the means by which the religious addict evaluates the quality of his or her relationship with God. When special talents are claimed, such as the ability to predict the future, the addict wins the approbation of other followers and gains prestige within the group. The addict becomes more and more dependent on exercising the gift in public to achieve the mood alteration necessary to feel loved and accepted.

All Christians have very real spiritual gifts to minister to others. Some have the gift of compassion, which is a supernatural ability to reach out to others, to make them feel accepted, and to meet their needs. Others might have the gift of teaching, making it easy for God's Word to be absorbed into the hearts of students. These spiritual gifts differ from the counterfeits of self-manufactured talents used to exploit others and elevate self-importance. And even genuine spiritual gifts can be perverted and exploited. Some religious addicts become so focused on the gift that they forget about God, the Giver of all gifts. They use their gifts to rise to the top of the organization, claiming to be specially anointed by God. But true spiritual gifts are exercised in humility for the service of the body. They are never used for self-elevation.

Increased Pressure

With increased involvement in toxic religion comes the added pressure of responsibility. The honeymoon eventually ends, and the religious addict becomes aware of the demands of the leader. The greater the demands, the more compelled the addict is to perform. As the leader holds the follower accountable, the religious addict responds with more intense effort and the desire to please. The stakes rise; the addict is asked to sacrifice self-identity, family, and what is known to be right and wrong. The leader's views are promoted in place of right and wrong. But the addict is so saturated with toxic faith, nothing seems unreasonable. The more that is asked, the more that is given. The goal is not to please God, but to please the leader.

What once brought relief from the pressures of life is now needed for survival. Without the group and its rules, the addict fears being set adrift. The religious addiction has become a trap not easily sprung. What once was an experience of liberation now enslaves.

Attendance and involvement used to bring a sense of belonging; now absence or lack of involvement bring tremendous feelings of guilt. The addict obsessively and compulsively defends against any sense of not measuring up. Hope becomes less of a prospect than ever imagined. The addiction provides less relief than before. The addict begins to act out; the behavior becomes more bizarre and ritualized to maintain the illusion of hope.

Deepening Denial

By the time religious addicts reach the middle stage of the progression, they have created their own world with their own rules and are unwilling to be with anyone who does not abide by those rules. They insulate themselves from those who challenge their toxic-faith system. Their denial of reality and their problems deepen as they hang on to their toxic faith. They lock into the system and their beliefs and go through the motions, waiting for a major spiritual breakthrough.

They want God to perform a miracle, just for them, to prove he is real. Their faith has died, and they cannot go on without some type of tangible evidence. In their denial, they claim that every coincidence is a miracle of God. They claim healing for problems that never existed. If these proofs do not come immediately, they wait. Some religious addicts have sat atop a hillside for months waiting for the Second Coming. The predicted date passes, but they stay put, denying that their date was wrong. Rather than come down the hill and rejoin society, they live in the protection of their denial and their false hopes. They become like compulsive gamblers waiting for the long shot to come in. Neither gamblers nor religious addicts see the price they are paying for their denial and magical thinking.

As the denial deepens, addicts eliminate all doubts about their faith and no longer question the validity of anything within the practice of their faith. They grow blind to the truth. Everything else is questioned in light of the toxic faith. Personal interpretation of Scripture becomes the standard, and all judgments are based on those self-conceived interpretations and standards. All problems are flatly denied. Denial prevents discussion on any issue that might crack the facade of perfection. Others' problems are addressed with pat answers and little concern. The clock of despair ticks swiftly, bringing addicts closer each day to the point when financial problems, illness, or emotional distress can no longer be denied.

The middle stage of religious addiction is full of activity and diversions from God. The addict is still able to function, believing the toxic faith is the real thing. But God is lost, and there is little chance of finding him until the addict hits bottom in the last stage of religious addiction.

Characteristics of the Middle Stage of Religious Addiction

- Immersed in the system. The person becomes an active member, iden- tifying completely with the group.
- Knows propaganda of the group. Many pieces from the leader's writ- ings are readily quoted.
- Outspoken. Little regard is shown for offensive comments made in the name of faith.
- Giving unusual amounts of money. Basic needs of the family are sacri- ficed to have gifts noticed by the organization and to win favor.
- Relates to few people outside the group. Relationships are limited to other toxic-faith believers.
- Recruitment of others. Motivated to recruit others to the toxic faith, the addict does not attempt to bring others closer to God.
- Self-medication. The religious experience becomes an intoxicating high that medicates the addict's pain. Each new day is a search for a new religious high.
- Disappointed if ecstasy does not occur. Longing for the emotional catharsis that brings relief, the addict searches for other forms of relief when the toxic faith does not produce it.
- Dual addictions. Other addictions develop, such as eating, drinking, and having illicit sexual encounters, as the pleasure from religious ecstasy wears off.
- Difficult to handle rejection. Those refusing to join the group are dis- counted to overcome the feelings of rejection.
- All-encompassing practice of faith. Every area of the addict's life is affected by the toxic faith.
- Always searching for ways to further the faith. Every activity is used as a means to talk about the group and its beliefs.
- Discovery and use of special gifts. Self-manufactured and authentic spiritual gifts are used to exploit and manipulate.
- Claims of special anointing. The addict believes God has provided a more unique mission and more unique gifts than the less faithful have.
- Increased pressure. The drive to perform and please does not stop.

- Involvement for survival. The addict becomes trapped in the system with no choice but to conform or risk mental upheaval. The addict is totally dependent on the system for survival.
- Deepening denial. Unable to see the price being paid for the magical thinking, the addict refuses to question the reality of the faith.

The Late Stage

After Faye reached the last stage of her addiction, it did not take long for her to hit bottom. She gave all of her savings to the group and lived from paycheck to paycheck. She believed she was trusting in God to provide for her and her daughter. But problems came and destroyed her.

First, problems developed at work. No one at work could stand to be around her since all she did was rant and rave about her group. And when her employer got in a bind, she was unavailable because she was attending a group gathering. Finally she was fired after an argument with her supervisor about religion ended in a shouting match.

Faye felt good about being fired—the price she had to pay for her faith. She loved playing the martyr. She lived on her severance money for two weeks, then she was broke. That was when her daughter became ill with a kidney disease. With no money for a doctor, and her child's fever raging, Faye called the leader of her group to ask for advice. The leader told her to bring her daughter to the gathering that night so they could pray for her. Faye took her daughter there and everyone prayed and touched her, but the little girl did not get better. They told her to have faith and God would take care of the girl.

As hope for a miracle passed, Faye watched her daughter drift in and out of consciousness. She questioned whether to trust the group. She questioned their motives. She realized she had no money because of the group. Her thoughts of doubt finally became strong enough to motivate her to take the girl to the county hospital. When she arrived, the girl was unconscious. The doctors hooked her up to a dialysis machine, but by noon the next day the girl was dead.

Faye became hysterical. God had failed her; the group had led her the wrong way; now her daughter was dead. Her family knew the reason for the tragedy was that she did not take the girl to the doctor in time. Faye felt humiliated, depressed, and ashamed. Her family tried to console her, but she did not want to be with them. She gathered enough strength to hold a funeral for her child. Each person in attendance was someone who had disappointed her in some way. She felt hopeless and alienated from the world. When the last shovel of dirt covered her daughter's grave, she drove home, sobbing as she made her way back to where the memories of her little girl lived.

At the house, a calm came over her. She regained her poise and her tears dried up. She felt a new peace about what had happened. It didn't matter what the others thought of her. It was irrelevant that the group had been a farce. She didn't care that they took her money. All that mattered to her was her little girl and being near her.

Faye cleaned up the house, took a bath, and prepared for bed. Before entering the bedroom, she went to the medicine cabinet and took down a bottle of sleeping pills that had been stored there for over a year. Faye went to the kitchen, poured a glass of water, and swallowed all the pills. She calmly walked to the bedroom, wrote a note to those who would find her, said her prayers, lay down, and never woke up again.

And so Faye became another tragic victim of toxic faith and religious addiction.

Religion Stops Working

Eventually toxic faith stops working for all religious addicts, just as it did for Faye. When religious addicts reach the last stage of the progression, the addiction consumes them and they feel isolated from anyone who is not part of the toxic-faith system. Anyone not buying into the delusions of the addicts is considered weak in faith or at times even the enemy. The enemy can include family members. No one is allowed into the private world of toxic believers; only those who are also consumed by the addiction are trusted. Addicts will not listen to reason, and they base all of their decisions on what the toxic-faith leader says or what they believe God has told them. Eventually the isolation and the false beliefs create a crisis that cannot be overcome by more denial.

Life does not feel good in the last stage of addiction. All is not fun and every religious experience is not enjoyable. The highs still come, but they are fewer and shorter. The less relief that comes from them, the more the addicts rely on other addictions. When the religious highs diminish, feelings of despair and distress replace them.

Addicts therefore try harder in hopes of working up relief. When relief does not come, they feel abandoned by God and the original guilt and pain they tried to cover begins to resurface. They feel lost and hopeless, abandoned by the group because the image of perfection is destroyed by their obvious despair. The religion in which they invested so much stops working, and they don't know where to turn.

It is never easy to act like everything is working when it is so badly disintegrating. The weight and burden of continually acting as if all is well compound the stress and disappointment. Under the strain, the addict experiences suspiciousness, distrustfulness, confusion, and psychological and emotional deterioration. Feeling like a victim, feeling persecuted and hopeless, the addict works to prove that the blessings will come. When they do not, the addict is convinced that the role of martyr is a good one to replace the role of superior faith warrior.

Resentment and Anger

Resentment and anger increase as nothing turns out as expected, and every day becomes a bigger disappointment than the day before. If the person has preached against a sin that continues to surface, the sermons fill up with bitterness and resentment. Growing feelings of inferiority produce anger toward others who appear to have their lives well ordered. No one is available to share these feelings with because the group rejects any toxic believer who doesn't appear to have a strong faith. This intensifies the emotions. Rage often overpowers the rational thoughts of the addict, and everyone nearby is put on the defensive.

Anger and rage are the first signs that toxic beliefs are starting to fall apart. When anger emerges, the addict can no longer fool others with a look of false peace or serenity. There are problems and they are obvious. At the root of the anger is disappointment that the toxic-faith leaders, beliefs, and system did not deliver. Relief did not come. Addicts are enraged by how they look to the rest of the world and that now reality must be dealt with, unprotected by delusional thinking.

Addicts are angry with themselves but throw their anger at everyone else. Problems are attributed to the devil, unbelievers, sin, lack of faith, lust, greed, and anything else that can be preached against those outside the faith. Although the dogmatic beliefs start to falter, still they are preached to others more dogmatically than ever before.

The angry addicts become so miserable to be around that most choose not to associate with them. This increases the pain, heightens the isolation, and moves the individuals closer to despair. As long as the anger continues, hope for change continues with it.

Projection

With everything falling apart, someone must be blamed. The addict will not accept responsibility, so a scapegoat must be found. That scapegoat will bear all of the anger and disappointment. The pain will be projected onto that person or institution as if that entity were the cause of the addict's problems. Every consequence of the compulsive religious behavior is depersonalized and considered to be the result of someone else's actions. If a person didn't cause the trauma, it must be sin, the spirit of lust, or the world. Anything other than self becomes a target of the rage and blame.

If addicts recognize a need for change, it will be in the area of behavior, not the heart. They will try to do things differently rather than change any thoughts or beliefs. By identifying the problem as a behavior, such as lack of prayer, addicts hold on to the toxic faith until the very end. They will try everything to produce the spectacular desired result. They become so grandiose about their faith that they see no need for a change in heart, maturity, or development of character. Since addicts believe they possess the truth, they are convinced that different behavior will isolate them from whatever is the source of their difficulties.

Crumbling World

When the world starts to crumble around addicts, they respond with disappointment, anger, rage, and more determined effort. Troubles come from many sources, and each one affirms that the faith system will not come through for them. It could be financial collapse that begins the fast slide toward bottom. Some have contributed and pledged so much to the group that they bankrupt themselves. Some sign notes, use their homes as collateral, and then give up their homes when the truth is known about the shady dealings of the ministry.

As the toxic world becomes more confusing, the addict searches out ways to change behaviors to fix the problem. Often too much time is spent away from work. Needed overtime is turned down so that compulsive religious activity can be continued. Because work can be converted into a time of sharing his toxic beliefs, a car salesman will witness rather than sell cars, or a hairdresser will talk about the faith so much that no one returns for hair care. This, along with alienating other employees with irritating sermons, may cause job loss and financial disaster.

Home life starts to crumble as the finances do. The angry addict becomes so caught up in "God's work" that all family responsibilities are neglected. Relaxing with the family or taking a child to Little League or ballet class stops so that the religious disaster can be worked out. This situation produces fertile soil for affairs and often leads to divorce. After living with an addict for years, the family finally becomes fed up and refuses to exist with the addict anymore.

Faith also starts to crumble. The addict, no longer able to maintain the denial, slips into brief moments of understanding. Glimpses of reality briefly enter the addict's mind, but they are quickly brushed aside with a frenzy of activity. The thoughts produce tremendous feelings of guilt, confusion, and pain. Still, the addict starts to realize that rules have been abusively enforced and that the rigid doctrines of the group have hurt, not helped, people.

Thus disillusioned, addicts begin to doubt. For the first time since becoming involved with toxic faith, they doubt themselves, their beliefs, and the existence of God. They doubt the sincerity of the leaders they follow. Confusion overwhelms them. Unable to trust their perceptions and unwilling to trust anyone else, they lapse into deeper and deeper depression. They realize they are powerless to control their lives.

Hitting Bottom

At the end of the progression lies desperation so intense that it forces change. Mental and emotional breakdowns are common among religious addicts. Some attempt to take their lives. Some take the lives of others and then their own. They do desperate things because their minds can't handle the incongruity between their beliefs and what they know to be real. They feel betrayed by God and the world, and they don't care who they hurt as long as they don't have to suffer further humiliation. Many see the only way to guarantee this is to die or be admitted to an institution.

In the end, the presence of a false god denies the addicts what they desperately need: a loving relationship with a loving God. Unfortunately, when they finally put down their work, performance rituals, and need for perfection, there often remains no motivation to seek the true God who could heal their broken hearts.

HOPE FOR CHANGE

The ultimate stage for religious addicts is recovery. People who have released themselves from the trap of addiction will find a loving God ready to receive them. They will also find loving people in traditional churches ready to forgive them and invite them back into the fold. The end of religious addiction does not have to be a disaster. It can mean returning to a relationship with a very patient God.

God allows us to become totally dependent on ourselves. He allows us to become totally dependent on other things, such as chemicals and rituals. He even allows us to be dependent on religion that leaves him out. He will let us exhaust all of our resources and explore every area of dependency outside his plan for each life. While we try to live every way except his way, he continues to wait.

No religious addict has wandered so far that there is no way back to this loving, patient God. One step toward a godly dependency is all it takes.

Characteristics of the Late Stage of Religious Addiction

- Despair. The addict begins to sense hopelessness because the toxic faith is not producing the desired results.
- Erratic behavior. Knowing something is wrong and refusing to change beliefs, the addict attempts to fix the problem by changing behavior rather than the heart.
- Resentment and anger. As the addict's world falls apart, everyone else is to blame, and everyone else is a source of rage.
- Obsession with beliefs. Continually wondering what is wrong with the faith, the addict questions, ponders, and thinks through each belief until the addict is completely unable to concentrate.
- Deep depression. Collapse of beliefs leads to the inability to function.
- Physical deterioration. Depression and stress take their toll on the body, resulting in fatigue, lack of appetite, and medical complications.
- Stagnation. Once faith is lost, all else seems lost, and the addict is unable to do anything but obsessively ponder past mistakes.
- Searching for another fix. Other addictions such as food, drugs, and sex intensify as the addict seeks relief from other sources.
- Fear. Experiencing major insecurity, the addict becomes afraid of everyone, seeing each person as a threat. The addict is afraid to continue in the toxic-faith system and afraid to get out.
- Financial collapse. Work-related problems and financial irresponsibility often result in financial collapse.

- Family deterioration. Stress and distrust destroys family relationships, resulting in affairs and divorce.
- Hitting bottom. Running out of self-will and manipulation, the addict must give up the addiction and turn to God.

CHAPTER 6

Ten Characteristics of a Toxic-Faith System

It is not hard to tell a healthy faith system from a toxic one. The toxic-faith system stands out with its obsessive people who victimize family members and destroy their own faith in God. The following comes from a journal of one who knows toxic faith from personal experience. Nothing worked for this young man until he worked out his faith.

> I accepted Jesus Christ as my Lord and Savior in April of 1974. I was sixteen and a sophomore in high school. Being raised in the Church I knew all the stories, but I did not know Jesus personally. A Sunday afternoon in the park changed all that. Then the fun really began.
>
> My parents were busy looking for a "deeper teaching," not a closer walk. This led them to a cult church. Like all cults it had some good, right-on Bible teachings. It also had even more interpretative twists, false teachings, and power-abusive leaders. There was even a seasonal prophet. By that I mean "HIS" prophecies always had something to do with what time of year it was. Easter had a bunny, Thanksgiving had a turkey, Christmas had a tree, etc.
>
> Most of all the decisions for the church and congregation were made at the weekly men's meeting. This was great if you were a man. Women did not enjoy many liberties, if any at all. They were constantly told to just submit and obey without question.
>
> The pastor, or shepherd as he was called, had final say in

everything in the lives of his flock, whether to buy a house, take a vacation, get married, and even whom to marry. Two of the women in the church were given permission to marry. One to her boyfriend, who was a member of the church, and the other one to an appointed gentleman in the church who had a small boy but had no wife to help raise him. Many people sold everything they had and gave it to the church. Then they would share housing with others in the church. My parents would later do this and live with the shepherd and his family. This eventually led to their leaving the church. It's one thing to go to church with somebody; it's another to live with them.

My spirit told me that this was wrong, yet I could not prove it when biblically challenged. It's sad that we sometimes need to be challenged before we start to read the Bible. But for me it was God taking a bad situation and making it good. People from the church (usually men) started stopping by the house unexpectedly with a word of correction for me. Everything I said or did was questioned and analyzed by my parents or their friends. I started asking God questions. Why me? What did I do to deserve this? Am I out of the will of God? God does not want his children fighting, does he? As I became more familiar with the Bible I was able to answer many of my parents and their friends' questions or statements with what was truly in the Bible and show them where it was in the Bible. I soon became known as the black sheep of the family. Unfortunately, my mother told many a tall tale about what was really going on in our house to my grandparents and other relatives. She rationalized that they didn't have as deep a walk as she had, therefore they wouldn't understand.

Discipline was many times handled at the men's meeting. The child offender would have to pull his or her pants down and be spanked with two male witnesses present. This was very upsetting to the young girl teenagers of the group. Fortunately, my younger sister and I were never disciplined in this manner. Being in our late teens and very strong-willed (we would not submit), we were just verbally reprimanded or grounded.

One month before I was to turn eighteen, I had a best friend chosen for me. It was the seasonal prophet. I was also informed that I was no longer allowed to date until I was eighteen. I could not date girls except those in the church, and I could not date them until I became a member of the church. Dating was also something the girls had no control over. You see, if a boy wanted to take out a girl, he didn't ask her. He asked her father. The girl had no choice.

Upon my eighteenth birthday I was given three choices:

1. Join the church, and live at home.

2. Move out and live on my own.

3. Move into the single men's home.

I had felt this coming on, so I had already accelerated my studies to graduate early from high school. This was not easy because I had to work thirty hours a week from the time I turned sixteen to pay for my own rent, gas, and car insurance. Also, 25 percent of my income went to the church. This was not by my choice but by my parents. I never complain now about giving 10 percent.

Two days after my eighteenth birthday I moved out of my parents' home with the help of four friends. My parents had gone out to a meeting, making this the most opportune time to leave without a fight. The next morning, though, I got my fight. My father had come to the grocery store where I worked. Before I clocked in he asked me if I would step outside so we could talk in private. We got outside and as I turned around he "sucker punched" me. Being sixty pounds heavier and four inches taller, he was able to knock me down with one punch. He then informed me that they (mom and dad) had given my soul over to the devil for the cleansing of my spirit and that I would be dead in six months. I did agree to talk with one of the elders from my parents' church. At the time, he was living in a trailer up on a nearby mountain. I prayed the whole way up that if I weren't sure of discipleship being right or wrong, that I would just drive off that mountain. Not a real healthy thought.

Well, I did go into that meeting all prayed up (the only way I knew to get some good answers). After three and one-half hours I was sure God was real. I looked at the elder and saw right through him. In fact, I was able to share with him about our loving God, the one we can call Father. I left rejoicing. Later, when my parents left the church, one of their friends informed me that the purpose of that meeting was to pluck my eyes out. They felt my eyes were causing me to sin. It pays to go into battle with your armor on!

Over the next eight months I lived with friends and other members of my family. I thought about joining the military, but I felt I was needed more as a witness to my parents than in a barracks somewhere else.

Then just before Christmas my parents left the church. I wish I could say that we all lived happily ever after, but I cannot. Not yet, anyway. My dad and uncle no longer talk to each other. In fact, my uncle won't even mention God now unless he is swearing. My parents feel that I deserted them when I left home, so they have very little to do with me or my family. I have tried to reconcile, but they do not wish to talk about it. But who knows, prayer does and will change things.

What a sad account of an actual experience with toxic faith. Too few understand that people are being exploited in this way every day. Religious addiction develops in a toxic-faith system and flourishes where other addicts build the system. Without the system that feeds into and off the addiction, the addiction would die. Every toxic system has identifiable characteristics that set it apart from healthy systems. These characteristics allow the individuals stuck in the system to play out their distinct roles in a predictable manner.

The characteristics of a toxic-faith system differentiate it from systems, churches, and ministries committed to growing people in faith and developing their relationship with God. Knowing the characteristics of a toxic system can be helpful in evaluating whether a ministry is poisonous or pure, addictive or freeing. Since we are all prone to addiction, it can also aid us in staying on track or bringing us back into balance.

CLAIMS ABOUT "SPECIAL" CHARACTER, ABILITIES, OR KNOWLEDGE

Toxic Characteristic #1: *The members of the toxic-faith system claim their character, abilities, or knowledge make them "special" in some way.*

Members of toxic-faith systems reach a point in their addictive progression where they make claims about themselves to set themselves apart from others. They may attempt to support these claims with Scripture. Each time Scripture is used, some followers are more motivated to serve, feeling God's special hand on the ministry and the people involved with it.

Some of the most clever deceivers in history have used Scripture to foster their toxic faith. Satan had no problems in quoting Scripture to strengthen his temptations of Christ. Matthew wrote about the incident as follows:

> Then the devil took Him up into the holy city, set Him on the pinnacle of the temple, and said to Him, "If You are the Son of God, throw Yourself down. For it is written: 'He shall give His angels charge concerning you,' and, 'In their hands they shall bear you up, lest you dash your foot against a stone.'" (Matthew 4:5-6)

Satan attempted to control Christ, manipulate him, and motivate him to do something outside the will of God. He used scriptures from the Old Testament as tools for evil. The good guys are not the only ones who use Scripture!

One pastor asserted his "specialness" by quoting the book of Revelation, where John writes:

> To the angel of the church of Ephesus write,
> "These things says He who holds the seven stars in His right hand, who walks in the midst of the seven golden lampstands." (Revelation 2:1)

Now, follow this reasoning: This pastor asserted that the angel mentioned in this quotation was the pastor at the church of Ephesus. Because he, too, pastored a church, the Lord also spoke directly to him, much like he did to the pastor (or angel) at the church of Ephesus. And so, since God spoke to the pastor at the church at Ephesus in order for him to pass on God's word to the people, God likewise spoke to him to communicate to the people of his church. Thus, he justified his special communication link with God.

This type of claim concerning divine direction is very dangerous. It places the leader above all others. Challenging the authority or accuracy of the leader is equated with challenging the very Word of God. How could anyone disagree with a leader who says he has a direct link with God? Who would want to be pitted against the Word of God? The leader knows this and uses it as a clever manipulation of the "ignorant" followers who believe in the sincerity of their toxic leader. When members of that organization challenge the motives or actions of the leader or persecutor, they are put off with statements like, "I was only doing what God asked me to do." For those under that type of manipulation, there is no way to challenge the persecutor's position. They either agree and obey or suffer the consequences. And religious addicts are more than eager to agree and obey.

The Claim of a Special Anointing or Calling

One terribly poisonous misconception claims that God has a special calling only for certain people and everyone else needs to find something "unspecial" to do. According to the misconception, the businessperson who tries to do God's will on the job is not as special as the leader of a church.

This premise contradicts the teaching that God has a special plan for every person's life. In a healthy church, a pastor will encourage individuals to minister as they discover talents and gifts that can be used in serving God. The minister of pure faith will encourage everyone to consider themselves special in the eyes of God. Each person has a very special place of service designed by God, and each person should be encouraged to find it.

In a toxic system, the toxic minister sets himself or herself up as having a special destiny or mission that can be performed by no one else.

This special anointing or calling is often nothing more than the pathological need to be valued or esteemed. It also takes some of the power that should be attributed to God and gives it to the toxic minister. It is a way to usurp God's authority, and it is a way to discredit anyone who disagrees with the direction of the ministry. If others will not value the minister enough to submit to his or her dictatorial rule, God's anointing is called in to make sure everyone understands that any waver of support is really a waver in faith in God. Those who have felt this type of manipulation should leave that church or organization immediately. But most religious addicts don't feel it; they thrive on it (for a while).

This claim of a special touch has caused problems for people I know. The abuse of a high position to build a self-serving ego has caused unhealthy marriages to continue without healing, finances to be wasted, time to be spent in hours of futile work, and individuals who feel forsaken by a God who does not seem to care. Under the guise of special direction from God, many individuals have compromised their faith and fallen into a trap that did nothing but establish one person's authority above any earthly accountability.

The religious addicts at the top always seem to profit from this misguided loyalty by being able to spend more, build more, or sin more, depending on the area of their lives that has deteriorated. The victimized followers—seeking a closer relationship with God but focusing more on the addicted leader than on God—lose contact with God and often fall away from faith permanently. Misguided loyalty allows the delusions of the leader to grow and destroys the faith of the loyal. The result may be financial or spiritual bankruptcy. The only hope to protect other potential victims is for the leader who claims to be God's special officer to be forced into accountability or dethroned.

Power often corrupts. When organizations develop with little or no accountability for the leader, tremendous potential exists for the leader to fall into corruption. One church I was involved with in Texas confronted a minister about his behavior. Many issues led to the question of whether the minister should stay or go. The minister responded by saying he had started the church and that anyone disagreeing with him should leave.

He claimed that God had given him a vision for the church and the means by which the church had grown. The leaders knuckled under to the pressure, and the minister retained his position. He continued with no form of accountability, and it was only a matter of time until he got into trouble again.

When ministers wield absolute authority, everyone loses, even God. This is always the case when religion serves a person instead of a person serving God.

The Claim of Special Powers from God

The claim of special powers from God is another way for a person to feel valued, regardless of whether they have anything to do with God. This claim is often used to manipulate people into believing the gifted one is a great person of God. One of the scariest scriptures for these toxic ministers is found in Matthew 7:21-23:

> Not everyone who says to Me, "Lord, Lord," shall enter the kingdom of heaven.... Many will say to Me in that day, "Lord, Lord, have we not prophesied in Your name, cast out demons in Your name, and done many wonders in Your name?" And then I will declare to them, "I never knew you; depart from Me, you who practice lawlessness!"

No more notorious abuse takes place than in the area of faith healing. At times God rips through the normal bonds of the universe and heals people miraculously. On some occasions he uses people to facilitate that process, and on other occasions he does not. The problem comes when some people use teachings about God's healing power to manipulate and exploit believers.

A perfect example is the faith healer from California who claimed to know people's afflictions, their names, where they lived, and other personal tidbits that only a miracle worker would know. Once he had established his credibility through such feats of knowledge, he would claim to heal the people of what he knew was wrong with them. The religious addicts who followed him loved to watch his magic and believed it was all real. He deceived his devoted followers into believing God revealed the needed information to him. In fact, supplied with a tiny hearing device and radio receiver, he got the information from his wife, who had gathered it before the "performances." Confronted about the practice, he admitted that it had been part of the family tradition passed down from his minister father.

Not only did he mislead loyal and would-be followers into believing that he was hearing God, but he deceived them into believing he healed those people with the power of Jesus. The power of modern technology was portrayed as the power of the Savior of the world. He used his supposed special power to prove he enjoyed a favored position with God.

This man's exploitation of the terminally ill, the sick, and the afflicted, and his ability to reportedly laugh about the exploitation of their finances, are unconscionable. Few things are more cruel than exploiting an individual's search for hope. To these persons God may well say, "I never knew you."

Sadly, the addicts who follow them may never know God either.

AUTHORITARIANISM

Toxic Characteristic #2: *The leader is dictatorial and authoritarian.*

Every church or ministry must have a strong leader if it is to meet the challenges of hurting people and help them grow in faith. The stronger the leader, the stronger the ministry, whether the person holds all the power or chooses to delegate everything.

Problems arise when the leader takes his or her leadership role as license to dictate whatever he or she feels is right or wrong. Those who work in such a setting find themselves either agreeing with the direction of the ministry or leaving. There is no room to compromise, since the dictatorial leader believes that everyone should submit to his or her rule without question. Those who fear for their jobs or feel they may not be able to find similar jobs will comply with the leader rather than challenge certain decisions or actions.

Often a strong leader mistakes a position of leadership for a position free from accountability. The leader will set up a toxic-faith system that allows for free rein and no accountability. There may be a board of directors, elders, or deacons, but when the authoritarian ruler picks them, he or she picks people who are easily manipulated and easily fooled. What appears to be a board of accountability is in fact a rubber-stamp group that merely gives credibility to the leader's moves. These board members become the co-conspirators of the persecutor and permit the toxic leader to persecute without interruption. Then when a practice is called into question, such as an extremely high salary, the persecuting dictator justifies it by saying the board made the decision or approved it. The illusion of accountability becomes more dangerous than those organizations that blatantly disregard accountability.

In a toxic-faith system, the organization revolves around a dynamic leader whose vision for the ministry launched it. Many solid ministries have been started by the vision of a dynamic leader, and they are able to continue or reorganize when that leader relocates, retires, dies, or is asked to leave the organization. In a toxic-faith system, the organization would sink or discontinue without the authoritarian ruler to tell the people what to do. His or her name is all over the ministry. Without the talent and charismatic personality of that leader, there would be no reason or motivation to continue the mission. The ministry is a short-term project centered on one individual, not God. When that individual chooses to exploit and manipulate the followers, the exploitation goes unabated since there is no accountability. And when for some reason the leader leaves the ministry, it dies.

Individuals who gather around a ministry of true faith use their talents to reach out to people and serve God. They fit in their talents and abilities where God can best use them. In a toxic-faith system, talents and abilities are used to meet the needs of the authoritarian leader. His or her needs come first and must be met for the ministry to continue. The persecuted victims, blind to the manipulation and egotism of the leader, line up to assist in serving the persecutor. When the victims find out they have not served God or other followers, they usually get very angry and often must deal with feelings of betrayal and abuse, similar to recovery from an incestuous relationship.

Underneath the raging ego of the leader is a suffering person who fears being unimportant. The position of leadership may have been the first and only time the minister had any authority. He or she uses the authority to prop up feelings of inadequacy. Anyone eager to advance in the organization must never challenge the authority of the toxic-faith leader. Additionally, followers must give their complete support to the leader—and to the leader's style of management—without criticism. Any negative comment or action is perceived as a threat. The threat is eliminated so the ministry can survive and the mission can be accomplished.

The authoritarian leader comes to power through a combination of a driven personality, tremendous talent, and loads of charisma. The individual has no problem establishing spiritual and emotional authority over religious addicts by using persuasion and manipulation. When followers see a dynamic presentation of beliefs and behaviors, they unquestioningly accept the teachings, doctrines, and dogma. The more they accept the teachings of the toxic leader, the more the leader feels the people's dependency, and the more license the leader takes in controlling the thoughts and beliefs of his or her followers. As long as people are willing to follow, that leader will feel supported by God in whatever he or she desires to do. The leader is completely unaware that the entire exercise is being conducted to build ego rather than to serve God.

The authoritarian and dictatorial style is found in more than toxic-faith churches. It can also be found in toxic-faith families. Tim's story echoes others where power takes control of a parent.

Tim came from a rigid religious background. His earliest memories were of his father taking him to hear a preacher who sounded more angry than godly. His father was as dogmatic at home as the preacher was at church. He thought of himself as a general in the army of God, and his family had better fall into line. Authority was not to be questioned; children were to be seen and not heard; mom's place was in the kitchen; and no one was allowed to express any needs or desires. Tim's father held God up as the omnipotent Overseer who waited for his children to make mistakes so that he could punish them. He portrayed God as a tyrant.

Tim's father also justified his absence in the home and the intensity and fear he instilled in the family by blaming God. Dad could rail on the family since he was the priest of the family and the voice of God for all those who were in "submission" to him, but for everybody else, anger was one of the seven deadly sins. Tim was not allowed to watch television or play with any kids outside the church. His world overflowed with toxic rules and regulations that were to be obeyed at all costs, else the wrath of his father and God could be expected. No one hugged or kissed in his family, especially between father and son.

Tim would wonder why he couldn't be like other kids and have fun. What was wrong with him? Why did Dad and God not like him? Why was he different?

As Tim got older, he didn't see how he could live up to his dad's or God's expectations. Though a part of him wanted to be close to his father and God, it caused too much pain to get close.

Tim drifted away from God and his family. Tim became a very timid and frail man, always fearful of "screwing up." He felt that he didn't fit in with his family, the family of God, and society in general.

Tim finally found that he could find relief from his pain, loneliness, and boredom in drinking and in sex. Tim had found a "god" that could meet his need to numb his feelings of insecurity and inadequacy. I met Tim in a chemical-dependency unit.

Tim fell victim to his father's toxic faith, religious abuse, and addiction. His toxic-family system allowed his father to perpetrate the delusion that God was a God only of wrath. This left Tim with a hole in his soul, a hole that Tim filled with alcohol and one-night stands with other men. For Tim, the alcohol killed the pain of never measuring up, and the sex filled the need for male attention and affirmation. The alcohol gave Tim the false sense of security; the sex and the absence of insecurity gave him the false sense of significance. If someone wanted him, even if only for sex, he still mattered. Someone finally cared for him in some way, even if it was only to use him.

To help Tim recover, we had to address the religious abuse of his past in addition to the alcohol abuse and sexual compulsivity. At this time

Tim was afraid to call out to God. Fearful of his heavenly Father's wrath, he ran from him. Tim had been running from God for a long time, and there was no reason for him to believe that God wanted anything to do with him.

Tim finally was able to identify the toxic characteristics of his family's faith. He saw how all the family members played their toxic roles to a T. He saw that he was not crazy but a victim of craziness and toxic faith.

Tim not only gained control over alcohol and sex, he also learned the characteristics of healthy faith. Finally he was able to establish a relationship with God free from the fear of punishment and grounded in respect and love. His father's tyranny stopped affecting his life when Tim refused to be victimized by it any longer.

AN "US VERSUS THEM" MENTALITY

Toxic Characteristic #3: *Religious addicts are at war with the world to protect their terrain and to establish themselves as godly persons who can't be compared to other persons of faith.*

In their attempt to maintain and protect their beliefs, religious addicts line everyone up in two camps; there is no middle ground. A person is either part of the toxic-faith system or against it; a person is either supportive or destructive. The toxic organization fosters this mentality until its followers believe that everyone on the outside is a threat to the ministry, has no understanding of what is "really" going on, and must be ignored if they challenge the beliefs of the religious addicts. At the point of any new threat, the leader and the religious addicts are ready to go to war. Individuals who have not made a similar investment will be perceived as enemies ready to strike at any moment.

The "us versus them" mentality is evident throughout the organization and its teachings. Religious addicts go to great lengths to stress the church's or organization's uniqueness. Other followers will be told of ways that each possesses special knowledge and insight unavailable to others. Some ritual or practice is often utilized as the center of that uniqueness and superiority.

Consider baptism, for example. I was immersed and prefer this form of baptism, but theologians have disagreed on this subject for centuries. At times it can become the focal point of disagreement between groups. God is more interested in the heart than in the form of baptism. Yet rather than accept the different concepts and realize that God will honor the act of public dedication, whatever its form, religious addicts will insist their way is better and that the other is a tragic mistake. This attitude will be carried over into other areas as well.

The form of baptism is just one distinctive that separates denominations from one another. Each denomination is based on certain differences that allow people to affiliate with congregations and worship styles with which they are most comfortable. But when those differences are used to support an attitude of superiority, they become a source of manipulation to keep people from deserting the organization. Toxic believers condemn others, not from a fundamental foundation of belief, but from convictions on peripheral matters—say, the simple act of using water to sprinkle or to immerse.

When toxic believers propagate the "us versus them" mentality and rail against the evils of the world, they make personal attacks on the "sinners" and glorify the existence of the "saints." They imply that they have risen above the mundane sins of the world. The message is often that this group of addicts has come to a new level of life unattained by others. When the addicts are finished with the "us versus them" teachings, no one is attracted to the group by faith. People enter into it only by manipulation.

Religious addicts often cease to react and operate like human beings. They show no compassion for the hurting or those who feel trapped in sin. Zealous addicts make sinners feel alienated and hated. The attractive, gathering nature of Christ is lost in the religious addicts' desire to set themselves above and apart from all the rest. Self-righteousness replaces the humble service to God that probably characterized their walk of faith at the beginning.

The more toxic the belief system becomes, the stronger the "us versus them" mentality of the organization grows. The larger the system becomes, the more the addicts have to protect. As the ministry grows, it will come under closer scrutiny, and some of its toxic beliefs will be revealed as such by those who suspect the motives of the leader, the addicts who follow, and the entire organization. When these investigations begin, religious addicts are manipulated into believing that they are being attacked by the enemy. The prudent course would be to admit the mission has gotten off track, confess the wrongs, and bring it back in line with biblical teachings. But religious addicts would never do that until every other option had been taken away.

Religious addicts set up an exclusive society of toxic-faith believers. Individuals prosper and succeed by supporting the beliefs and practices of the persecuted leader. Like any other society, its rules govern and control every aspect of the society and its people. Anyone not adhering to the rules is considered an enemy of the society and everyone in it. Religious practice loses its focus on God and becomes a complicated process of furthering the society and its rules. Those in the exclusive society believe they are serving God, but they are serving a human leader and that individual's concept of what should and should not be. Unwillingness to serve that concept will bring on the wrath of all the religious addicts.

Punitive Nature

Toxic Characteristic #4: *Toxic-faith systems are punitive in nature.*

Toxic-faith systems don't have to be big to be toxic. In small churches across the world, congregations are led by toxic ministers every bit as manipulating and controlling as the head of a toxic mega-ministry. When a minister gains control of a small group, it seems that control can produce some of the most punitive forms of faith practice in existence.

One example comes from a small church in southern California. The minister was a small man who saw himself in a big way. He wanted total control over his congregation, and they allowed him to have it. The control often took very negative and punitive forms.

An unmarried woman told the pastor she had been involved in an affair with a married man in the church. She felt terrible about it and had broken off the relationship. She felt guilty and wanted to confess this to the minister and receive his help in moving back to a close relationship with God.

He was willing to help—but only after he had put her through some very stressful situations. He forced her to go to the man's wife and confess the sin to her. He forced her to go before the congregation and confess her sin before them. He forced her to agree not to date for one year as a sign of true contrition. Rather than offer her hope, he offered her a set of iron hoops that destroyed her personally as she jumped through each one, trusting they were the way back to her relationship with God.

Contrast that to the approach Christ took when confronted with the adulterous woman. He told her accusers to search themselves, and anyone who was without sin could hurl the first stone. No one moved. Then he refused to provide a punitive system for the woman; he simply told her to go and sin no more. The woman felt the compassion of God, not his wrath (which too many ministers take upon themselves to inflict).

Another incident in the church occurred when a group questioned the minister's morality and his relationship with a woman in the church. They did not accuse him of adultery; the group was concerned about the undue attention and affection he obtained from the woman. The pastor attacked the main accuser and demanded that anyone having anything to do with the man be removed from the church. Sides were drawn immediately to support the faithful and to punish those who doubted the minister's integrity.

In the name of righteousness, this and other minicrusades have been carried out countless times in the church. Each punitive action divides the congregation and removes those who would attack the minister's power. A minister addicted to power punishes and purges the system of anybody who would upset the status quo.

Those on the inside believe God is tough to follow—and the leader is willing to go to great lengths to ensure the congregation pays the price to follow. To those on the outside, the whole ministry appears negative and punitive, out of balance, and distorted—light-years away from the love, acceptance, and forgiveness freely given by God and his Son.

Overwhelming Service

Toxic Characteristic #5: *Religious addicts are asked to give overwhelming service.*

A toxic-faith system does little to counter the compulsive worka-holism of career seekers. It refuses to do this because it is so guilty of the same sin. Religious addicts are requested to serve, serve, and serve some more. They respond by becoming involved in numerous groups, com-mittees, and meetings. They are badgered into signing up and sacrificing their families and friends to meet the system's needs. They believe they serve God, but really they serve their own egos as they seek greater noto-riety within the system's hierarchy.

This level of service often becomes overwhelming. People become so drained that they can't think clearly. Their emotions distort. Over-whelmed religious addicts commonly suffer from deep depression, extreme anxiety, and a general numbness. Activity takes precedence and dries their souls, leaving many feeling hopeless and some the victims of total breakdowns. Leaders in the system wonder why so many become involved but then fall away from the faith. Why? They burn out through the service demands of the system.

It is hard for addicts to see that activity has become central to their practice of faith. They are caught up in doing things rather than serving God. Not everyone is Mother Teresa; not everyone has her gifts or her support system. Leading lives of overwhelming service does not put addicts in the religious hall of fame; it puts them in the hospital or breaks their relationships. Only when the whirlwind stops can God reenter as the focus of faith.

Followers in Pain

Toxic Characteristic #6: *Many religious addicts in the system are physically ill, emotionally distraught, and spiritually dead.*

Many toxic systems claim to free people from all problems: emo-tional, spiritual, and physical. The irony is that the systems accomplish just the opposite. Yet religious addicts are determined to hide their real feelings and thoughts and present a happy, peaceful glow. They suppress all discomfort to maintain an image of perfection.

The pain that is buried is buried alive, so it surfaces in the form of emotional despair and physical illness. Religious addicts often suffer from chronic back pain, headaches, eye problems, arthritis, asthma, and hundreds of other complaints. They fight to deny their physical and emotional conditions, often until it is too late to provide effective treatment.

It is not easy living in an unreal world. Addicts have to do drastic, desperate things to maintain unreal beliefs. Denial becomes a quick and easy tool until both physical and emotional trauma break religious addicts' facades of perfection. The followers in pain find relief only when they break down and are forced to examine their true condition and limitations.

Sharon came from a rigid religious background and was a pained follower. Throughout her life church authorities reminded her of her "total depravity," which she interpreted to mean that she had no worth or value and that all she needed was Jesus. Unfortunately, the only Jesus she knew was the one of religion. The more she failed to find emotional relief, the more she thought her sin and depravity were to blame. The more she tried to be perfect, the more she failed. Sharon's religion highlighted her inadequacies rather than taught her about the Christ who loved her. Her toxic faith focused on performance rather than on a relationship.

Sharon numbed her feelings with overeating. The more she ate, the more she repented and asked Christ for deliverance. The more she sought Christ's acceptance, the more she invested herself in her toxic faith. She worked hard at church to find her salvation. The more she tried to be perfect to merit God's intervention, the more she saw the hopelessness of ever being good enough. The more she saw the fruitlessness of ever being good enough, the more she ate. The more she ate, the more she believed that she needed Christ to deliver her. And so the vicious cycle of addiction took root. Like the hamster on the hamster wheel, the more she tried, the faster she went nowhere, until exhaustion forced her to begin looking for help outside her toxic family of faith.

When Sharon initially sought help, she had no idea that her toxic faith was a major factor in her feelings of inadequacy and hopelessness. She believed that if she could get her eating under control she could be "more perfect" and that God could then accept her. Her toxic thinking suggested that if she could get this "sin" out of her life, then God could love and accept her.

Since her eating disorder was firmly entrenched in religious addiction, part of her treatment had to address her toxic faith. It was difficult for her to acknowledge that she was hurt and angry with God and that she was bitter at having to perform for him to merit his acceptance. Breaking through her denial about her feelings toward God allowed her to open up to the idea of a loving God.

She began to realize that the God she knew was the god of religion, the god of her toxic faith who demanded performance for acceptance, the god who demanded that she clean up her act before he would hear her petitions.

We explored how her faith overflowed with toxic thinking. Sharon thought in terms of all or nothing. She was either in or out of God's will, with no gray areas. She never considered the truth that as we learn how to live and know God, we are going to make mistakes—and that it isn't bad, it's human. Much learning is the process of trial and error. The issue is to learn from our mistakes and not judge them.

Though Sharon knew the scriptures on grace, she never was able to experience it. For her, grace depended upon behavior. Relief swept over her when she began to realize she didn't have to earn God's grace. Since she could reach out and find someone who understood and could help, she realized that God *had* heard her petitions and *had* extended his grace by directing her to a place where she could get help.

Sharon found comfort in her eating-disorder group and discovered that many of its members were also running from the same feelings she had. Some shared how their toxic faith had incapacitated them and kept them in bondage.

She began to explore how her toxic faith had enslaved her. She began to question. She began to identify, with the help of others and a trained professional, the toxic characteristics of her faith and how they tied into her need to alter her mood and to stuff her feelings. She began to see how her faith did not free her, but in fact, condemned her—which worsened her feelings of inadequacy.

With the help of others, Sharon began to identify how the twelve-step process could help her understand and gain freedom from bondage. For the first time, Sharon began to experience unconditional acceptance from group members and from the loving God of the Bible. She gained strength and courage to live life more freely and fully, no longer a pained follower.

CLOSED COMMUNICATION

Toxic Characteristic #7: *Communication is from the top down or from the inside out.*

Communication in a toxic-faith system isn't a two-way street. Information is considered valid only if it comes from the top of the organization and passes down to the bottom, or issues from within the organization and is shared with the outside. Religious addicts stake out their positions and refuse to honor differences of opinion. Those at the top no longer hear of the perceptions and needs of the people, and the addicts on the inside no longer care about the needs of those on the outside.

Religious addicts develop extremely selective hearing and respond only to those things they perceive as important. Anything that doesn't fit into what they already believe will probably go unheard. With an attitude of spiritual superiority, religious addicts tell themselves that they are always in greater touch with God's truth, more sensitive to God's will, and more worthy of being listened to than anyone else.

A similar system of closed communication exists in many families, and religious addicts often come out of these family systems. Closed communication is especially common with fathers and children. A father may not take the time to communicate with his children because he considers their opinions insignificant. A father with "more important things to do" will not plug into the needs, thoughts, and feelings of his children.

So he remains ignorant of them. He values only his words to direct and punish them. The children feel inadequate to express themselves and their desires. A religious addict raised in this type of home recreates it in the organization. The organization eventually becomes ineffective because it loses touch with the people it is designed to serve—just like a father loses touch with his children.

In many toxic organizations, someone is "assigned" to close off unwanted communication for the leader. This individual is to placate those who disagree and satisfy those who want a direct voice to the leader. The person running interference knows that his or her job is to never tell the leader anything other than what is desired. The toxic system discounts the importance of the individual.

Open communication values people and allows them to be heard and feel heard. They are treated as equals and the organization or ministry truly listens so it can focus on those needs. In closed communication, the top of the organization loses touch with human needs because those at the top do not care about the people they are supposed to serve. The religious addicts who follow also cease to care for people in need.

LEGALISM

Toxic Characteristic #8: *Rules are distortions of God's intent and leave him out of the relationship.*

When religious addicts create a toxic-faith system, they lose God in the process. In God's place, they implement rules that serve only to further the empire of religious addiction. As new recruits enter the toxic-faith system, they are indoctrinated into the rules rather than strengthened in a relationship with God. The rules reinforce addiction, not faith. Addiction leads to conformity to a predictable pattern of behavior, often blocking any faithful following of God.

One toxic-faith system takes great pains to ensure that dress and hair styles conform to antiquated beliefs about what is becoming to God. All group members dress the same, wear their hair the same, and look the same. There is no room for individuality. Parents squelch an adolescent's desire to find uniqueness and develop a separate personhood. Conformity is paramount. So little room for individuality exists that the kids rebel by the droves. When they do, they are considered outcasts and of little importance compared to the few who are willing to stay inside the system, follow the rules, and reproduce the addiction structure.

Some toxic-faith systems place less value on appearance than on behavior. They believe their rules accurately interpret God's standards, and they expect others who participate to adhere to the rules. Such faith systems are based on "don'ts" rather than a faith centered on God. What one does is valued more than who one is. Because many young people never discover who they are, they develop into robotic duplicates who believe life is found in the implementation of rules.

It is hard for these toxic-faith practitioners to realize that Christ rejected the rigid, legalistic religious system of his day. He would pick grain on the Sabbath if it meant meeting a need. When the rules said not to heal, he healed anyway if it would bring a person closer to God.

Faith always has been more than a list of dos and don'ts. Standards make up only one part of faith. When they become the main focus, faith grows rigid and legalistic.

No Objective Accountability

Toxic Characteristic #9: *Religious addicts lack objective accountability.*

Lack of objective accountability is a central theme for all areas of toxic faith. If religious addicts entered into healthy, accountable relationships with others, toxic faith could not flourish. Anyone who claims to be so tied into God that he or she does not need to be tied into people is a religious addict guaranteed to fail in faith and in ministering to the needs of others. God never intended for anyone to be so focused on him that they had no need to stay connected with people. No one's faith can be free from accountability to others. Lack of accountability is a clear sign of lack of faith in God and the presence of a faith in self.

When toxic-faith practices come under scrutiny, the religious addict reacts predictably: "I am accountable only to God." *No one* is accountable only to God. We are all accountable to the government. A married person is accountable to a spouse. Anyone asserting accountability to God alone either is not thinking clearly or has a terrible sin to hide. When a religious addict makes such an assertion, followers should clear out of that ministry if change is not immediately implemented. A person accountable only to God is a person out of control.

Under the reign of a toxic-faith leader operating without accountability, religious addicts also tend to avoid accountability. They become little generals in a toxic army that they claim no one outside the organization can understand. This cuts off all others and arms them with the right to do as they please. These little generals follow orders from their leader, believing they are on a mission from God, and refuse to listen to any input from outside.

Severing accountability eliminates much of the possibility of turning toxic believers away from the organization and back to a true faith in God. They continue as part of the system and at times are driven into total disbelief in God.

Labeling

Toxic Characteristic #10: *The technique of labeling is used to discount a person who opposes the beliefs of the religious addict.*

Labeling attempts to dehumanize critics so that dismissing them or their opinions becomes much easier. The religious addict chooses not to address a critic individually but places a negative label on all who would disagree with his or her personal habits. Rather than say that John Smith has asked some questions, the addict proclaims that there are "detractors," "traitors," or "malcontents" who would destroy the ministry or organization. The labels become rallying points used to squelch a revolt. Once the label is in place, it becomes more difficult to see that person as a human with real needs and the potential for good judgment.

John had been with the church from the beginning, and all ran smoothly until he began to disagree with the pastor about certain interpretations and applications of Scripture. Suddenly, although John had faithfully taught Sunday school for years, he was labeled a trouble-maker.

John drafted a letter to the pastor about his concerns, but before sending it he asked an elder for his response. Before John had decided what to do, the elder informed the pastor about the contents of the letter. And that was it. The pastor determined John had gone too far and that he was trying to undermine the ministry. Hadn't he shared his concerns with an elder, and didn't that prove his guilt? The pastor immediately called John at his place of work and informed him that he was no longer going to be allowed to teach. Neither was he welcome at church any-more. He was a traitor and needed to repent of his rebellious spirit. Because the pastor called John a traitor, the church staff forgot they were dealing with a person who had been a part of the congregation since the beginning. If John believed something contrary to what the pastor believed, they felt John's belief had to be traitorous.

From the pulpit the pastor preached on how a little leaven spoils the lump and how the congregation needed to expel those who would cor-rupt them. In an instant, John and his family were no longer friends of those with whom they had fellowshipped over the years. They were "trai-tors" who had "betrayed" the pastor and therefore needed to be expelled. Yet what John had done was simply to disagree with authority. At no time had he condemned anything the pastor had preached, and he had shared his concerns with only a select few in leadership.

This nasty turn of events devastated John and his family. Their lives had revolved around the church for so long that they had cultivated very few friends outside the church. Rejected and abandoned by those they had trusted and cared for, John's family felt broken and in pain because the system could not tolerate difference. John was no longer a person with feelings and intellect, but a traitor with a rebellious spirit. This toxic faith enabled the delusion that each person has a right to his or her own relationship to God—as long as it lines up with the system. By labeling John and by persuading other church members to believe that label, the insecure pastor was able to avoid dealing with disagreement.

The military uses labeling to enhance the "killability" of the enemy. The last thing a military leader wants a soldier to think about is that the person in his rifle sights may be a father of five little girls who will starve without a daddy. The enemy is given an ethnic label in an effort to dehumanize him. The soldier is better able to kill one hundred of them than one father or husband.

Religious addicts use the technique well, and when they use rumor and innuendo to kill the reputation of a sincere critic, other followers are more apt to go along if a label can dehumanize the dissenter.

The purpose of labeling is to separate and divide. In our society, someone who has conservative beliefs is labeled a fundamentalist. The label no longer describes the approach by which that person evaluates life; it now describes the person. Someone who considers fundamentalist views to be narrow focuses on the holder of those views and labels him narrow-minded. The approach is transferred to the person's individuality. The person is shamed and demeaned for beliefs that have little to do with the person's value or unique gifts from God. Disqualification by labeling hurts the victims and allows persecutors to continue in their toxic faith. It is sheer poison.

I believe abortion is a sad choice; I'm not for it. Because I care deeply about this issue, I have been sensitive to the use of labeling within the abortion debate. Those who stress the woman's right to choose label their pro-life opponents "anti-choice" and "anti-women." Those who stress the personhood of the unborn label their opponents "pro-abortion" or "pro-death." The technique works well to form sides and rally the troops, but the labels don't reflect the true depth of belief on either side.

Most people labeled pro-abortion don't really think it's a good method of birth control. Some will even admit that they consider it a form of killing. They believe a mother should not take illicit, addictive drugs during pregnancy, so naturally they would not agree to kill the child during pregnancy. They're not really fighting for abortion. They perceive a world where men make all the decisions for women, and they want out of that world. They take a stand for abortion because they see it as a move to independence from male-dominated thinking. They do not hold abortion but the independent right of a woman to control her body to be most dear.

For the most part, those labeled anti-choice don't believe a man should make the decisions about a woman's body. They wouldn't condone a man force-feeding a birth-control pill down a woman's throat. They are not out to use submission as an excuse for exploitation. They believe in choices for women. But just as they do not believe that a child should be murdered when it is one week old after birth, they do not think a human life should be willfully terminated before birth. The freedom to choose is eliminated by the law after birth, and they want it eliminated before birth. The complication comes because the child grows within a female's body. They would say they are not anti-choice, but all choices must have restrictions, this one being the taking of life.

Because it is difficult to rally against rational-thinking people who have distinctly different views, labels must be used to polarize the opponents and energize the followers to fight those opponents. The enemy is disqualified so the difficult issue underlying the enemy can be avoided. The potential to find truth in the opposition's argument is destroyed when labels are used. Who wants to listen to a narrow-minded bigot? Since a narrow-minded person challenging your position is of no consequence, that person is eliminated as a competent opponent.

Labeling discounts and dismisses the opposition and establishes the superiority of religious addicts. It does not invite the exploration of the beliefs of others; it reduces them to objects of scorn. Labeling becomes the perfect weapon to attack the enemy or defend the toxic-faith system, its beliefs, and addictive practices. Labeling allows religious addicts to define truth, uphold that truth as defined, and destroy anyone who would dare to question that truth.

HOPE FOR CHANGE

Knowing the characteristics of a toxic-faith system enables individuals to evaluate the characteristics of their church or organization. When members of toxic-faith systems identify them as such, there is hope that multiple generations of abuse will discontinue.

At last, followers can see and feel manipulation by religious addicts. The persecution will stop when they refuse to be victimized. When many victims move away from the system, the toxic leader may be forced to become accountable, while other addicts may recognize the reality of their compulsions. This may force religious addicts back into a real relationship with God, free of ego, manipulation, and the victimizing of those outside the system.

Toxic-Faith Characteristics

- The members of the toxic-faith system claim their character, abilities, or knowledge make them "special" in some way.
- The leader is dictatorial and authoritarian.
- Religious addicts are at war with the world to protect their terrain and to establish themselves as godly persons who can't be compared to other persons of faith.
- Toxic-faith systems are punitive in nature.
- Religious addicts are asked to give overwhelming service.
- Many religious addicts in the system are physically ill, emotionally distraught, and spiritually dead.
- Communication is from the top down or from the inside out.
- Rules are distortions of God's intent and leave him out of the relationship.
- Religious addicts lack objective accountability.
- The technique of labeling is used to discount a person who opposes the beliefs of the religious addict.

CHAPTER 7

The Five Roles in a
Toxic-Faith System

Toxic faith exists when one or more dysfunctional systems provide false concepts of God, faith, and the individual. It often develops among those who grew up in a dysfunctional family. It also develops when a church, denomination, religion, minister, or televangelist teaches half-truths that susceptible members are required to believe.

Wounded individuals are easily caught up in systems that promote toxic-faith principles, progressing to the point of victimization and addiction. In a dysfunctional system, whether it be a family or a religious organization, roles evolve to support the system. Each person must be willing to play the roles that become more keenly defined as addiction intensifies.

In a dysfunctional system that breeds toxic faith, each person, no matter what role he or she plays, becomes addicted to the system, its beliefs, and its behaviors. The individual becomes trapped in predictable behaviors that remove God and faith, replacing them with dependency on a set of rules and dictates. Any deviation from the respective role is taken as a sign of rebellion and is dealt with quickly through shaming and rejection. Although each role is difficult to maintain, it is even more difficult to leave the safety and predictability of the role and act independently. A person who takes this step toward reality becomes an outcast of the toxic-faith system.

Examples of Dysfunction

When people are admitted into New Life Treatment Centers, they rarely identify their problems as religious addiction. They come to us depressed, anxious, or with some other major dependency. As we work with them, we often find that below the stated problems are layers of family dysfunction, toxic faith, and religious addiction.

One man stands out as a classic religious addict whose faith poisoned his relationship with God. He grew up in a very rigid home where things were done his father's way or not at all. His dad—a demanding, disciplined workaholic—counted on his son to live up to his expectations. But since the boy never could do so, he carried deep feelings of inferiority into adulthood.

In our patient's attempt to measure up to God, he transformed his dad's workaholism into his own churchaholism. He did everything he could to serve God. He was careful to abide by the rules of no drinking, no smoking, and no dancing; he avoided anything with the appearance of evil. He considered himself pure in every way. He felt he was measuring up.

After being married one year, he and his wife had their first son. A year later they had their second. He wanted to spend more time with his sons than his father had spent with him, so he determined that he would not be as tied to his work as his father was. The hours he worked at the church, however, took away just as much time. When the boys entered high school, they both became drug abusers, and one died from a drug overdose.

Two years later the man came into New Life Treatment Centers, a broken and hurting figure. He couldn't forgive himself for his son's death. He believed it was a result of his sins passed to the next generation. His obsession with thoughts of not measuring up put him in a major depression. He victimized himself with his unrealistic expectations until finally he could no longer function.

In this sad case, a father turned a son into a victim. That son took the dysfunctional core of family relationships and passed them to his own family. His rigidity victimized them. When a drug overdose took a boy's life, the father further victimized himself and taunted himself with thoughts of guilt and shame. He couldn't live up to his dad's, God's, or his own expectations. His self-defeating behavior almost destroyed him.

The roles in a toxic-faith system indelibly mark personal development and are often repeated in various forms from one generation to another. Unless the victim obtains help, there is little hope to break the chains of dysfunction and stop the multigenerational trend. The roles of the system powerfully predict a future generation of problems and trauma. Only when a person hits bottom and evaluates his or her self-destructive behavior does that person begin to see better alternatives.

The man who came to us worked through many layers of grief to crawl out of his toxic role. He grieved over never having the father he wanted or needed. He grieved over his son's death. He grieved over the loss of his perfect image of himself, shattered by the problems with his boys. When he finished the grieving process, he was ready to look up again and find God's love without conditions or unrealistic expectations.

In a toxic-faith system, the person playing the role of persecutor heads the group. The persecutor is supported by co-conspirators, enablers, and victims. These individuals have one primary function: allow the persecutor to function, insulated from reality. Each person believes the system, organization, or family must continue, and it is each person's job to distort, manipulate, hide, or deny reality so the toxic system can continue. Each person in a different way protects the persecutor from outside disruptions.

These people create a false reality by distancing and isolating the persecutor from contact with the real world. As they grow more committed to the persecutor and the toxic ministry, they become addicted to the behaviors of the role and the feelings derived from them. Once they stop supporting the false reality that allows the persecutor and the group to continue, they are no longer needed and are thrown out.

Individuals connected with a toxic-faith system must be able to work under the authoritarian, manipulative rule of the head of the family or organization. They become order takers and must blindly follow the leader. The leader, the persecutor, becomes so strong that he or she replaces God in the lives of those in the toxic-faith system. This poisons everyone's faith. It also poisons the organization or family and everyone who comes in contact with it. The job of each role in the system is to process the poison into a palatable form that is sweet and seductive enough for the victims to swallow. Anyone not willing to help with dispensing the poison becomes a threat to the authoritarian rule, is no longer needed, and is removed.

Jim Jones provided a tragic and graphic example of how men and women become involved in a poisonous system, even to the point of death. He took hundreds of people to Guyana to create their own world where they could practice their own brand of religion. He poisoned his people with lies, deception, false hopes, and dreams that would never come true. Finally, he poisoned them with cyanide.

Jim Jones manipulated, brainwashed, and controlled the minds of his followers until they believed anything he said and did anything he asked. Somehow the women justified having sex with him because he needed it and their duty was to provide it. How Jones distorted the Bible to make it appear right, only those women knew. Somehow he was able to poison the values of everyone who made the trip with him. Before he was finished, he had robbed them of their God, of their faith, and for many, of their very lives.

The colossal power of a persecutor was vividly illustrated at the end of Jones's reign. An investigation into the ministry began when authorities became suspicious of all of the money and property that had been donated to it. The more threatened Jim Jones felt, the more desperate he became. His followers believed that the investigators were sent from hell to destroy what God had created. They believed so strongly that they were willing to kill a congressman to protect the ministry.

With his back to the wall and his options at an end, the desperate and suicidal Jim Jones convinced his followers to join him on a trip that was supposed to end in heaven. His loyal co-conspirators and enablers lined up the victims to take a drink of "eternal life." When it was finished, hundreds of bloated bodies lay dead from the poisonous cup of Jim Jones.

That a man like Jim Jones could poison his flock with a toxic brew leaves little doubt that other deluded leaders can poison their followers and fanatical parents can poison the faith of their children with toxic beliefs and ideas. But they cannot do it alone; they must have the help of their co-conspirators and enablers.

In a toxic-church system, a persecutor dictates the rules to the rest of the followers. He or she uses a strong inner circle to carry out the mission. In a typical church, this could be made up of associate pastors, deacons, and elders; cardinals, bishops, and priests; members of the board, directors of ministry, or assistant directors. The titles vary from system to system, but in toxic-faith systems, the structure is always the same and it propagates the poisonous beliefs of the persecutor.

The persecutor establishes a rigid hierarchy so that everyone knows his or her role. As each person fits into the structure, identity and individuality are sacrificed to meet the demands of the system. With the faithful followers willing to do anything to support the persecutor, the organization becomes dysfunctional and unbalanced, leaning heavily toward the top. The more unhealthy the system, the more unbalanced it becomes—guaranteeing that it will not last forever. It will fall apart unless enough people force the persecutor and others in the system to turn from their egocentric plans and move back to a focus on God.

Toxic faith in a family produces a dysfunctional system that destroys a relationship with God and traps the family members in unhealthy roles. Dysfunctional systems have been around ever since the first family. The first family was so disturbed that one son, Cain, killed the other, Abel. Because the world is not a perfect place, every system, family, or nation has the chance to function in an unhealthy way. The roles of the toxic-faith system are consistent with the roles traditionally identified within dysfunctional families. If a person can come to understand how dysfunctional families work to protect and uphold an addicted family member, it is easy to see how the toxic organization works to protect the persecutor.

A healthy system is made up of individuals with a full range of emotions, intellect, free will, and the ability to function independently. In a dysfunctional system, each individual plays out a role needed for the system to function. Since individuals lack the capacity to function independently, they depend on one another to play out their roles and allow the system to continue. Those roles have to be played so that those in the system can remain in their denial and avoid the overwhelming fear of insignificance. Individuals desire a relationship with God, but on the spiritual journey they become snagged in a system that takes away the relationship with God and poisons the faith of all who participate in it.

THE SUFFERING WHITCOMBS

The Whitcombs illustrate how toxic faith can be handed down from generation to generation. One generation reacts to the dysfunction of another, but it is so locked into the unhealthiness that the same problems repeat themselves in a similar form. This story begins with a deceased grandfather, the father of Lee Whitcomb, the central figure in this toxic-faith family. When Lee Whitcomb's father died, he did not leave his grandchildren money or property; he left them a legacy of abuse and family instability.

Grandfather Whitcomb was a farmer who worked hard to feed his family of five children. As the oldest child, Lee worked the closest with his dad. They plowed the fields and harvested the crops together, doing whatever it took to feed the family and make enough money to plant the following year. As Lee reached his fourteenth birthday, he witnessed changes in his father. He became more moody and detached and fell into fits of rage and horrendous arguments with Lee's mother. It grew worse and worse until everyone was terrified of the elder Whitcomb and what he might do if he ever lost control.

Lee's father did lose control, gradually descending into abuse and violence. He began by grabbing Lee's mother and shaking her. He did the same to Lee. One night Lee heard an argument between his dad and mother that climaxed in yelling, screaming, and physical abuse. When

Lee heard his mother being slapped, he ran into the room and stood between the two. His father broke his jaw, then ran from the house. Lee and his mother went to the hospital to have the jaw fixed, where it was wired up and set, causing Lee extreme pain and discomfort.

Lee had never been extremely fond of himself, but the broken jaw removed the self-esteem he had left. He loved and hated his father at the same time. His father's pleas for forgiveness did nothing to restore Lee's feelings about himself or the relationship with his father. He felt that he was getting what he deserved, that somehow he must be very bad and in need of terrible punishment. Although his father seemed remorseful after the jaw-breaking episode, his remorse led to more anger, more depression, and more incidents of abuse. Each time he hit Lee, the blow reinforced Lee's beliefs that he did not deserve to have a good life.

Lee came to believe that a God somewhere was trying to punish him for being a bad person. Each outburst of his father's anger represented the anger of God toward Lee. The God he created in his mind lacked all kindness—a vengeful, angry deity. Lee considered himself the victim of God's wrath in addition to his father's. Lee didn't get his ideas from Sunday school, because Lee's father never took the family to church. He didn't believe in God, and he left the rest of the family to develop their beliefs apart from the Bible. Each child, especially Lee, developed a tainted view of God that affected every aspect of life.

Lee and the rest of the family lived in terror of their father for three more years. When Lee was seventeen, his father succumbed to one final fit of rage over a tractor part that had worn out. When he discovered the problem, he became enraged, blaming Lee for not taking better care of the machinery. He held the worn metal piece in his hand, shoved it at Lee's face, and yelled at him. Then he retracted the metal piece and cocked his arm. The moment he lunged forward to hit Lee with the evidence of his incompetence, Lee struck first, slugging his father so hard he dropped the tractor part and fell to the floor. Angry and humiliated, he lunged at Lee again, only to be thrown back to the floor. At seventeen, Lee was too big to be physically abused. He fought back and overpowered his father.

Lee's father ran from the barn to the car. As he drove madly down the dirt road to the highway, Lee watched a dust cloud spiraling behind the old green Chevrolet. By the time his dad approached the highway, a huge truck was lumbering down the same stretch of road. Blinded by rage, Lee's father never saw the onrushing vehicle. He pulled directly in front of it, and in an instant a huge ball of flame rose from the road.

Lee raced toward the wreck, knowing his father was dead. Huge flames engulfed both the car and the truck, the two drivers beyond any earthly help. Lee's heart filled with both guilt and relief. His family's terror had ended, but he felt responsible for his father's death. Feelings of relief only confused him more about himself and a God who would allow it all to happen. At seventeen, he hurt terribly and needed answers he couldn't find.

Lee struggled with his guilt feelings for many years. After his dad died, he picked up the responsibilities of the farm and worked it as his father had, but his brothers and sisters grew up and moved out. At age twenty-three he married a young high-school dropout who he felt would be satisfied to live on the farm. They had four children and raised them while they took care of Lee's mother until she had to be moved to a skilled nursing facility. When she left, an exact replica of the family she had started remained behind to produce food from the farm and turmoil from an abusive upbringing.

At the request of a friend, Lee attended the local church and felt comfortable there. The old organ sounded like a dying cat, the preacher fumed with anger as he poured out his message, but Lee liked being there. He found something he missed as a child, and he felt a void being filled. Some of his guilt pangs seemed to quiet down in the pews of that small church.

Lee became a Christian about a year later and greatly increased his involvement with the church. He began as an usher and then served on the Sunday-school committee; within three years he became an elder. If there were a meeting, he was at it and probably running it. Other than the pastor, he became the most prominent personality in the church. People would comment that they were amazed such a faithful follower had come from the likes of his unbelieving father. He loved the attention he received as a poor farm boy made good. He loved the power he felt from being a leader. He loved the work and the feelings he had from serving God.

But Lee's background led him to an unbalanced faith, and his family suffered from it. He poured everything into the church, and it wasn't long until Lee was serving his ego rather than God. It was as if he spent each hour at church in an attempt to erase some of the guilt over his father's death. It also seemed to him that church work guaranteed that his own kids would not turn out like their grandfather or like himself. So he worked off his guilt, worked off his father's old ways, and as he worked in a frenzy of church activity, he could deny his own problems.

Lee so fixed on his image as a church leader that everything he did revolved around the facade of wholeness. Lee felt empty, even as a Christian, but the church work made his life look rich. He suffered as many adult children of abuse suffer, but no one could imagine the truth as he worked each week in the service of the church. He looked good to everyone, especially to himself.

Lee's four children all felt abandoned by a distant father. They felt tremendous resentment over often being without a father for school events because he was too busy to be there. When they complained to their mother, she always demanded that they stop being selfish and instead be grateful to have such a wonderful father, a true man of God. It was clear the children's feelings were considered irrelevant. All that mattered was the church.

As resentment of the church and Lee grew, the children rebelled. One son started getting into trouble at school. A daughter began dating boys whom Lee labeled "sleazy." As these embarrassments continued to erode Lee's image of himself, he became even more rigid in his demands, adding to his long list of "don'ts." He would not allow his girls to be seen out of the house past 9:00 P.M. He would not allow his boys to hang out with other boys in a corner of town. He demanded Bible study and family prayer time. Nothing would stand in the way of Lee's creating the perfect family.

No one could live up to Lee's rules and the regulations of the church. Every time a child did not meet his expectations, Lee became enraged and demanded adherence to all his rules. Each time a child stepped out of line, he saw it as a personal affront and beat the child in the name of disciplining the transgressor back to the faith. He had an image to uphold, and any family member not willing to support and protect that image was punished severely.

He replaced discipline with total punishment that involved severe beatings of all four kids. As their father's anger increased, the children's resentment and bitterness grew. Each year the children fought to survive while longing to be free from the perpetrator of terror.

Each family member handled the father's anger and rigidity in a different way. Each one locked into a survival role to protect against a complete emotional and spiritual meltdown. The mother saw the problem but refused to deal with it. She patched up the hurts of her children with little regard for their dysfunctional futures. She paraded her crew through church and upheld the false image of a wonderful husband and father. She became as hooked on the facade as Lee was, and while she kept his image in place, she lost touch with her needs and identity. Eventually, a host of illnesses put her in bed. At age fifty she lived like a sickly eighty-year-old woman.

The oldest son became a successful businessman. He excelled in school and college and worked his way to the top of a large manufacturing company, a classic workaholic who shunned anything to do with the church. If there were ever a child out to save himself, it was the oldest boy. His drive and perfectionism made him difficult to live with. All three of his former wives would attest that he was extremely rigid on the outside while out of control on the inside. As he aged, he became more withdrawn from family and friends, content to spend almost every waking minute absorbed in his work.

The oldest daughter reacted to the dysfunction in a very different way. She grew up quite normally with a strong faith in God. Rather than avoid church, she used the church as a healthy bridge back to a real God, not the demanding God of her father. She married and had children and lived what most would consider a blessed and fulfilled life. She was the exception to the other kids of her family and other religious-addict families. Yet she, like her siblings, avoided her father and mother. She understood them and forgave them, but she chose not to be around them.

Her sister didn't make the same wise decisions. She rebelled, just as her younger brother rebelled. At sixteen she dropped out of school and out of the family, moving in with one of the "sleazy" boys her father hated. She became a regular drug user and quite a boozer. Everything her father stood for, she opposed. She built an image for herself at the polar opposite of his facade—the child from the other side of the tracks. She held nothing but menial jobs and never turned from the environment of filth she created. Each day she lived was an insult to her father, who never had time to love her. Her only pleasure came in knowing how he seethed with revulsion each time she came to mind.

The rebellious son was in constant trouble with school officials until he finally graduated a year late. The summer after his senior year, he seemed to mellow and mature and enrolled in a local junior college. There he found some new friends who supported his more mature lifestyle. He graduated from college with a degree in sociology and went to work in a health clinic. He had no place for a God made in the image of his father. He was a good man, but he never tapped into the saving grace of the Creator. He married, had children, and did all the things middle-class families do—and never filled the spiritual void left by his father's problems. Life remained incomplete, and although he could identify sociological problems, he did not know how to fix his spiritual one.

RELIGIOUS ADDICTION FROM
FAMILY DYSFUNCTION

The example of the Whitcomb family shows how family dysfunction gives birth to religious addiction. The addicted create their own dysfunctional families, full of individuals who will do whatever it takes to survive. Unfortunately, survival involves unhealthy roles that are difficult to change. These roles separate the members, break the family apart, and produce individuals who no longer are connected or even appear to be related.

These relationships are not rare. As we identify how they develop and the roles members play in developing them, we see how desperately families need help and what they need to change. It is possible to break through denial and assist in our own recovery, the recovery of another, or an entire toxic-faith system.

The following material details each role of a toxic-faith system. In the religious addict, each role is a prison that locks away the real person behind the bars of obsession and compulsion.

The Role of the Persecutor

The first and most dominant role in a toxic-faith system is that of persecutor. Persecutors don't start out to victimize their followers or families. They start out as unhealthy individuals who often were deprived or smothered by their parents as children. Rather than move beyond such a dysfunctional background, they compensate in ways that victimize others.

These individuals need to defend against their own sense of brokenness and fallibility, and they often do so through outrageous behavior. They end up hurting many, especially those who possess a true faith and sincerely seek God's will for their lives. Though the behavior may be outrageous, behind it is a very sad existence, a person who feels forced to carry on a role, forced to be something he or she does not want to be and was not meant to be.

Lee Whitcomb, like many abusive fathers, was a persecutor. He found an answer he thought to be right and pure. He believed his practice of faith focused on God. Since it did not, God became an afterthought to religion. Without a growing faith in God—just more rules and restrictions—Lee could not help but victimize his children. He loved them and wanted to help them, but he lost them to the practice of religion. Lee didn't start out to destroy his children, but his victimization produced some very destructive results. What made him perverse made his children wander. His failure to finally tap into a real God kept his children away from him and, with one exception, away from God.

Evils of the Soul

Although his parenting fell out of balance, Lee Whitcomb really did want the best for his children. He tried to protect them from evil by implementing rules that made him look good. He really did believe the protection would help his kids.

Often people full of problems project them onto others, especially their children. Lee attributed his weaknesses to his kids and almost injected those weaknesses into them. A daughter chose sleaze because her father did everything he could to insulate her from it; it only made the sleaze more attractive and the perfect source of punishment to inflict on her father. If there had been balance in his parenting, most of Lee's children would not have deserted him and the faith for a lifestyle of sin and rebellion.

Childhood Problems

Lee Whitcomb began to serve the small church because he felt God wanted him to do so. He wanted to use his few gifts for God's glory. In the beginning, all he wanted to do was serve God. I believe God was quite pleased with his initial dedication. But as he progressed to power and prestige, his motives changed, and he gradually went from one of God's humble servants to an egomaniac demanding to be served. If he had been raised in a healthy home, there is a good chance he would not have turned his practice of faith into a toxic system.

What led Lee to God also led him away from God. That is why those in the church must not seek simple solutions to every personal problem. Sometimes a relationship with God needs a cleansing of the past, a cleansing that will not occur without professional help. Those who most oppose this type of help are often the ones who need it most. Not everyone suffers because of childhood problems, but those who do often need help in resolving the sins of the past.

Self-Reliance Versus Godly Dependency

God can take the worst possible background and use it to draw people to him. When the world and parents and the system have all failed, God waits, ready to assist. Too often, rather than turn to God or persevere through God's help, we turn to our own devices, as corrupt as they may be, to resolve conflict and ease the discomforts that come with living.

The Lee Whitcombs of our day have found in their faith a place where they can obtain what they always wanted and needed: acceptance, a way to be valued and esteemed. They find security: a growing trust in God. When they no longer focus on God, however, their faith becomes toxic. Then everything is done for self in the name of God. It is like falling in love with the gift, not the giver. What was the fruit of being in a healthy relationship becomes the purpose of the relationship; the individual worships or idolizes the by-products of the relationship rather than God.

This is an idolatry of altered moods. Self-obsession leads to idolatry and the worship of those feelings that develop through faith. Searching for the feelings, not God, becomes an addictive obsession. The feelings were not bad, but they soured when they became the sole motivation for the relationship with God.

Living in a False Reality

All Lee Whitcombs create a false reality, which is the purpose of any addiction. They invest their skills and talents in creating and feeding the false reality. They use the power given to them to gain prestige and control of the environment around them. This self-constructed creation mirrors to them a sense of security and significance separate from a true faith and relationship with God.

Persecutors like Lee Whitcomb are usually very talented and capable of leadership. Believing that they are called of God, they feel invincible. Are they not backed by God and his Word? They preach their rules and regulations and target anyone unwilling to follow those rules. Any challenge or attempt to confront is disqualified and dismissed with a tirade that appears to be an accurate interpretation of God's Word but actually is just a distortion of the truth, designed to support the toxic system established to meet the needs of the persecutor's ego. Using a tainted interpretation of Scripture in this way makes the persecutor tough to reach and his unreal world almost impenetrable. He takes his own tenets and turns them into teachings believed to be of God. Sadly, they are not.

The Value of Performance

Persecutors are usually great performers and place a lot of emphasis on performance. Because they were often rejected when younger, they don't want to risk rejection when they are older. Rather than trust God and risk being rejected or betrayed by God, they focus on what they do in the name of God and what they perceive to be the instant rewards sent from God. In this way they lose all faith in God and totally rely on their abilities to find God's favor. Their performance becomes everything, and they surround themselves with people willing to say that their performance is outstanding.

Aside from the persecutor's performance and the applause of men and women for a job well done, he or she feels worthless. Performance validates the persecutor's worth and being. Every day brings a new battle to regain self-worth.

Although able to perform, the persecutor rarely feels good about the performance and must be lauded to compensate for a sagging ego. The persecutor constantly fears that whatever he or she does, it won't be enough, and no one will be able to pick up the pieces this time. If things are going well, the persecutor fears that the other shoe will drop. This fear leads to harder work and more effort. Guilt burdens the persecutor to do everything possible to push the ministry closer to the vision he or she created.

The persecutor feels accepted only when followers express pride and compliment the performance. Each new crisis becomes an opportunity to reestablish self-worth by being commended for performing well under pressure. The persecutor takes great pride in rising to the occasion, handling the new challenge, and proving to the family or followers that they are following a capable leader.

The persecutor appears to the world to be satisfied with being driven to achieve, obsessed with success, and compulsive about everything. Deep inside, however, the persecutor is not happy with the performing role, resents it greatly, and is very angry about having to do so much while feeling so little for all the effort. The only time anyone sees that anger is in a rare loss of temper or in a regular outburst of intolerance from the pulpit. The persecutor lives with the anger, unable to express it, because there exist no intimate relationships with whom he or she could share it. The persecutor fears that if anyone knew he or she was angry, it would dispel the myth that God's will was being done and the persecutor was happy. So the pulpit is the only place the anger can be released. When a persecutor preaches, most rational people stop and ask, "Why is that guy so angry?" What the persecutor would pass off as righteous indignation is in reality pure, unresolved anger, poisoning the faith of the minister and the followers.

Developing an Addiction

Addictions develop because of a lack of self-worth and a need to feel good about one's self. Addictions are about finding safety and relief from feelings of worthlessness and pain. Some find safety in alcohol, some in drugs, and some in sex. Religious persecutors find it in the utilization of religion.

A god, not the true God, serves the need to hide pain and insecurity. A god, not the true God, is developed to hide feelings of rejection and abandonment. Religious persecutors need shelter, and they find it in religion rather than God. They become addicted to the feelings they can contrive out of manipulating people and the religious system they construct.

Everyone needs a source of protection in time of need. Without it, a person becomes overwhelmed with the pressures of life. God is that shelter, and faith is the way to that shelter.

Putting religion in place of faith in God is evidence of no faith at all. Persecutors are afraid to trust God and find shelter in him. In fact, they don't trust anyone. They trust their addictive relationship with the system and will do anything to protect that system. They are at war with themselves, and everyone becomes the enemy. Until they finally learn to trust God, they live a life full of fear and anxiety, wondering where the next attack will come from. They become addicted to the perception, believing that they are being attacked by those who have less faith in God.

When addiction sets in, the addict learns to trust the source of addiction for everything. The addiction, be it religion or alcohol, becomes the god of the addict. The persecutor finds religion to produce good feelings, prestige, and the ability to feel in control. This god of ungodly religion is the persecutor's entire world, where every new day brings a new victim to come under the destructive power, control, and manipulation of the persecutor.

Persecutors manipulate their victims with guilt, shame, and remorse, projecting their guilt and shame onto others. Feeling they have disappointed God, their parents, and everyone else, they bring people to their level by allowing them to feel what it is like to disappoint someone important and powerful.

An unreasonable father says to his children, "If it weren't for you, I could make it. After all that I've done for you, don't you feel bad about being a hindrance to me? You need to pull your own weight, or I can't make it. It will be all your fault." An unreasonable father persecutes his children by making them feel responsible for the persecutor's image and future.

Disappointment

Persecutors are full of disappointment. They are disappointed in God and what he has provided them. They are disappointed in themselves because they are not as great as the others to whom they compare themselves. They are also disappointed in the people around them because they believe if those persons had worked harder, they could have gotten further.

Persecutors set out to fulfill their dreams, call them God's plans, and then are disappointed in everyone when they don't produce the expected result and feelings. Each new accomplishment becomes an addiction, producing less and less gratification. It takes larger doses of challenge, just like the heroin addict needs larger and larger doses of heroin. Each time the accomplishment does not produce the reward, the disappointment intensifies.

A disappointed persecutor is always in search of relief from the source of disappointment. He or she will do anything to experience an emotional high and break through to that state of existence where false pride can override the disappointment.

The persecutor appears to be self-sufficient and self-satisfied. Yet those close to the persecutor know differently. The persecutor looks for compliments, begs for attention, and is willing to reward anyone for some bit of good news. Efforts that counter the disappointment build up the persecutor's sagging ego and ease the pain of insecurity. Those who work with a persecutor know that the way to his or her heart is through compliments, flattery, and praise. Anything that supports the delusion that "I'm okay" provides relief.

Materialism

Although it was not true of Lee Whitcomb, persecutors often believe that individuals should be rewarded for their labors. They also think that no one labors like they do and no one should be rewarded like them. A $2 million salary, a second home, and a jet are all considered honest fruit of honest labor. They rationalize owning so much and living so luxuriously by saying, "Isn't a workman worthy of his hire? Doesn't the Word of God promise abundant blessings? After all, I've worked hard for God. I did good. Can't you see how pleased God is with me?"

Persecutors attempt to convince themselves that they are pleasing God by amassing many material goods and by claiming that God always blesses the faithful with material goods. Is it possible that Satan sends these material things so they can continue on their binge of self-obsession, all the while imagining that God is doing the blessing? The persecutor certainly would never entertain such a thought. Instead of supposing that material things could be mere distractions, material excess is viewed as proof that God himself is pleased with his or her work. Each new toy becomes another excuse to find more signs of God's approval.

But when material things begin to provide less and less relief (as they always do), persecutors must pursue things outside the material realm. That may mean more power through politics. It could mean an affair. There are numerous alternatives.

Hidden and Observable Compulsions

Persecutors are very compulsive people. Their religion becomes an obsession, motivated by compulsion rather than conviction. Most individuals who are compulsive in one area are usually compulsive in other areas. That is why so much caution should be used when working with or supporting someone who appears to be driven to achieve for God. Being "called" is entirely different from being driven. Driven people exhibit blatant compulsive behaviors that usually indicate something is being hidden.

It is unusual for religious compulsion to stand alone. Usually, a secondary compulsion reinforces the primary one, and vice versa. One compulsion stands out for the world to observe. It is an "admirable" compulsion, such as work or a hobby or religion. The other compulsion is usually hidden, one that few people (if any) would consider admirable. The covert compulsion could involve sex, theft, or something else illegal or unethical. Until the persecutor allows faith in God to resolve issues of pain, insecurity, and abuse, a new compulsion will form to replace the last one abandoned.

Eating is a common cross-compulsion that comes with religious addiction. Many people in our churches are overweight and cannot stop eating excessively. Rather than eat to live, they live to eat. Their compulsive religious addiction produces no lasting meaning, and they try to compensate with food.

One case of cross-compulsion did not involve food. A man who was a pastor came to the New Life Treatment Centers with many problems, one more obvious than the others. Each time he shook someone's hand, he would become anxious and irritated until he could find a place to wash his hands. He also showered several times a day and kept his room immaculate.

As he revealed his hidden sins, it became obvious why the pattern existed. He had had an affair with a woman of his church. It occurred early in his ministry, and it never happened again. His marriage stayed intact, but his behavior grew more and more bizarre.

The affair began when this woman met him after church one day. She found her place in line to greet the pastor, but when she extended her hand, he reached to shake it, her eyes fastened on his, and she held his hand and would not release it. He became obsessed by the seemingly insignificant meeting. Eventually, his obsession led to infidelity.

Long after the affair had ended, the pastor couldn't stop thinking about that original handshake. He believed his life would have been entirely different if that handshake hadn't taken place. His obsession led to his compulsive hand washing and other cleaning behaviors to free him from filth.

The man's obsession persecuted both him and others around him. He became a tyrant who needed to have everything perfect. His mental obsession drove the compulsions of his body and turned his life into a mess.

Manipulating with Contrition

Persecutors need forgiveness, and when in a bind, they ask for it. While they are asking, they appear quite sincere. But they are not. They ask for forgiveness only when they cannot talk their way out of a jam. When someone finally produces evidence of imperfection, the persecutor shifts his or her emphasis. He or she talks of the need to forgive instead of holding a grudge. Tearful confessions usually do the trick to win back the doubting Thomases whose faith in the persecutor started to wane.

With the persecutor's admission of guilt and request for forgiveness, most victims find themselves more than happy to continue their support. Family members are willing to accept the act of contrition as evidence that change will occur. But they do not hold the person to a new level of accountability, and eventually the problems resurface.

When persecutors are in charge of ministries, a plan for change should follow their acts of contrition. They should also consider their position and future. If they don't, those in the church should force them to. Persecutors *are* forgiven. But that does not mean they should continue in a place of leadership. In the role of persecutor, they are caught up in a most deadly and sinful condition called self-obsession. They also need help from wise and godly people. If they are allowed to continue in their ministries, they will go on victimizing people until they run out of locations. And when that happens, they will change professions and victimize people in other ways.

The greatest thing anyone can do for a persecutor is to force that person to seek help. The deplorable behavior that is visible only reflects a deplorable and broken heart in critical need of repair. Certainly, behavior must change, but more important, there must be a change of heart. Allowing the persecutor to continue without change sentences that person to a lifetime of misery and pain. So hold him or her accountable to make those changes! Although it is painful, it will save many future heartaches.

Hope for the Persecutor

The hope for persecutors lies in identifying their sense of persecution. Deliverance from this torment comes from a willingness to feel the pain of being treated unjustly. The way out is through the pain and grief of being treated unjustly by people the persecutors cared for the most. Just as Christ bore the pain and grief of being unjustly beaten, scourged, and crucified, persecutors (and all of us) must forgive their own persecutors as they share in the fellowship of Christ's sufferings.

The pain of resolving these issues and giving up old, familiar behaviors is not easy to bear. It won't happen unless the persecutor is forced to make it happen. The evil behind many persecutors is that though the way out is through pain and confusion, that way is safely hidden by toxic convictions. These poisons are supported by those who share the toxic-faith system and depend on its continuance. Those equally confused people are called co-conspirators.

Characteristics of the Persecutor

- Frequently defends own problems
- Feels the need to embellish the truth and make things appear more grand than they really are
- Feels the need to be in control
- Seeks power and control
- Speaks boldly about sinful behavior, even when involved in that same behavior
- Projects own wrongs onto other people
- Sees things in terms of very black or very white
- Believes people are extremely wonderful or bad, usually depending on the amount of support offered to the persecutor
- Has an attitude of superiority
- Appears very angry with those involved in sin
- Often is motivated by greed
- Fears sexual inadequacy
- Was probably born into an abusive or neglectful home that appeared wonderful to those outside the family
- Feels owed something
- Feels persecuted
- Is extremely self-centered
- Lives in false world where person is convinced he or she is right
- Usually possesses special talents
- Contorts God's Word to fit own beliefs
- Surrounds self with people who are insecure and easily swayed
- Manipulates others using guilt, shame, and remorse
- Blames others for own failures
- Attempts to make others accept responsibility for own mistakes
- Feels disappointment in God, self, and others
- Usually is impressed with material goods and those who own them
- Is very angry
- Has compulsions in several areas

- Possesses an observable compulsion such as hard work that appears admirable to the world
- Possesses a hidden compulsion that would disgust most people if it were known
- Places great value on performance
- Deeply resents having to perform
- Is not involved in any accountable relationships
- Has no intimate relationships
- When in a bind will ask for forgiveness and appear sincere doing so
- Fears not measuring up or losing image
- Fears that if no longer able to perform for the masses will be useless to God
- Needs professional help

THE ROLE OF THE CO-CONSPIRATOR

The Ultimate Team Player

For every persecutor there exists at least one co-conspirator who manipulates, plots, and plans to keep the persecutor in power and position. The persecutor and the co-conspirator work as a unit; they operate as one. Both are addicted to religion as the means by which they feel accepted and significant. In a family, if the husband is the persecutor, the wife is most likely the co-conspirator.

In large organizations, more than one co-conspirator usually exists. Several co-conspirators work together to form a team of yes-men and yes-women who will do anything to protect and defend the persecutor. They feed into the persecutor's ego and further blind him or her from reality. When conflict arises, they usually find a way to agree with the persecutor and support his or her position. They are loyal and supportive of the persecutor in every way. If it were not for them, the persecutor's empire would fall quickly.

In a toxic-faith system, these are the most dangerous followers. They are as driven and misguided as the persecutor, and because they are close to power, people trust them. Because they so deeply believe in the persecutor, many will continue to support that person when trouble, rumor, or admission of wrong surfaces.

In a family, the co-conspirator differs from the enabler. As will be detailed in the next section, the enabler passively allows the persecutor to continue to victimize others. The co-conspirator has a more active role.

The primary role of a co-conspirator is to make the persecutor look good. The co-conspirator is the caretaker of the entire system and also has the especially important task of being the caretaker of the persecutor's image. If the persecutor lacks compassion, the co-conspirator will supply it. He or she makes sure that the persecutor is identified as compassionate. When the persecutor praises the co-conspirator, usually it's because the latter made the persecutor look good by covering up or compensating for some major flaw.

In a typical crisis, the co-conspirator comes to the rescue of the persecutor, thus gaining special favor in the latter's eyes. The dynamics look the same in a family or in a ministry.

First, the minister confesses to the co-conspirator that a great wrong has been done. He or she admits that sin has been committed and that "Now, more than ever, I need your love, support, and forgiveness." The co-conspirator is told that the persecutor has endured relentless persecution. There are admissions of working too hard and burnout. Perhaps there is the slight hint that if those around the persecutor had been more helpful, the disaster could have been averted.

In a family, the co-conspirator is made to feel guilty for the persecutor's act, while at the same time being assured of worth and value. With the persecutor's dramatic and tearful confession, the co-conspirator is hooked, becomes addicted to the emotion, and with the intensity of the crisis rallies to save the persecutor, the victim of this "dreadful" situation.

Developing the Delusion

Co-conspirators believe their actions are genuine. They say, "I know God's hand when I see it, and his hand is on this person." They see everything from the point of view of the persecutor, that he or she has been called of God to head the family or run the ministry and that everything must make sense in light of that divine calling. Co-conspirators delude themselves and others and further enhance the delusions of the persecutor.

Each co-conspirator sees the evil plot as out to get the persecutor and takes it as a personal mission to protect the persecutor at all costs. If it means that lies and distortions must be propagated, then lies and distortions will be devised. If it means lying to prevent the authorities from taking children out of the home, then lies it will be. For this willingness to lie, thus continuing the delusion of sincerity and purity, the co-conspirator is rewarded with gifts, power, money, and prestige.

The Search for a Loving Father

Co-conspirators are often adults who have felt inferior all of their lives. Because they have never felt the love of a father, they search for significance from the love of someone else. They seek God's love, but during the search they discover that the love of a human is more tangible. Their sincere desire to seek God is derailed into a desire for the favor of man.

When they find that favor from a powerful leader or dominant spouse, they will die to protect their source of self-worth. They defend the persecutor and protect the empire or family because they know their own feelings of self-worth will die when it crashes. Their desire for right and wrong is replaced with the desire to feel good because they are part of something big. Desiring security and significance all of their lives, they finally have found someone (or an entire organization) who gives them that value—and there is no way they will allow that value to deteriorate.

Family Co-Conspiracy

A co-conspirator must be treated much differently from a person caught up in enabling behaviors. The co-conspirator is in a different state of denial and often lives with greater barriers to reality.

One case brought the severities of co-conspiracy to the surface. A female in terrible shape was admitted to our treatment center. She had collapsed emotionally and spent hours crying, isolated from everyone else. Although she contemplated suicide, she was too weak to commit the act. She survived long enough for us to help her.

It was one of the most bizarre cases we have ever seen. She was raised in a repressive home where her father ruled with an iron fist. She and her three sisters obeyed him without questioning. He was demanding and rigid and never revealed his emotions. He always seemed angry and never had time for the girls. This woman spent her life looking for a place to belong and someone to belong to. She felt like an outcast most of her life.

The man who would later become her husband had a strong personality, just like her father's. Rather than be repulsed by it, she was attracted to it. From the beginning of the relationship, he controlled and dominated her. His spell of manipulation charmed her, and she fell in love with him. They married and had two children.

They shared conservative views in their practice of faith. Both believed that the husband should be head of the home and that the wife should submit to his authority. In practice, this belief became very distorted and gave the husband a license to exploit his wife. He told her what to do and when to do it—and she loved the control. She loved not having to make a decision and so went along with his autocratic rule. She told her daughters they must do the same. She demanded that they never question their father's actions, just do what he said must be done. They complied.

Our patient was addicted to a lifestyle in which she didn't have to accept responsibility for anything. She did everything at the instruction of her minister or her husband and never made an important decision; she just followed orders. When her minister yelled at her and the rest of the congregation, she felt cleansed. It was so similar to her childhood; she was comfortable there. Everything was fixed with an order, a prayer, or a miracle. That existence allowed her to deny the reality of her broken childhood and her problems of inadequacy.

Her co-conspiracy began when her husband started to control every aspect of their daughters' lives, a control that began to destroy both girls. Due to his uneasiness with himself, he refused to let other men be with his daughters. He convinced his wife that in our society, dating was evil, and all boys wanted only to abuse girls. While others were allowed to date, their girls were forced to stay home. They still were not allowed to date when one was a senior in high school and the other a junior. Each day the mother took the girls to school and picked them up in order to prevent any outside social interaction. The girls grew miserable, and their misery turned to despair and depression.

The co-conspiring mother played an active role in the persecution initiated by the father. He made the rules, and she enforced them. She tried to convince the girls it was for their own good and pleaded with them to honor their father's demands. She helped her husband trap the girls, and she kept the trap fastened tightly. Without her help, her husband would not have been able to victimize the girls. The more withdrawn they became, the greater her resolve to force them to comply with his demands.

The crisis occurred when a school counselor intervened. The younger daughter went to the counselor and told her how she and her sister were being raised. The girl explained that the dating prohibition was merely a symptom of a larger problem of control, manipulation, and victimization. The counselor had been worried about the depression of both girls and got both into counseling at school. Each session led closer to the confrontation that would collapse our patient.

The counselor called the mother to the school to talk about her daughters. She laid out the facts the girls had presented. She said that this type of parenting was as abusive as physical abuse. She explained that the girls had no social skills and were completely dependent on their parents, while other kids were learning to separate themselves from their parents. The counselor told the mother that the girls were withdrawn and severely depressed. They had no friends, and many other students laughed at them. She declared that if something were not done, she would intervene and try to have the girls placed in a home where love was more important than rules.

The meeting broke through the delusions that the mother had carried for years. She realized she had been part of hurting the girls. She realized she had made excuses for her husband. She knew her own problems reinforced his. But she did not know how to fix it. She felt as if she were facing a wall of fire that she knew she had to climb. She collapsed into tears and could not stop crying. Her sobs grew deeper and she became hysterical. *She* was trapped, not her daughters. She felt the pressure of her self-inflicted trauma and could not continue with reality. The counselor brought her to us for fear that she would commit suicide after her strength returned.

The story doesn't have a completely happy ending. In this case, the husband refused to work on his problems and divorced his wife. She did fairly well in treatment, and through ongoing therapy regained control of her life. Her daughters also entered therapy, but it will take years to rebuild what their victimizing father destroyed. The key to the mother's recovery is her ability to forgive herself for helping her persecuting husband to create a family where he did as he pleased while the rest of the family ceased to exist as individuals.

Hope for the Co-Conspirator

Co-conspirators are addicted to religion, the religious system that gives them importance, and the embodiment of that religion, the persecutor. Co-conspirators invest a lifetime of effort supporting the persecutor, so it is not easy to turn from the system or the person who created it. Buying into the strong existence and lying to cover problems make it difficult for co-conspirators to turn away from the persecutor and the addictive relationship with religion. But it can be done.

Co-conspirators can remove the obstacle that hinders their relationship with God. Co-conspirators can gain a clean slate by confessing the need to feel secure and the willingness to deny, distort, and lie to protect their place of security. Co-conspirators must be willing to face themselves, see what is really there, and stand alone without being propped up by a devious and controlling persecutor who has victimized the co-conspirator (along with everyone else).

Co-conspirators can be greatly used by God to bring people to him. But first, they must be willing to pay the price of giving up or changing their relationship with the persecutor and confessing wrongs to those who have been victimized. Then they must forgive themselves and start over. When this occurs, there is tremendous hope for a new life, free of control and the need to control.

Characteristics of the Co-Conspirator

- Assumes the role of the ultimate team player
- Shows total dedication to the persecutor
- Always finds a way to support the position of the persecutor
- Feeds the persecutor's ego
- Is addicted to the power granted by the persecutor
- Keeps things going within the toxic-faith system
- Ensures that everything is taken care of responsibly
- Typically is a small person who feels big when in on the action
- Willingly deceives to maintain the persecutor's power
- Is good at lying
- Enjoys being rewarded for willingness to distort the truth
- Usually felt inferior as a child
- Ties personal feelings of value to another person rather than to God
- Protects sense of self-worth by protecting the persecutor
- Appears unassuming and grateful to be number two in the organization
- Enjoys material things
- Is sincerely deluded
- Feels weak
- Lacks the strong charisma and leadership abilities of the persecutor
- Feels extremely inadequate
- May have had a large ministry that was lost due to the revelations of own immorality
- Works as a single unit with the persecutor
- Lives to be appreciated and recognized by the persecutor
- Needs to feel safe in work and relationships
- Is viewed by outsiders as trustworthy, conscientious, competent, mature, and reliable
- Needs professional help

The Role of the Enabler

While the co-conspirator is actively involved in delusion and connives to keep the persecutor in power, the enabler allows, rather than promotes, victimization. In a family, the enabler is normally the spouse of the persecutor, usually the wife.

Enablers are also found within toxic organizations. They have lesser positions than those of the co-conspirators and are not active in the decision making of the organization, but they willingly support those decisions. They are ready to rescue the persecutor and placate whenever possible.

Addicted Caretakers

Enablers are the primary caretakers of the persecutor. Often they are asked to do the behind-the-scenes dirty work of the persecutor and co-conspirators. They resent being placed in these roles, but they rarely complain. They are religious addicts, addicted to the persecutor, the toxic system, and their role. They are addicted to the feelings of worth they obtain when they are called on to fix problems or cover up the wrongs of the persecutor.

They lose themselves in the life of the persecutor. The more they have invested in the persecutor, the more they resent themselves. Rather than break free of the system, they cling more tightly as they lose more and more of their self-worth. They cannot view themselves outside the role of enabler. They become so dependent on the persecutor and the system that they will believe any lie or rationalization if it will maintain peace and the status quo.

Addiction to the persecutor takes precedence over everything else. The addiction poisons them and robs them of their faith. They leave their faith in God and place it in the persecutor. They rationalize supporting evil and a victimizing system out of the need to be submissive. Addiction to the person is the single most important factor in allowing the wrongs of a toxic-faith system to continue.

Enabling Thoughts and Behaviors

Throughout a toxic-faith system—whether a ministry or a family—many exhibit enabling behaviors. One always has a primary role of enabling, and this person exhibits more of these behaviors than anyone else. These behaviors form the very identity of the person, who is insecure and unable to think for himself or herself. The primary function of the enabler is to allow the persecutor to continue and the toxic-faith system to survive. Each behavior makes sense only in light of the drive to support the toxic system.

One of the most enabling behaviors is going along with the group consensus. When this occurs in a toxic ministry, thousands of people can be harmed. Despite the carnage, the enabler goes along and complies, as if there were no problem. Thoughts such as these fill the enabler's mind:

Others are more knowledgeable about the situation than I am. I must go along with their decisions.

It is my place to be supportive, not to confront. My faith demands that I be obedient and loyal.

These people are so nice, especially to me. Their motives must be pure.

Perhaps I don't really know the pastor well enough to discern whether he is right or wrong.

Since they are closer to the situation, I will go along with them.

He must be "special" with special needs. Who am I to rock the boat? I must be a faithful follower and not allow others to hurt the ministry.

Such thoughts paralyze the enabler and prevent that person from seeing the reality of the problem and confronting it. Instead, the fearful enabler allows the problem to grow until someone else intervenes.

In the family of an alcoholic, the husband and the wife may take on the roles of the addict and the enabler. The enabler could cause the drinking patterns to change course by seeking help or conducting an intervention. The enabler could be the catalyst for change, since the addict depends on the enabler. But the enabler becomes comfortable in the role and allows the drinking to continue. In fact, the drinking is no more addictive than the enabling role. Instead of being able to intervene, the enabler must be intervened upon.

The same is true for the enabler of a persecuting religious addict. Until a friend risks rejection and intervenes, the enabler will go on assisting the persecutor in his or her victimization. As long as the enabler remains convinced there is no hope to change, the toxic system will continue.

The behaviors of the enabler insulate the toxic system and the persecutor from reality. When someone criticizes the persecutor, the charges are denied and covered up. Similarly, the enabler silences anyone inside the alcoholic family who would be so bold as to suggest that something is wrong. The children in the alcoholic family or fellow workers in the organization soon learn that it is not safe to talk or express feelings, especially when those feelings doubt or question the persecutor's behavior. As long as the enabler pushes criticism aside or silences those who want to speak from within, the persecutor is free to continue, unabated in the quest for power.

Survival Mode

Unlike the persecutors and the co-conspirators, who act out their addiction to conquer, the enablers act out their behaviors to survive. To them, the world is cruel, and the persecutor is a victim. They believe that if someone as strong as the persecutor can get in trouble, they would be destroyed quickly. They will do anything not to have to face the world alone. They rationalize that they are acting in their children's best interest. They state that their decisions are made in accordance with their faith. They are actually holding on for dear life, doing anything that will prevent them from having to endure the painful process of change and facing the world alone.

Because they are so determined to keep things as they are, they feel responsible for everything. They take the entire burden of the family on themselves. They work harder and harder to keep the family going and the persecutor in power. They neglect their needs for the sake of meeting the needs of the persecutor. They consider every new development a threat to their existence; protection becomes their only means to survive.

When the persecuting head of the family falls, the enabler believes if a little more effort had been given, everyone would have been happy.

It is very similar in a ministry. When ministries fail and ministers fall, the enablers believe that a few more sacrifices would have saved the day. The co-conspirators fuel this thinking with manipulative comments in time of trouble. If the minister has an affair, the co-conspirators confront the enablers about doing a better job of meeting the needs of the minister. Others will ask for greater sacrifice and understanding from the enablers. These unrealistic expectations trap the enablers into believing more work and more effort must be extended. Sometimes they break under the pressure. When this occurs, people rally behind the persecutor, pointing out what a burden a sick wife must have been for all those years.

Enablers carry the weight of the world, especially the weight of the delusional world of the persecutor. Everyone around the enablers seems to imply that more must be done to help the persecutor and the ministry, and the enablers fear they may not survive if they do not comply.

Hoping for Change

Enablers know that what is happening is wrong. They want it to change but are too afraid or don't know how to facilitate change. Enablers feel so powerless outside the world of the persecutor and are so dependent on the persecutor that they believe they are unable to face the consequences of change. They are different from the co-conspirators, who know things are not right but fight to keep them as they are. Enablers are so burdened by guilt that they want things to change. They never stop hoping that somehow the persecutor will decide to live differently, the ministry will go back to serving God, and everything will be wonderful.

They increase their efforts to support and love the persecutor, hoping this will result in the needed change. Their increased efforts, however, only feed the ego of the persecutor and allow the persecution to go unabated. The enablers feel sorry for all of the deceived victims, but not enough to risk forcing change on the system. They hope and pray for something to make a difference, while refusing to do what they can to change it. Enabling continues when confrontation would help the most.

Responding to the Toxic System

Enablers are responders. They respond to each new crisis and all of the subtle hints of the toxic system to do what is needed to protect that system. The system, especially the co-conspirators, blackmails the enablers to stay in a supportive role, whatever the price. Each enabler acts for different reasons, but most are prone to respond to the "poor me" appeals of the persecutor. An enabler who has been in the role for a long time will quickly move to feel sorry for just about anyone requesting pity. The persecutor presents a "poor me" facade and requests rescue. Trained enablers quickly respond to the rescue call and move in to support and save the persecutor. Rather than take care of their own needs, they assist the persecutor in his or her helplessness.

The key response of the enablers is to support. Even when they doubt the persecutor and the mission of the ministry, they continue to offer support. They know few responses other than to defend and support the person being criticized. The persecutor's world may become more unpredictable, but at least he or she can count on the constant support of the enablers. This support allows the persecutor to believe he or she is right and fuels the delusionary existence that exploits many victims. Only when enablers withdraw their support does the persecutor see any need to change or at least to consider change.

Hope for the Enabler

The only hope for enablers is reality. They must face the reality that the system continues in large part due to the support they offer the system and the persecutor. Enablers must admit that they are playing out an unhealthy role that has trapped them in a system doomed to failure. The hope comes from ending the charade before more people are hurt.

The huge codependency movement, which began over a decade ago, has helped many destructive relationships change into productive ones in which accountability for both partners is a priority. When enablers stop enabling, they can enter a new type of relationship where needs are met rather than ignored. The price is the loss of an enabling identity that is hard to sacrifice. Thousands of enablers have made the difficult move out

Characteristics of the Enabler

- Allows victimization rather than promotes it
- Supports victimization with silence
- Is dedicated to not rocking the boat
- Does not trust God enough to allow family turmoil or destruction of a ministry
- Appears powerless
- Receives praise for sainthood in being able to survive under severe persecution
- Can be perceived by co-conspirators as the enemy or a threat to the co-conspirators' position
- Allows the persecutor to be in denial
- Covers up the harm done to the family or the organization
- Eases the persecutor's pain
- Outwardly appears loving and supportive of the persecutor
- Inwardly is angry at living an unfulfilled life
- As a persecutor begins to lose credibility, will start to develop other skills, such as obtain a degree in counseling, knowing the system and the family may fall apart
- Feels very little self-worth
- Becomes a caretaker of the persecutor
- Is addicted to the persecutor and the system
- Has the primary goal of maintaining peace and the status quo
- Has great difficulty thinking for oneself
- Goes along with group consensus
- Acts to survive
- Feels extremely responsible
- If the ministry fails, blames self
- Neglects personal needs for the sake of the ministry and the persecutor
- Never stops hoping things will change
- Never stops fearing what will happen if things do change
- Needs someone to intervene

of the role, and the world, especially *their* world, is a better place for it. When enablers do the courageous thing, victims are spared further victimization.

THE ROLE OF THE VICTIM

The most unfortunate of all the roles in a toxic-faith system is that of the victim. Victims don't know what they're doing when they blindly support a toxic-faith system and its persecuting leader or parent. They do everything out of a desire to know God and worship God, but their actions are misguided. They trust their parents and leaders to be people of integrity and will shun any mention that it is not so.

Victims sacrifice their time and money and faith to support the system. The persecutor, co-conspirators, and enablers manipulate these people to keep the family or toxic-faith system going and the persecutor in power. When the toxic-faith system is finally exposed for what it is, victims must bear the feelings of being used to meet the needs of those in authority.

Victims are compliant people. They cause no problems because they believe every word that is passed down from the top. From their positions in the background and with the blind support they offer, they make everything appear okay. Each victim who stays inside a sick family will sacrifice individuality, just like an enabler. Their blind allegiance is taken for granted because victims lose themselves in the family or the organization. They never make a fuss and never rock the boat. They merely wait to carry out the next assigned duty. Victims sacrifice personal needs and desires so that they can be part of the system.

The silent and invisible victims sacrifice their need to be significant in order to be valued by the system. They fear rejection and abandonment so much that they would rather be exploited members of something than be on their own and part of nothing. The leaders and parents in the toxic system know this and exploit it regularly. Victims hide from each other any sadness and pain from feeling insignificant. Everyone acts as if it is a great privilege to be taken for granted and lost in such a worthwhile mission.

Spiritual Molestation

Victims place their complete trust in the parents or leaders of the toxic-faith system. They count on their parents and leaders to take care of them and nurture their spiritual well-being. At the time when the loyalty of these spiritually needy people is the strongest, the persecutors of the faith spiritually molest them. Spiritual molestation rapes the victims' minds of reason and strips them of direct access to God. It takes away their self-respect and leaves them feeling broken.

Some turn completely away from God after they realize they have been so badly abused. If they lack support after the victimization, they often lose their desire to know and draw closer to God. Left with feelings of betrayal and lack of confidence in their ability to identify a trustworthy person, they abandon their spiritual journey.

Once victims have been spiritually molested, persecutors and co-conspirators attempt to manipulate them into keeping the secret. Hellfire and brimstone and other tools of God's wrath are used as threats against rocking the boat or revealing the problems within the family or toxic ministry. Victims who succumb to the threats bear the pain of existing in a world of lies. When they are perceived as willing to go along with the lies and deceptions, they are repeatedly abused by being asked to adhere more closely to the rules of the family or ministry.

Tragically, these victims feel they deserve the abuse. They feel as though they don't measure up, are bad, and should be satisfied to go along and be accepted. Rather than stand up for what they sense is right, they continue to work hard to measure up and meet the needs of the system that molested them.

Examples of Victimization

Victimization can occur in a family or in a ministry. The results are the same—lack of identity and loss of faith—but the form is quite different.

In a family, a child can be victimized by believing that following rules will result in a relationship with God. The less these rules are rooted in the Bible, the more likely they will block the child's faith and rob the child of identity. Each time a parent tells a teenager what God wants (so that parent can obtain what he or she wants), the teen suffers. So parents use God as an excuse to guide a child into a career they want rather than a career the child would love. Others victimize to feel some degree of power, since they experience none in other areas of life. The victimization can even become sexual, using God as an excuse to molest children, telling them this is a way to protect them from the outside world.

One man did exactly that. When his daughter reached age fifteen, he began to fondle her and eventually had sexual intercourse with her. He told her of an evil world, full of disease and abuse. He told her that it was his job to protect her from it, that she should remain with him instead of seeking a husband who could be violent. He even told her if she did marry, God would punish her. This depraved man continued in this way for three years until the girl finally found the courage to tell her mother. Though it was not easy, the mother believed her daughter and took action to stop the abuse. The girl's view of God was incredibly distorted, and it took many hours of counseling to help her see that God is not a victimizing God.

When victimization occurs outside the family or in a toxic-faith system, it can result in churchaholism. The victim's addiction to religion is most evident in the hours of sacrifice given to develop the ministry. When trouble arises, even more time is spent attempting to fix the ministry. Just like the alcoholic who spends many hours at the bar and away from the family, the workaholic wastes time in countless meetings to cover the wrongs of the persecutor.

Victims sacrifice time almost as if they are Christian martyrs who, out of faithful duty, must go down with the persecutor. While the victims attempt to make a name for themselves as sacrificial believers, their children wonder why God would take up so much of their parents' time. When the ministry goes down and the victims realize all the work was for nothing, it is difficult to remain faithful and continue to draw close to God. Most would do well to obtain counseling once they discover they have been abused so badly.

Sexual victimization can be very damaging. A faithful secretary, dedicated to meeting the needs of a minister, may become trapped in a sexual affair without ever intending it. She may be manipulated and seduced and then convinced that for some reason it was okay to meet the "special" needs of the minister. It is so sad to see families destroyed by the uncontrolled lust of a persecuting minister who cares about nothing more than his own personal gratification. Anyone caught up in an affair of this nature needs to confess the involvement to another person of leadership and get out of the relationship immediately. The minister will meet his "needs" and then leave her for another as soon as he is through with the exploitation. No matter how the relationship evolved, it must be seen for what it is and stopped.

Victims make great sacrifices. They sacrifice their happiness and self-respect to feel important and gain acceptance. They unknowingly sacrifice their needs so that persons they esteem can be saved from suffering the consequences of their own actions.

Although they are unaware of it, the victims' attitude of sacrifice has more to do with a lack of self-worth than anything else. In the name of God, they sacrifice far beyond what God would ask. The ways in which they give of their time, money, and themselves perpetrate the exploitation. The more the victims sacrifice, the more victims the ministry creates.

Hope for the Victim

The result of spiritual victimization is often a hardened heart and many unresolved feelings of anger and resentment. Victims have bought into a false system of conditional divine love and have tried to meet those conditions of sacrifice. When the toxic aspects of faith are revealed, the victim concludes that an unloving God cannot be reached.

Hope for the victim comes in seeing the unconditional love of God, a love that does not depend on performance. When this is understood, feelings of resentment and anger can be resolved. God's unconditional love is always available to radically change the victim's heart. There comes a point in recovery that the risky dimension of faith must be accepted. That dimension requires forsaking the confusions of trusting in a person or an organization and trusting in God alone. When this occurs, many victims find a true and pure faith for the first time.

Characteristics of the Victim

- Makes tremendous sacrifices out of a combination of a desire to serve God and very low self-esteem
- Wants to feel a valuable part of something important
- Was often victimized as a child
- Looks for someone to make salvation easy
- Often experiences loneliness
- Actually believes money and effort will buy favor with God
- Willingly sacrifices time, money, and self for a cause considered to be of God
- Is easily manipulated by persecutors and co-conspirators
- Is spiritually molested by toxic-faith leaders or parents
- Feels victimized when the truth about toxic-faith ministry is revealed
- Often abandons spiritual journey upon discovery of abuse by an exploitative leader or parent
- Is often threatened by co-conspirators and persecutors to keep the victimization a secret
- Bears the pain of existing in a world of lies and deception
- Sometimes leaves one toxic-faith system and moves to another
- Frequently is very emotional in the practice of faith
- Becomes isolated and lonely once disillusioned about a ministry or family
- Though astute in business and other affairs, naively practices a blind faith
- Refuses to doubt questionable activities; instead rationalizes why exploitative things would be necessary for the ministry's survival
- The more money given to a ministry, the greater the resolve to protect and defend it
- Gives untold hours to develop the ministry and then sacrifices further in attempts to fix it
- Sacrifices a wonderful family for the sake of a toxic leader
- Often has a martyr complex

- May be seduced into a sexual relationship to meet "special" needs of the minister
- Is reluctant to stop the victimization for fear of looking foolish
- Often is involved with the toxic-faith ministry out of a desire to be or look important
- Willingly pays a high price for acceptance
- Frequently needs counseling after discovering exploitation

The victim's hope must come through exercising the gift of free choice given by God. Free choice is never made in the midst of emotional blackmail or pressure to conform. The free choice of faith is made out of love for God and the desire to serve him.

Through this service and unconditional love, the victim can gain significance and security. The victim is then freed to meet the needs of others out of love and service to God, rather than manipulation and coercion.

The Role of the Outcast

Of the five roles in the toxic-faith system, only one is not a religious addict or bound by toxic faith. In most toxic systems, someone can usually see the problem and confront it. Unwilling to play the games of the persecutors and co-conspirators, the person becomes an outcast.

These people who stand up for what is right and challenge the system lose their jobs, friends, and church. They become lone voices in the wilderness, crying out for change that will not come as long as the persecutor dictates power, the co-conspirators manipulate the system, the enablers allow it to continue, and the victims fall in line with blind faith. When outcasts surface, they are identified as troublemakers and pushed out of the system as soon as possible.

Forced to Rebel

In a healthy system, individuals respect the person and position of leadership. For it to remain healthy, there must also be respect for the workers.

Without respect, the "hired hands" are not allowed to disagree. If they don't like something, they are labeled complainers, negative thinkers, and not team players. The toxic-faith system has no place for anyone who challenges the integrity or disagrees with the methods of the leader. In a toxic-faith system, loyalty is equated with blind faith and complete agreement with the leader.

Allegiance that requires overlooking the truth must be pledged daily. When that allegiance evaporates, the confrontational workers or church members are labeled as outcasts and rejected by the organization. In this way they are forced to rebel, since the organization allows no room for disagreement.

Outcasts who challenge the delusion of the system are discredited immediately. The toxic-faith system creates a lose-lose situation where the outcasts must give up perceptions of reality or be willing to face complete rejection. Abandonment becomes the reward for trying to correct the ministry.

Outcasts can interpret reality for themselves. Even when their perception of reality contradicts that of hundreds or thousands of followers, they can clearly see the problems and press for solutions to those problems. Outcasts are unimpressed by position or personhood. They love God and want to protect his people and his institutions from spiritual fraud.

Those who are so dedicated to God have little difficulty seeing others' dedication to egos and empires. Yet they are forced to suffer for what they see because they refuse to watch people live a lie and abuse others. No toxic-faith system can handle this keen insight and dedication to truth. They must place their jobs and the church they love on the altar of sacrifice as they are forced to move on to a place free of toxic faith.

Hope for the Outcast

God honors those who are willing to sacrifice their comfort at the altar of what is right. God has a special place in his heart for the heroes of a toxic-faith system. Those who stand up for God and tell the world the emperor has no clothes will receive their reward sooner or later.

I have talked with some of these courageous outcasts, and I know of the pain and suffering they endured when they rejected the toxic-faith system. But all is not terrible for the outcasts. They feel good about finally making a stand. They also feel the respect of others who value their courageous acts.

The hope for these outcasts is that many great men and women of God and many great churches exist where God can be found. Rejected in one place, they will be welcomed in another, where pure faith is upheld and God is honored through the integrity of the organization's leadership.

Characteristics of the Outcast

- Is not a religious addict
- Does not possess a toxic faith
- Willingly stands alone
- Stands up for what is right
- Is willing to be rejected by others in the toxic-faith system
- Can discern right from wrong
- Commits to leaders having integrity
- Refuses to be victimized by false teaching and lack of integrity
- Speaks out for truth
- Usually loses a job within a toxic organization over concern for it
- Suffers rejection by friends after challenging the leadership of those in the toxic-faith system
- Often is treated as a leper
- Is begged by others in the toxic-faith system to support the persecutor
- Endures shame for actions
- Refuses to respect or be manipulated by those in the toxic-faith system
- Sees the truth and acts on it even if it produces great personal pain
- Interprets reality for self
- Is motivated to protect people from spiritual fraud
- Is very dedicated to God and the people who seek a relationship with him
- Commands respect of others for courage

Life Beyond the Roles

Toxic faith exists within an unhealthy family or system of people trapped in roles that addict them and destroy their relationships with God. The persecutor starts the delusion and invites others to live within a false reality to increase the ministry and his or her prestige. Co-conspirators reinforce the false reality and are rewarded for their assistance in manipulating others to follow. Enablers fail to question the false reality and cushion the blow of consequences when the immorality of the persecutor and the entire organization is revealed. Victims who fail to question reality succumb to the deception and sacrifice their time, talents, family, sexuality, money, and self-respect to support the toxic-faith system. Only the outcasts dare to be different and question the false reality in which they find themselves. For the sake of what is right and their true faith in God, they suffer rejection and abandonment.

Where toxic faith exists, everyone is affected. Everyone is hurt by the counterfeiting of faith in an all-powerful, loving God.

Toxic faith is all about addiction and victimization. Each person in his or her role becomes addicted to the type of power or security offered by that role. The longer the person remains in the role, the more difficult it becomes to stop the addictive behavior unique to that role.

The tragedy of a toxic-faith system is that everyone is a victim. Most people are victimized for profit and gain. They are asked for their money and their lives to support the toxic leader and his or her lavish lifestyle. They sacrifice out of a belief that bigger is better, and they become bigger victims as the organization grows.

Each person in the system views the persecutor and the mission as more important than himself or herself. The persecutor is thought to be so important in the kingdom of God that nothing is too great a sacrifice for that person and his or her vision. Grandmothers like mine will send in their pension checks. Husbands and wives will send in their vacation and grocery money. People will lie and steal and give up their self-worth for the sake of the misguided leader. Children will fall in line after a parent's demands for conformity destroy their identity.

The promises of God and heaven's special blessings will be used to manipulate the masses, much like Adolf Hitler's promise to restore the former glory of Germany. Deliverance from earthly sorrow and oppression is the hook, and the price is nothing short of prostituting the faith.

Every toxic system must have willing followers who will play their assigned roles without question. They become the caretakers of the system as it grows and the scapegoats as it falls apart. They are held in bondage by their toxic convictions and beliefs. They martyr themselves, not for a loving God, but for a toxic religious system that demands sacrifice as payment for services rendered.

All toxic systems grow through an illegitimate desire for profit, power, pleasure, and prestige. Followers become addicted to the instant rewards of toxic faith and a sense of belonging to something. They become compulsive in their practice of a faith that is supposed to quickly bring rewards of earthly gain. The compulsion for gain and the greed behind it allow the toxic system to grow. Rationalization, justification, minimization, denial, and projection all are used to distort the real causes and motivations of toxic behavior. This distortion is necessary to avoid the reality of conscience, inner fear, and an overwhelming sense of shame.

Regardless of the roles one plays, the misuse and abuse of religion constitute the primary addiction in this toxic system. The system and the players within the system take precedence over a relationship with God. In the name of God, one person—a manipulative persecutor—can create a religion where he or she serves as god. This self-made religion is used to avoid the reality of life, not as a means to a healthy relationship with God. The religion drives a wedge between believers and God and becomes the most eternally deadly toxin of all.

Toxic-Faith Pecking Order

The toxic system has its own pecking order and uses certain toxic roles for keeping that pecking order in place.

- The religious persecutor is bound by the fear of giving up the power-and-prestige position, lest he or she has to face failure and insignificance.
- The religious co-conspirator is bound to the system to have a purpose in life and to avoid the fear of letting the persecutor down.
- The religious enabler is bound by the fear of ridicule and shame.
- The victim of religious abuse is bound to follow and blindly believe.
- The outcast is bound by the desire to let the truth be known and to be free from the toxic system.
- The roles, except for that of the outcast, are driven by the fear of not belonging to the toxic-faith family. The only thing more fearful than not belonging to the toxic family is the fear of not belonging to anything at all.

CHAPTER 8

Ten Rules of a Toxic-Faith System

Any system, whether a family or ministry, must have certain rules to maintain it and keep its members in line. The rules form the distinct character or culture of the organization or family.

Systems infected by toxic faith are no different. Their rules are not written down, but they exist. Sometimes they exist only in the minds of the religious addicts who thrive on the system. Everyone within the system understands the rules and abides by them. As the system grows, new challenges arise, and the rules are periodically changed at the whim of the leaders. The followers of a toxic leader who do best quickly figure out what rules have been eliminated and which ones have been put in their place. The following are some common rules of toxic-faith systems.

CONTROL

Toxic Rule #1: *The leader must be in control at all times.*

When someone becomes addicted to something, he or she is completely controlled by it. Deluded by the addiction, the addict is unaware of this loss of control and believes that he or she is in control.

Control is a primary issue for most individuals who suffer from an addiction. Toxic faith is no exception. When the toxic-faith leader struggles with control on a personal level, he or she also attempts to be in the center of control within the system. The leader desires to have the final say in every decision, whether minimal or monumental. When a religious addict is a parent, the children grow up with little ability to think independently. Anyone not adhering to the leader's tough standards is immediately dismissed so that total control, or at least the illusion of total control, can be maintained by the leader.

Control is really an illusion. No parent has complete control in any family. No leader can predict all the circumstances and stresses that the ministry will confront. The more the person seeks to control all details, the less likely that person will be able to maintain a clear vision of the larger issues. The more control is sought, the less there is to be had.

Individuals addicted to alcohol and drugs are keenly aware of how this paradox works. The Alcoholics Anonymous program has several sayings that illustrate the paradox of control: Let Go and Let God, Easy Does It, One Day at a Time, and the Serenity Prayer. Each saying is a reminder that to stay in control, a person must every day give up control to God. Seeking to maintain control serves only to sink the person deeper into addiction.

If faith is toxic, it exists outside God. It creates a god much different from the Creator of the Bible. There is little or no trust in the almighty God. Faith in self and the ability to keep things under control replaces a true trust that God is in control. Both persecutors and co-conspirators are very controlling people. Throughout the system, individuals fight for control while attributing complete control to the leader.

It is no wonder that so many leaders who try to exercise complete control break under the pressure. Some probably act unconsciously in a self-destructive manner to relieve themselves of their overwhelming position. They lose the power they fought for by attempting to maintain more power than they can handle.

The Serenity Prayer is a powerful tool for learning to relinquish control. This prayer of faith directly contradicts the persecutor's attitude toward problems. Until the leader relinquishes control, the ministry will continue to teach through example the philosophy, "I must take things into my own hands." That is exactly what religiously addicted followers do.

Blame

Toxic Rule #2: *When problems arise, immediately find a guilty party to blame.*

Almost every toxic believer caught in a public scandal has relied on this rule to explain or minimize the scandal. Two religious addicts were caught in illicit sexual acts outside marriage. In the end they both confessed and accepted responsibility for their behavior, but they did so only after trying every other option.

The first blamed Satan. He claimed that if his ministry were not so important, and Satan had not worked so hard to trap him, the affair would never have occurred. It was as if he had no choice but to succumb to the devil's evil influence. His faithful followers also were willing to blame Satan. They didn't force the minister to step down or obtain special help. He declared he was determined more than ever to fight Satan, and they were willing to let him.

In another case, blame was placed squarely on the woman, who was labeled a seductress whom no man could resist. Her sexual powers, combined with the minister's burnout, led to the sin. The congregation also received some of the blame; he claimed his parishioners were so needy they took everything he had. With no reserves left, he was unable to resist. Faithful followers rallied around him and prayed that he would find relief from the pressure. They also removed the temptress from the congregation to protect the minister. Blaming saved his position and the toxic ministry he developed.

From the example of addicted leaders, addicted followers learn to blame others, circumstances, and situations for all problems. No problem cannot be discounted by the words "Satan took hold of me and would not let go until I had sinned greatly." By denying and dodging personal responsibility, whenever possible, the religious addict can avoid the reality of needed inner changes. Also, the object of blame is shamed and rejected from the toxic-faith system.

Families are more powerful than ministries in affixing blame. When dad is a persecutor, all problems will be pushed off on the wife and kids.

It's amazing that the wife or children can exist in a system where any mistake could be a reason to punish everyone. This was the case in one family. If a light was left on and no one admitted responsibility, all the children were beaten. The father believed those acts of irresponsibility explained why he could not get ahead financially. He believed he would succeed financially if his family would cooperate better. The reality, however, was that he lost more money in reckless stock investments than his family could ever save. Refusing to see this, he placed the blame wherever he could, usually with his innocent children.

Many times the persecutor in a family system will gamble on God. The persecutor will take money that is owed to creditors or other people and give it to ministries in the name of God, hoping God will return it tenfold so he can pay his family's bills. Even though it is the persecutor who is "tempting God" (Matthew 4:7), he refuses to believe he could be at fault. The persecutors in any toxic system will find somebody or something to blame rather than look at themselves and challenge their own beliefs. Be it the innocent children in a family system or the congregation in a toxic-faith system, the persecutor takes no responsibility in the things that go wrong.

PERFECTIONISM

Toxic Rule #3: *Don't make mistakes.*

A toxic-faith system traps all its religious addicts into the tyranny of perfectionism. Because they are taught that they belong to an elite system, followers believe they can attain perfection, think they need to attain it, and feel terrible shame when they fail. They all strive for perfection and make themselves sick in the process. They shift from believing in God to avoiding failure, ridicule, and criticism. They believe irrationally that if they can attain perfection, others will not be able to find fault with them. Then, once they have measured up, they will obtain acceptance, love, and the feeling of belonging.

This rule against making mistakes increases shame and fear and motivates members of the toxic system to deny and repress their humanness.

A mistake is considered a reason to fear that their faith lacks strength. Fear becomes the motivation to work harder to compensate for a lack of faith that has produced the mistake. Perfectionists are driven by the desire to measure up to a standard that can never be obtained. Failing to reach that standard, religious addicts increase their involvement in the system as a means to measure up.

Embracing sin, not denying it, allows people to learn and grow. Accepting the reality of sin means accepting one's full humanity, which leads to the realization of our need for a divine Savior to make up for what we cannot do. In accepting Christ, Christians acknowledge that personal perfection can never be obtained in this life. The person who denies that truth lives in constant fear of not measuring up. The fear of making a mistake, the fear of sinning, keeps the victim of perfectionism from experiencing the grace of God and traps that person in a toxic religious system.

The toxic-faith system has no room for error and no room for people who make mistakes. Since people in need, people who mess up, and people who reveal their humanness glaringly point out the weaknesses of the toxic-faith system, they must be removed. Their expulsions also motivate others to measure up to the perfect standards of the organization. They try harder, lest they be thrown out too.

But the system expects something that cannot be delivered. As long as the leader knows how to manipulate, erring perfectionists will stay locked in their positions within the organization—until they commit one of the unpardonable sins and then they will be thrown out. They lose if they stay in the system and don't measure up, and they lose if they are thrown out and rejected.

The rule of perfectionism denies the follower the right to embrace the limits of the human condition. If the individual has never dealt with feelings of inadequacy and inferiority and never accepted individual limits, each mistake will seem devastating. The victim will be driven to perform, measure up, and do things "right" to avoid feelings of inadequacy and insecurity. The practice of faith becomes obsessed with performance.

The perfectionist practice of faith becomes product-oriented; the relationship with God becomes less important than the product of acceptable behavior. Anything short of perfection elicits the shame of not being quite good enough. Shame is the religious addict's reward for endeavoring to be Christlike. The toxic believer, never knowing the freedom of having one's struggle valued, endeavors endlessly to avoid the shame and pain of not measuring up. He or she always hopes that "this time I'll do it right."

Pure faith is not product-oriented, but process-oriented. For Christians, the struggle to become Christlike is important. Although we can never be perfect, we endeavor to grow toward maturity because we feel acceptable to God, self, and others. Failing to measure up does not bring shame, but repentance from sin. Failure validates the believer's inability to be perfect and his or her need for a saving God.

Perfectionism denies our humanity, with shame as its reward. Pure faith accepts our humanity, with peace and serenity as its rewards. In a healthy system where failure and mistakes are accepted as parts of the human condition, believers value the endeavor to grow closer to God and stronger in faith. Fulfillment and satisfaction replace shame and remorse. They expect that mistakes will be made and corrected with the help of God.

In a system of religious addiction, works—how much one gives, knows, worships, prays, meditates, and so on—become the measuring stick of one's spirituality. Faith is based on the fear of disappointing God.

In a healthy system, acceptance is based on love. Our Father, who is love, accepts us because of who he is and not because of what we do. The believers in a healthy system accept individuals because of who they are and not because of what they do or don't do. This acceptance frees individuals from the bonds of perfectionism and shame.

DELUSION

Toxic Rule #4: *Never point out the reality of a situation.*

Religious addicts aren't interested in reality. They don't want to know how things are. They are interested in how things should be and how everyone can work together to create the illusion that everything is the way it should be. Anyone not creating that illusion will be discounted or removed. To talk of reality is to commit organizational suicide. If more faithful followers were willing to commit organizational suicide and become outcasts, all the other religious addicts would be forced to face reality and change to meet the needs of the people the ministry is supposed to serve.

No one wins, and everyone is a potential victim, where this rule exists. No one is willing to speak up. Everyone becomes a submissive servant. A family is no longer a family, but a military unit of commands, orders, and obedience. If some issue becomes so important that someone must speak the bad news, tremendous effort is expended as everyone tries to figure out how to best present the facts—a most painful experience. An entire organization can be destroyed when tremendous energy goes into protecting the religious addicts instead of ministering to the people.

One organization ministered in several locations. The leader counted on the offerings taken in each satellite organization to cover ministry costs and to provide additional funds to support the headquarters. The leader told the board of directors that the plan would work and that expansion would be no problem, but the organization's accountant knew that each month the ministry fell deeper and deeper into debt. Payments to vendors went out later and later to continue the illusion that enough cash was available. No one wanted to break the news to the leader because he became a tyrant when things didn't go well. A messenger with bad news often was identified as the source of the problem; so it was no wonder the accountant took a long time to muster the courage to deliver the bad news.

When the leader finally heard about the problems, he flew into a rage. He couldn't believe that things were in such bad shape. Why had he been left out of the information loop? He fired the accountant for not keeping him informed and refused to acknowledge that it was almost impossible to inform him without being punished for it. The accountant broke the rule of never being the person to deliver the bad news.

He lost.

PERPETUAL CHEERFULNESS

Toxic Rule #5: *Never express your feelings unless they are positive.*

Religious addicts don't care about people. They don't care how people feel or what their needs are. They care about their own feelings and their own needs. Addicts who know the rules will never reveal a thought, feeling, or doubt that would make the toxic leader feel uncomfortable. The leader wants to be reinforced only with positive feelings and statements of affirmation. No room exists for those who are negative, depressed, or worried about a problem. In a toxic-faith system, followers must always wear pasted-on smiles. Individuals who make known their problems are considered outcasts and are ostracized.

Toxic systems deny men and women the chance to feel what they feel. "You can't be angry with God" is the mantra of the toxic-faith system. If individuals feel sad, there must be something wrong with them. Either they don't have enough faith, they aren't praying enough, or sin is in their lives. Whatever the words, the message is that they can't feel what they feel without being shamed or being made to feel inadequate. Be it the church of the "frozen chosen" or the church of the "eternal smile," certain feelings aren't allowed. Feelings must be hidden if the toxic system is to render adequate support.

Many churches today lack openness. They are gathering places for fakes who look good, talk well, and support an image of perfectionism. Every problem must be wiped away with a quick "Praise the Lord!" Real feelings must be abandoned for the "good" ones supporting the myth that the truly faithful have no problems. Any revelation of problems indicates weakness and a lack of faith.

Religiously addicted parents become frustrated easily. They don't want to be bothered by problems that interrupt their busy schedules. They get involved only when it will make them look good or at least make them appear to be interested in people. Parents often have a messiah complex that leads them to believe they can and must fix everything. An individual repeatedly in pain demonstrates that some problems can't be solved by the parent or that faith isn't working. But that hurts too badly, so the person with problems must be removed.

Toxic-faith parents and leaders of organizations don't want to face the reality of human needs. They want to live in a world where everything can be fixed with a great sermon or a quick prayer. The illusion that allows the organization to grow, the family to look good, and the leader to continue to be out of touch from people and their needs, takes precedence over real needs and real feelings.

Blind Loyalty

Toxic Rule #6: *Don't ask questions, especially if they are tough ones.*

Religious addicts must be blindly loyal. Questions, especially the tough ones, reveal that a follower has some doubts and lacks faith. Any questioning is considered resistance to the organization or the leader of the family. Questions are met with responses that indicate certain issues are not to be mentioned. Expenditures of the organization, for example, are said to be beyond the understanding of the followers.

A father who spends unaccounted hours away from home is not to be bothered with "why" from anyone in the family. Actions can be understood only if people know the big picture, which is portrayed as too complex for the "common" members of the group or children in the family. Religious addicts learn either to follow blindly or be punished.

Questions are difficult for persecutors to handle. Each one is viewed as a personal affront and a threat to the ministry or family. A person intent on getting accurate answers will not remain part of a toxic system. If a person struggles to find the truth, it will be nearly impossible to locate. If a person wants to move up in the toxic-faith system, that person must not ask questions when things do not add up or make sense.

There was a time when everything in the solar system was said to revolve around the earth. Those who questioned this belief were cast out, and some were punished. In a system of religious addiction, the toxic-faith leader believes that the ministry or the family should revolve around him or her. Anyone questioning that approach, or suggesting that the ministry revolve around people's needs, has no place in the system.

Conformity

Toxic Rule #7: *Don't do anything outside of your role.*

A toxic-faith system doesn't permit personal growth. Those who remain in the system must learn their roles and not deviate from them. Otherwise they will be perceived as rebellious and unstable. The toxic-faith leader doesn't want individualism; he or she wants predictability and conformity. If a person can't adhere to the rules of the assigned role, that person must be ejected from the system. Either learn to play it safe within a role, or don't play at all. Either play the role assigned, or leave and don't look back.

A toxic-faith system is intent on maintaining the homeostasis of the system, that is, keeping the boat from rocking. "Don't do it differently." "We know what is best for you." "Just play it safe and do what we tell you." All are guidelines for acceptance. To risk, to dare, to imagine being something other than what the system wants one to be, to behave in a manner different from the "norm" for the system—all bring the swift judgment of the system.

The toxic-faith system gets victims to stick to their roles by shaming them. Those at the top encourage followers to shame the rebel to intimidate him or her back into submission. To someone who dares to be different, the toxic system responds, "You're selfish." "You're stupid." "You're crazy." "You're in rebellion." "You're a sower of discord." "You're not committed." "You're not in God's will." "You're not fulfilling God's call for your life." "You need to learn to be obedient." "You need to learn submission to authority." The shaming can be so effective that no one dares to remain in the system after being humiliated.

Co-conspirators have a tough role. They are in place to meet the needs of the toxic-faith persecutor, but when their contacts or resources dry up, the persecutor will replace them with other religious addicts, with more money or influence, or with people more willing to do the persecutor's bidding. Co-conspirators are also removed if they appear to be a threat to the persecutor. This is especially true of those who serve alongside the persecutor. These individuals can begin to threaten the leader's authority. If they are perceived as more talented or more respected, they will be discredited and replaced.

The only individuals who can exist over time in the toxic system are those who stay within the bounds of their roles and continue to find new ways to serve the leader. The more a person can accomplish for the toxic-faith leader, the longer the person will stay and the more respected the person will become.

Toxic families have little difficulty keeping their members locked in their roles. Most do not want out of their roles because they so depend on them for survival; they feel insecure outside the roles. Self-defeating behavior is all the person knows, so it is instantly repeated. A lost child will quietly exist alongside the other family members without rocking the boat. The toxic-faith family leader has little problem with compliance, because the members have staked out their roles and refuse to give them up.

MISTRUST

Toxic Rule #8: *Don't trust anyone.*

The rule of mistrust encourages isolation and alienation from human emotions and discourages intimacy in interpersonal relationships. It seeks to block risking, vulnerability, and self-disclosure. Trust is discouraged so that the system's leader maintains allegiance and power. The one to be trusted must be the leader of the family or organization. Each member is disconnected from other members, and everyone depends on the leader. Family members will be less likely to bind together to thwart the system, and organization members will be less likely to get together and discover the truth.

Trust cannot exist where reality is created "as you go." Just when a person starts to become comfortable with the way things are, the leader changes the rules or perceptions. The follower or family member immediately responds with the awareness that no one but the leader or parent should be trusted to interpret or direct what is going on. Everyone else is unaware of the changes until the leader explains them. Only the head of the system can be trusted to prepare the family for the future.

Religious addicts exist inside a system based on false reality. Rules are made up, and those living within the rules are unreal. No one can trust in a system where no one is being real. When people do not say what they think or express what they feel, no one can be trusted. Where one must sacrifice the reality of what one thinks, feels, hears, and sees, trust is impossible. In the absence of trust, manipulation and fear grow. Victims allow themselves to be manipulated as long as they remain in the system. Unable to rely on anyone but the leader, they permit that leader to reign over them.

AVARICE

Toxic Rule #9: *Nothing is more important than giving money to the organization.*

Giving is an important part of anyone's faith. You don't really experience the depths of faith until you are able to give a portion of your money to God rather than spend it all on yourself. Christ often talked about money because it so clearly indicates what lies within a person's heart. Canceled checks and credit card expenditures point to what an individual is like. When a portion of one's income is freely given to God, it indicates that the believer's heart and mind belong to the Lord. Someone who does not yet understand the role of giving in the practice of faith has missed many blessings.

Toxic-faith organizations do not keep giving in perspective; they do not view it as an act of worship, but as a means of funding. Religious addicts believe that nothing is more essential than the organization's continuation, which is funded by the gifts of followers. The more toxic the organization, the more manipulative it becomes in obtaining money. Continual, desperate cries for money are sure signs that the organization depends on human manipulation, not on faith in God.

At one point, I was somehow placed on the mailing list of a very toxic religious organization. Its leader had become a master at raising money. His organization sat at the top of his list of concerns; he could have cared less how much someone had to sacrifice to keep his group going.

I pay my taxes and have never been sued personally, but when a yellow slip is left in the mailbox telling me to pick up a registered letter the next day, I worry. I wonder if it will inform me about a tax auditor or something equally official. This toxic organization sent me a registered letter.

The next day when I opened it, I was furious to discover it was a fund-raising letter. It started with, "No one likes to receive a registered letter." I can't imagine how much money was spent on that clever manipulation to raise funds. I can't imagine how many people fell into the trap of thinking that since the organization had to resort to registered mail, it must be in the biggest need ever, so they wrote out a check immediately.

When ministries meet our needs, we must support them. But we must do that out of love and worship of God, not manipulation. The gift of money must not stand in the way of widows having enough food to eat, children having clothes to wear, or money being available to pay for heat in the winter. Yet thousands of horror stories tell of people who have given so much money under pressure that their health and well-being have been jeopardized. Toxic-faith ministers don't care about those people; they care about their empires and their egos. People are seen as sources of funds to keep the organization going, not as individuals worthy of service.

Many ministries do a commendable job of communicating their needs and requesting support appropriately. The church I attend does not take up an offering. Those who give either send it in by mail or put it in a box at the back of the church. The church has never had a problem with money. People have never been manipulated to give, and God has blessed it. There is another reason it has never had a money problem. One board member is a financial manager who holds the pastor, the staff, and the other leaders of the church accountable to a budget. It has not been easy for the pastors to stay within the budget, but because they have stuck with it, the church experiences the blessings of financial freedom. That is an example of doing it right.

Another ministry of great service to many people is Focus on the Family, led by Dr. James Dobson. This organization raises money without manipulation. Very little of its radio airtime is devoted to asking for financial support. Each month a four-page letter comes from Dr. Dobson, communicating the realistic goals of the organization, personal insights into problems, and a gentle request. The ministry has not gotten overextended and has not needed to resort to desperate means of fundraising. If it does get in a pinch, additional help is requested and the ministry's budget is cut; supporters are never manipulated into giving more. Individuals are encouraged to give to their church first and to Focus on the Family second. It is all done with balance and a godly perspective. No promises of instant relief or wealth are ever offered.

A toxic system is off balance and desperate for your money. Those in the organization will do anything to get your money. They waste funds, overextend the resources of the ministry, and then expect you to make up the difference. Nothing is more significant than raising money and manipulating you into giving more than you rationally should. If the organization you support begs for your money and seems to place greater importance on your money than on you, stop supporting that organization.

SPOTLESS IMAGE

Toxic Rule #10: *At all costs, keep up the image of the organization or family.*

The toxic-faith organization and the toxic-faith family exist in a world of denial. They deny everyone's humanity, including that of its leader.

One foundation for the growth of a toxic organization is the image of a godlike leader. The leader must be presented as having a level of perfection that others cannot attain. A father of a sick family will not admit to problems or ask for forgiveness. Protecting the image of the leader protects the image of the organization and the family, and it becomes a major priority. No one must know of marital problems, unless somehow the secret leaks. Then everyone must work to ensure that the leader is perceived as the ultimate mate, able to resolve the crisis of marriage with godly wisdom that no one else could have had. The co-conspirators and enablers around the leader work together to create awe in the minds of the followers. Every problem must have a solution that makes the leader appear sacrificial, loving, and serving beyond the capabilities of most others.

The flaws of a toxic organization must be covered at all costs. Anyone who rebels against the system must be personally attacked so people will think the problem is the person, not the system. People are not allowed to discuss negative aspects of the organization. If a financial crisis arises, the co-conspirators must work closely and quickly to figure out a way to communicate the problem without destroying the image of the organization or the leader. Deception and lies may be the only way to uphold the image.

When an organization exists in a false reality, image is integral to its success. Without an image of perfection, reality sets in, and people stop supporting the toxic-faith system. Everyone must work hard to ensure that the image and the false reality are upheld. Perception becomes reality, and image is the key to continued support from followers. The leader's job is to fool as many people as possible into believing that the image is reality.

This rule is never observed 100 percent, however. Some members of the organization or a family always come to see the group for what it is and challenge the false perceptions. They become outcasts, but as they go out, they force a crack in the delusive image of the leader, the family, or the organization. Eventually, enough cracks destroy the facade completely, and people recognize the organization for what it is.

A healthy system provides for the needs of its members. They feel confident that the system is there for them. In a toxic system, the members are there to keep it going. If they are willing to stick to the rules, the system can expand. If they sense a problem and begin to break the rules, the system falls apart. The toxic-faith leader ensures that all the other addicts—co-conspirators, enablers, and victims—know the rules and abide by them. Anyone who hints at not following the rules is dealt with quickly so the organization or family will not be damaged.

All rules in a toxic system have something to do with maintaining religious addiction. Rules are designed to fuel the addict's ego, protect the addict's position, and perpetuate the status quo. This is the central poison in the family or organization and in the faith of the addicted followers. Self-obsession and self-aggrandizing leaders replace God. Yet addicts believe their motives are pure; they are not willing to admit they contribute to a toxic system that leads them away from God.

In a healthy system, individuals are safe to explore how they act and what they think, feel, hear, want, or imagine. Members of the system are not judged and measured but guided and supported. When an individual who felt trapped by a problem of the past comes to a healthy organization, he or she feels a new freedom. The struggler opens up to other strugglers and, from the support offered there, receives help. The love that is freely shared leads individuals to a stronger faith.

A toxic system usually starts out good. Everything looks wonderful. As involvement increases, however, rules emerge, and the struggler starts to comply, becoming a victim in the process. Freedom is replaced by restrictive rules.

The toxic system convinces each member that the way to a stronger faith in God is through the organization or the head of the family. The rules exist so that a person can make it through, as long as the individual strictly complies with the rules.

In a healthy system, each person goes by the rules of God, not the dictates of people. Each person is freed to develop a relationship with the Creator, not with an organization. Each person is responsible for individual growth in faith. And each person has the capacity to reach for God and find him reaching back. The only rule is perseverance in seeking him.

Ten Rules of a Toxic-Faith System

1. The leader must be in control of every aspect at all times.
2. When problems arise, immediately find a guilty party to blame.
3. Don't make mistakes.
4. Never point out the reality of a situation.
5. Never express your feelings unless they are positive.
6. Don't ask questions, especially if they are tough ones.
7. Don't do anything outside of your role.
8. Don't trust anyone.
9. Nothing is more important than giving money to the organization.
10. At all costs, keep up the image of the organization or family.

CHAPTER 9

Treatment and Recovery

Since the beginning of New Life Treatment Centers, we have helped many individuals afflicted with religious addiction. Yet they never come to us saying they are religious addicts. Instead they are depressed, alcoholic, overweight, anorexic, suicidal, and despairing in many other ways. They don't know *what* they have; they just know they're miserable.

What a joy it has been to watch these people discover that at the roots of their other problems lie toxic beliefs and a toxic faith. Awareness dawns as they discover they have been chasing an illusion, a dream, rather than seeking God. While they are with us, they grow by leaps and bounds. They gain a renewed focus, and they understand who God really is for the first time. When they change their core toxic beliefs, many of their other problems subside immediately. As they turn their lives and will over to God, they find the serenity that has so long eluded them.

All of these individuals get involved in a recovery program where they work out their toxic beliefs in God and their distorted views about themselves. In addition to recovery groups similar to Alcoholics Anonymous, they enter into group therapy with other patients, led by therapists. As they describe their problems to each other, they identify their character defects and gain insight into how to correct them.

Therapists have certain objectives in mind for each individual. As each objective is accomplished, the patient moves closer to being able to function normally, free of conflict and depression. Specific areas must be addressed for these objectives to be achieved. The following material covers some areas vital to regaining a pure faith.

BREAKING THROUGH DENIAL: BEGINNING RECOVERY

The number-one objective in the recovery of the religious addict is to break through the denial that addiction exists. We must help the addict identify that involvement in religion has become of primary importance. The addict must accept that the religion is so toxic it has hurt relationships with family and friends.

This process of breaking through denial begins with the first confrontation or intervention. When those close to the addict finally express how they feel and how they see the toxic faith, the denial begins to fade in the addict with a good chance for recovery, and acceptance begins to take its place. If the addict will not admit that a problem exists—and many fight to the end to deny that there is one—there is little hope for recovery. Once the addict can identify how the religious addiction is abusive and destructive to relationships with God, self, and others, the number-one objective is achieved.

Then treatment can begin. Although they know they need help, most addicts are reluctant to let go of the addiction; it has become a reliable friend. When others rejected the addict, the addict could turn to the practice of toxic faith and those within the toxic-faith system who always seemed so accepting. When the world became too painful, the religious addict could count on the addiction and other addicts to create a delusional reality that felt a lot better (for the moment). It always made life tolerable, and though it never completely satiated the addict's need, it remained there always to provide comfort, a sense of belonging, power, and a feeling of being right or righteous. It is impossible to give up all of those benefits in an instant. The process takes time, effort, and a willingness to be vulnerable.

Bill came to us severely depressed. Divorce proceedings had shattered his plans to be a minister. Feeling that his friends, family, and God had abandoned him, he was on the brink of suicide.

During treatment it was disclosed that Bill spent most of his time in the church. He was heavily involved in missionary work, Bible studies, and all church functions. He was a religious addict, driven by his need to please God. For the most part, he had abandoned his wife long before she filed for divorce.

Religion for Bill was a way to escape his fears of intimacy and vulnerability. If his family or friends needed support or emotional intimacy, he simply didn't have the time. He believed it was his wife's job to raise the family while he served the Lord. He used religion to remain distant from those who loved him most.

Bill's toxic faith deluded him into believing that he was being persecuted because of his faith. The more his family complained about his absence, the more he quoted the scriptures on submission and the Great Commission. He believed that God would make his wife and family understand—after all, wasn't his absence biblically justified? Whenever someone confronted Bill, he would simply defend himself with Scripture and retreat into prayer. His prayers allowed him to avoid conflict in the family and delude himself into believing that God would make everything okay.

Bill had quit his job in a "step of faith," believing that God would provide. He had invested the family's savings "in the kingdom of God" and the missionary work that so consumed him. The more the bills piled up, the more time he spent in prayer and worship.

Finally the bill collectors foreclosed, his wife left him, and he shut down emotionally. He no longer found relief in prayer; he felt unworthy to have God answer his prayers. Bill had hit rock bottom. He no longer had the answers, and he sought help.

In treatment, we put Bill into a support group. Though he still maintained that God was all he needed, the group was able to lovingly confront his delusion that if he continued to hang on to the same toxic perceptions of God, things would be different. Group members told how toxic faith had nearly destroyed them and how they had finally challenged their toxic beliefs. They all knew what Bill was going through; they accepted him where he was and valued him. Anytime Bill reverted to the old pattern of biblically justifying his position, they understood. They knew that eventually he would see how his self-justification only led to defeat.

Eventually Bill began to feel understood and at the same time see the need for change. He began to identify the toxic thinking that surrounded his addiction. He was able to see how he used his addiction to avoid feeling and being intimate with his family, friends, and even God. He saw how his religious dogma separated him from the people he loved the most.

The people around him saw the change in Bill. He no longer tried to use Scripture to defend himself and shame others for "not understanding." He was able to move in humility. As Bill continued his treatment, the family also entered into therapy. The wounds of addiction began to heal and Bill's anxiety lifted. He was able to develop friendships with those who did not share his religious beliefs. He was able to explain his faith without cramming things down their throats. In doing so, he began to identify the characteristics of healthy faith and incorporated them into his belief system. He made great progress because he was able to start at the beginning by finally surrendering to God.

SURRENDERING TO GOD: SPIRITUAL RECOVERY

Often the initial motivation to change is not to find something better, but to eliminate something that feels worse. The religious addict may be motivated by a desire, not to find God or grow toward God, but to eliminate the guilt that goes unresolved in religious addiction. The addict may have recognized how he or she was using religion or what it was doing to others. These thoughts may leave the addict feeling so depressed, worthless, powerless, and guilty that any alternative is considered better than continuing without change. The feelings of guilt and failure may be the pain needed to get that person to surrender to God.

Surrendering to God is a process. The length and the difficulty of that process depend on how long the addict was involved with the addiction and how far it progressed. The more hidden the addiction has become, the more difficult the surrender process will be. Before something can be surrendered to God, it must be uncovered, revealed in all its terror, and acknowledged as real. Private, repressed sins are very difficult for the egocentric to admit. It is even more difficult to admit to not knowing what to do about them or how to fix them. This is the point of surrender where an addict is finally able to say that life has become unmanageable. Without a relationship with God, there is no power available to change. Surrendering is the process of letting go and trusting that God can and will handle the admitted problems.

This was an extremely difficult step for me at a traumatic period of my life. I had paid for an abortion for a woman whom I had made pregnant. The guilt felt incapacitating because I felt solely responsible. Guilt crushed me until I was able to accept God's forgiveness. Even with that acceptance, I did not fully surrender the problem to God. I implemented a system of hard work that led me to hours of Bible study, prayer sessions, and church attendance. If anyone asked a question, I had a spiritual answer. I felt great about myself because I worked hard to feel that way. Others, however, did not feel so great about me. I was worthless to them. I had become so pseudospiritual that I did not communicate with them. Someone had to spell out what I was doing before the situation sank in. Only then was I able to surrender to God completely.

Working on Toxic Thinking: Mental Recovery

Toxic thinking is one key way the addict maintains a delusional reality. Quite frankly, the religious addict's thinking is disordered. Treatment involves confronting toxic thoughts and replacing them with thoughts based in reality. The following are some common toxic thoughts and thinking patterns that we confront in treatment.

Thinking in Extremes

Toxic thinkers believe that people and issues can be viewed totally in terms of white or black, all good or all bad, completely right or completely wrong. This thinking drives the religious addict and fuels crusades against the corrupt.

Everything is extreme to the addict. One mistake and the religious addict feels like a failure, so all errors are denied. This leads to the denial of even small problems in an effort to defend against feelings of total failure. People will comment, "I cannot understand why that man cannot admit even one mistake." If one mistake is admitted, that person will feel like a complete failure. The act is so internalized that making the mistake moves the addict to believe he or she is capable only of making mistakes. Since no one can exist this way, denial becomes the defense. The addict denies the one extreme of bad and creates the illusion of living at the opposite extreme of perfection.

Treatment involves confronting such thinking. Religious addicts, though members of churches for years, must be reprogrammed. They must be told over and over that making a mistake does not make them mistakes or produce failure. Additionally, a person who makes one mistake or disappoints them in one way is not all bad. There are still some very wonderful things about that person.

Sin is an act; it is not a description of every facet of your character. You do not have to be perfect to be good. You do not have to be perfect to be accepted. God does not accept you based on your perfect performance, and it is futile to attempt to gain further acceptance from him. God is interested in a relationship, not hard work and trying harder. God cares about you. You, with all of your imperfections, are the focus of God's love. These thoughts must replace the extremes of toxic thinking.

The religious addict needs to change from a product-orientation to a process-orientation. The addict needs to recognize that life is a learning process and the product of who you are is ever-changing. Sin must be perceived as a part of fallen humanity that can be overcome through the power of God. People can recover from failure. People can change. Accepting these truths reduces the fear of making mistakes or falling short. After the mistake, a process exists that can restore the person to a growing relationship with God and others.

Religious addicts are very hard on themselves and everyone else and are driven by their all-or-nothing thinking. They must have mercy on themselves and on others. They must relax their perfectionism and allow it to be replaced with an acceptance of their humanity. Christ spoke of this ability to not see things in terms of extremes. When confronted about breaking a law on the Sabbath, he told his critics that he desired mercy rather than sacrifice.

Pure faith is full of mercy. We have the benefit of a merciful God. The addict must be helped to incorporate that mercy into views of other people and self. This can bring great relief to the addict and begin the process of reestablishing relationships that had been rejected due to thinking in extremes.

Drawing Invalid Conclusions

Religious addicts have the ability to turn anything into a negative. From their feelings of inadequacy, they can contort any set of circumstances into a doomsday scenario. If they sin, they think they have knocked themselves out of any chance of going to heaven. If the boss has a negative opinion of some work, it must mean that dismissal is imminent. If something happens one time, it must mean it will happen every time. If a father deserts me when I am young, every male will desert me. If I fail at one job, then I will fail at every job. They make all-inclusive statements: "God never answers my prayers" and "God never listens to me." *Never* and *always* are integral to their statements about themselves and their expectations of others. Things are *never* right; they are *always* bad and becoming worse.

The conclusions of religious addicts are not based in reality.

Not all of the addict's conclusions are negative. A religious addict can use the same technique to avoid reality. Instead of saying, "God never takes care of me," an addict might say, "God takes care of every area of my life." Although the statement is true to the degree that God cares about every area of our lives, it is not true that he will magically make a car payment or always heal a baby who could be easily treated by a doctor. Drawing the wrong conclusion—if I do nothing, things will work out anyway—can be just as destructive as drawing a negative conclusion.

Treatment becomes a process of confronting these thoughts of unreality. Group time is spent in identifying unreasonable and irrational conclusions, and the sources of those conclusions are rooted out. The addict comes to see life as it really is. Every event is not considered an indictment on the future. Each day is handled one day at a time, without projecting hardship on tomorrow.

Faulty Filtering

When individuals focus on the irrelevant and the negative, they focus on only one part of reality and thus distort the whole. They become so selective in what they will respond to that they discard much of what is good. One negative detail disqualifies the rest, even when that negative detail is less relevant than the more positive whole.

Suppose you take a blank piece of white paper and draw a dot in the middle of it. Nine out of ten people will tell you that they see the black dot. They have effectively selected the dot and abstracted it from the context in which it was seen. In actuality, they saw not only the dot on the paper, but most probably the person holding it and all the peripheral scenes surrounding the person holding the paper.

That is the way many religious addicts live, except their filtering does not involve a harmless piece of paper and a dot. Their faulty filtering revolves around their faults and character defects. They see only personal sin or the sin in the world and refuse to look at all of the good and positive things. Addicts focus on the negative of the world, and the world becomes too depressing and uncomfortable to live in. Addicts must then escape into the addiction of religion for mood alteration. Religious addicts who do not properly filter information are easy to spot. They are hypercritical and negative about everything, including themselves. When they come into treatment, nothing is right. The bed tilts, the walls are the wrong color, and the food is terrible. Although the food usually *is* terrible, they focus on all the wrong things.

Staff members must bring them back to reality. They are reminded that they called us for help with the one overriding problem that has been filtered out; we didn't call them. There was a reason for the phone call. They are confronted with the need to work on themselves. Eventually, they begin to filter back in some of the important issues. They are asked to look at the lives affected by the treatment and to talk to grateful patients who survived the food. When the filter starts to let reality sink back in, religious addicts become ready to concentrate on personal issues of change.

Invalidating the Positive

Invalidation does not ignore information; it just disqualifies the facts or distorts them, usually toward the negative. The religious addict loves the phrase, "yes, but," and this must be confronted through the treatment process. Suppose someone says to a religious addict that he looks wonderful today. The dedicated addict will retort, "Yes, but I feel terrible. And I know if I feel this bad, I am going to look much worse tomorrow."

Every positive can be contorted into something negative and wrong. If they cannot think of a proof that the compliment is false, they will rationalize the motives behind the statement: "They're just being nice to me," or "That person is out to get me or wants something I have."

The most dedicated religious addicts use a technique designed to look good while it degrades themselves. If a woman makes a wonderful flower arrangement and someone comments on it, she retorts, "It wasn't me; Christ did it." But let's face it—Christ didn't buy those flowers, put them in a vase, and arrange them in such a way as to have beauty and symmetry. The addict has such a hard time acknowledging what might be a special talent that she feels the need to invalidate any statement that compliments the talent.

When people show appreciation, religious addicts will say, "Don't thank me; thank God," or "It was God's will." This is not humility; this is something very terrible. As the addicts invalidate the information, they invalidate themselves. They support their self-defeating conclusions about themselves by discarding anything counter to that negative image.

Treatment confronts the self-defeating statements and actions. First, the person must see the pattern. Then the person discovers why he or she feels the need to do this. The next step is to replace the disqualifying statements with accepting statements. In this way an addict may learn to accept a compliment for the first time. Cracks in the negative facade let through some good feelings about self, based on the reality of God's love and sacrifice. The recovering addict recognizes the good that has been created within and appreciates it. The person accepts being created in the image of God and feels God's love for the first time. As these positive thoughts take root, the person's misery lessens, along with the need to resort to the addiction.

Discarding the Negative
The flip side of invalidating the positive is the religious addict's discarding of negative behavior to maintain a toxic sense of self-worth. An example would be the promiscuous follower who filters out his negative behavior by seeing only his positive actions, thus allowing himself to do immoral things that he would condemn as immoral if he saw others doing them. This is done by claiming special needs or being the exception. Some say they have the freedom to experience things that are clearly immoral. The religious addict is able to "yes, but," into continuing the most destructive and negative behavior.

For these people, treatment includes facing up to their wrongs, who they have hurt, and the restitution that must be made. These people are often the most resistant to treatment, because when they face who they are and what they have done, their world crashes around them. Sometimes they become so depressed they are difficult to motivate. These cases require more time than most.

Thinking with the Heart
Thinking with the heart occurs when feelings, not facts, form the basis of reality. "I feel bad; therefore, I must be bad." "I feel hopeless and powerless; therefore, I must be hopeless and powerless. If I am hopeless and powerless, there is no reason for me to go on." "I feel like a disappointment to God; therefore, I must be a disappointment to God. There is no sense in trying to have a relationship with him. He won't like me anyway." Addicts caught up in their emotions interpret the world only by the way they feel. In this self-obsessed existence, the only thing that matters is how they feel, not what is real.

This emotional reasoning reflects the toxic believer's basic belief system: "I'm basically a bad, unworthy person." An addict who feels this negatively about himself or herself will not have many positive thoughts about anything. Treatment involves separating the evidence of reality from feelings. The recovering addict is able to identify a thought or perception based on emotion versus one based on the evidence. This separation allows reality to sift into the person's thinking and eventually erodes some of the negative thoughts.

A woman dated a very wealthy man for more than five years. Every year she went to Europe with him and his family, and she loved mingling with the upper class. One day she suggested they marry—and he immediately rejected her. He demeaned her and said he could never marry her because she was too large and unattractive.

She felt like a failure. Because she felt so negative about herself, she became negative about everything else. She felt God disliked her. She did not know what she had done to offend God, but she believed she must have done something very bad because he had yanked away her future. From that time on, all her decisions revolved around those terrible feelings about herself and God. Her thinking had to be changed before she could find peace with her emotions.

Surrounding Oneself with "Shoulds"

An addict creates self-induced pressure with internal "should" statements, a predominant reason for mood alteration. Thoughts such as *I should have done better* and *I should have done more* drive the addict deeper into the addiction. The addict never measures up to the expectations of old thought patterns that play a recurring theme of "never good enough." These unrealistic measuring sticks become more and more demanding.

Addicts truly believe that these unrealistic demands must be met. They drive themselves to meet the demands in an effort to avoid disappointment or failure, but their only rewards are disappointment and depression.

Some believe that Christians should be happy all the time. If the Christian addict feels sad, there must be something wrong. This type of toxic thought drives the addict into more and more compulsive religious behavior in search of happiness. The addict reasons that since he or she should be constantly happy (but is not), he or she should expend greater, more intense efforts to find the elusive happy goal.

Other religious addicts insist that others should be more Christlike. Frustration and anger mount when individuals fail to meet the unrealistic expectations. These negative emotions drive addicts further into the addiction to alter their mood of destructive anger. They will act out compulsively.

Long hours of supposed intercessory prayer or intense witnessing (which many times is Bible bullying) take precedence over everything else. The addicts work to push others to live up to the expectations of what the addicts think they "should" live up to.

Their need for others to live up to these expectations is based not on spiritual concern for them but on the addicts' need to avoid feelings of frustration and anger.

Many "should" statements are not reality based. They leave no room for being human, and their purpose in the addictive process is to build up feelings of guilt, disappointment, and inadequacy. They must be replaced with thoughts based more in reality: "It would be nice if Christians were more Christlike." "I wish the pastor understood." "I wish I were (or it would be nice if I could be) more obedient." Such statements are taught as replacements for the tyrannical "should" statements.

Treatment helps addicts remove the illicit "should" statements from the thought processes. Repeated confrontation provides the impetus to rethink the demands. Each addict learns a whole new way of thinking about performance. You can almost see the relief come over them when they finally accept that their standards were too tough and they can relax.

Maintaining Hyper-Responsibility

Religious addicts will take responsibility for anything. Pastors will feel responsible for the problems and sins of the whole congregation. Parents will feel responsible for their adult children, even though they have been out of the home for years. Every terrible thing that someone else does provides an invitation to personalize the act, take responsibility for it, and feel shame over it. This compounds the low self-worth that plagues the addict.

At the heart of this hyper-responsibility is the addict's desire to be in control. Treatment focuses on the person's giving up the desire to be in control and giving up the egocentric feeling of being responsible for so many things. The addict also needs to refocus. Feeling responsibility for everyone else allows the addict to lose touch with his or her problems. Treatment takes the focus off everyone else and brings it back to rest on the religious addiction. Some have labeled this hyper-responsibility as codependency. Others call it a self-defeating personality disorder. It can be changed with repeated confrontation and the addict's turning over control each day to God.

The initial therapeutic endeavor, after the religious addict has acknowledged the problem, is to identify the toxic thought process. Treatment becomes a training ground for teaching the religious addict how to think. Mental circuits that have been shut down get turned back on. The religious addict's toxic thinking has become a way of life and an irrational way to interpret life. Treatment helps the religious addict identify what is real and how to act on that reality by thinking in a different way. If the religious addict does not choose to think differently, there is little hope for change.

WORKING ON NEW INFORMATION

Religious addicts often have fallen victim to a lifetime of propaganda. They don't know what to believe about God, the Bible, faith, or Christ. They usually know nothing about addiction and other dependencies. Treatment uses books, tapes, and lectures to reeducate religious addicts. Many books on the market explain the dynamics of addiction, codependency, counseling, and recovery. Carefully selected materials, including the Bible, provide each addict with a new foundation of information that can lead to overcoming the addiction.

While religious addicts are learning to process and resolve their emotions, new information saturates them each day. This is why a treatment center must be carefully chosen. When the religious addict starts over, a whole new value system evolves. If that person enters a center where destructive values reign, irreparable damage will be done. The information fed to the patient needs to accord with solid biblical principles. If it contradicts the principles of the Bible, it will hurt the process of coming to know God. Hours of acquiring new information help to alter the addict's toxic beliefs and eventually the compulsive behavior. The religious addict must learn to question rather than disqualify.

One purpose of information in treatment is to change a naive believer into a questioning seeker. Most religious addicts have sought easy solutions and what appeared to be the quick fix. They wholeheartedly believed anyone with what sounded like a good idea. Treatment attempts to change this. All material must be carefully evaluated, otherwise we return a person to the world just as susceptible to manipulation as before.

Case managers constantly ask, "What do *you* think?" They emphasize this basic skill because the religious addict has often been victimized by controlling persecutors who do not like to be questioned. The support group, both in treatment and after the patient is discharged, helps the addict to evaluate information. The group becomes a safe place to check out the validity of new information. The transformation from a convinced knower to a questioning seeker provides the recovering addict with a safety shield against toxic information.

Addiction is not merely something the addict does; addiction is a part of the person's character and nature. An inseparable bond forms between the person and the addiction. The bonding grows strong because it has become a form of survival for the addict. The addiction becomes the person, and the person becomes the addiction.

The bond to the addiction must be transferred to other individuals. If it isn't, the recovering addict will merely intellectualize the problem, and knowledge will easily become the new addiction. That is why a person cannot merely read a good book and have a radical life change (that is, without divine intervention). The group provides accountability and a new bond to replace the old one. New information needs to be acquired within and alongside a support group so that the information can be assimilated in a balanced and healthy way.

Working in a Support Group

I can't overemphasize the importance of support groups. If an individual is to recover from religious addiction, it will require the assistance of a caring group. *It cannot be done alone.* Millions have attempted to recover from addiction without the assistance of a group, and although they may stop the addictive behavior, they will not develop a balanced recovery. Sooner or later they will trip up and either fall back into the addiction or find another one to replace it.

At New Life Treatment Centers, all patients are introduced to a support group. Those groups that work with the twelve steps seem to be the most helpful. Some groups develop their own steps—maybe ten or eight—and they work also. The number and the type of steps are much less significant than what happens in the group. The group must provide a combination of support and accountability. It must supplement the entire recovery program, not become its single focus. If it becomes the single focus of recovery, it can become a substitute addiction and be just as unhealthy as a toxic-faith system.

Members of the recovery community are quick to find points of division and superiority. Sometimes this centers on whether the twelve steps, originating from Alcoholics Anonymous, are helpful or harmful. Some believe they are wonderful steps back to a full relationship with God and a restored relationship with others. Others believe they detour people from a relationship with Christ and replace the church and a pastor's leadership role.

Both sides are right in some cases. The twelve steps can be a wonderful guide to spiritual growth and maturity. They can also become an obsession that prevents people from achieving complete spiritual recovery. Some recovering addicts use their twelve-step theology to replace involvement in a church. This is just as destructive as having no recovery program at all. The church is a special place where spiritual gifts can be used to serve and worship God. There is no good excuse to avoid church involvement. Since religious addicts are susceptible to latching on to systems, they need to be extremely careful that the steps are used in a balanced manner.

Some people believe that the twelve steps are the only route to recovery. They discount the church, treatment centers, counselors, and everything else not related to the twelve steps. Sometimes the suggestion of another source of recovery is too big a threat to accept for these rigid recovering addicts. They can become toxic members of the group and hurt others in that group. Whether a group has eight, ten, or twelve steps, it is important that the group can serve the dual roles of encouragement and confrontation.

I was speaking at a conference where many Christians get together each year to rally for the cause of recovery in churches. It was obvious after talking to just two people that a major rift had arisen between two factions. One believed that the twelve steps were terrible, while the other believed they represented biblical principles. Each felt the other was out of line and wanted to convince the other of his error. It struck me as ironic that all those people were supposed to be recovering.

Recovery never focuses on someone else's problem, but always focuses on the self. Recovery is never "working on someone else's program"; it is always working on your own. These people were judging each other rather than appreciating the thousands each year that each group was helping.

Often people in need of a support group will use some philosophical basis for a reason not to join—they attended a bad group or heard bad things about another group. Such excuses enable these individuals to avoid doing the work required to get well. If the addicts would focus on their problems and their need to recover rather than on the group's problems, they would find most groups helpful and healthy.

CHARACTERISTICS OF A HEALTHY SUPPORT GROUP

Certain characteristics of a support group need to be evident if it is to provide a healthy environment for growth.

Acceptance

A healthy support group is made up of loving and accepting people. It welcomes a struggling addict into the group and assists as the addict develops a new identity free of addiction. The group will lovingly assist the person in cultivating a new relationship with God and his Son. If it is a mature group, it will not reject the person because of differing beliefs, but it will patiently work with the person in the search for truth. If the addict feels rejection due to personal beliefs, appearance, or any other peculiarity, he or she may leave the group and never return to another support group. In a healthy group, each person is allowed to be different and make mistakes without being shamed.

Unconditional Positive Regard

True love values individuals for who they are rather than for what they are able to do. True love—the experience of unconditional positive regard—is an extremely healing force. Receiving true love from the group enables addicts to love themselves, God, and others. Addicts in a group where true love exists are free to love others in that same freeing manner. It becomes an emotional and spiritual bond without equal.

Love is the central theme of Christianity, yet sometimes it is difficult to find around Christians. Christ demonstrated his love when he gave his life—not because of what we did, not because of what we deserved, but he loved us as we are. As we participate in recovery groups, we need to stick to the model set by Christ. We must provide the same unconditional love to other recovering strugglers. If we are not able to provide that for a recovering addict, we are doing much more harm than good and have formed our own toxic-faith system.

Freedom of Expression

Addicts need a place to express emotions without having to worry about living up to someone's expectations. They need a place where they are free to explore perceptions, thoughts, and feelings. They need a forum where new ideas and new forms of communication can be practiced with the support of the group. Members of the group should feel freedom to be who they want to be without fear of retribution.

In the group, addicts practice for the real world, where rejection is commonplace. Just like a loving family, the group needs to be a safe place where addicts find relief by saying the tough things rather than holding them in.

Nonautocratic/Noncontrolling

The addict needs to experience a "new family" or group where he or she has equal power and rights. This will be a new experience for the religious addict who was indoctrinated in a toxic system that operated from the "one-down" or "one-up" position. The addict, having learned how to control or be controlled, needs to learn how to accept responsibility for his or her behavior only. The addict needs a group where no one gives the orders and no one person is in control.

When all of these elements occur in a recovery support group, the attenders can grow and mature. They grow in their recovery and in their faith. When they stop growing, the group lovingly confronts them and moves them back into the recovery mode.

All groups are not wonderful like this. No group is like another, and an addict should attend at least five different groups, if possible, to determine which one would be most beneficial and comfortable to encourage spiritual growth.

I have a friend who is a recovering alcoholic. More accurately stated, she is an alcoholic who no longer drinks. This person does not attend AA or any other type of support group. She is a miserable person who always has another reason to be upset about some other imperfection in her life. She is an extremely sad case and hard to be around.

My friend loved the camaraderie of the bars she drank in, but she won't gather with those who have shunned the bars for a time to grow. She loved to tell her drinking friends of her problems, but she refuses to share her problems with those who could help. She spent hours drinking and taking drugs with friends, but now she has no time to spend on her own recovery. She had a lot of excuses for not joining a support group, none of them good.

No one in need of recovery can ever find an excuse good enough to justify not being part of something that has helped thousands of people restore their relationship with God. Addicts, whether drug or religious, can benefit from the support of a group whose purpose is to help individuals find a way back to a loving, caring God.

WORKING ON THE FAMILY

Like all other addictions, religious addiction hurts families and destroys many. Frequently an addict will move away from the family, feeling justified in doing so in the hope of finding a deeper faith. Many family members give up on ever having a normal relationship with the addict.

When the addict begins recovery, the broken family must also begin recovery. Any effective treatment must involve the family. If it cannot be facilitated at the time of intensive treatment, it can occur later. If it does not occur at all, however, the family will surely disintegrate. While the addiction developed, everyone in the family took on a particular role. The family became dysfunctional, just like the addict's family of origin in which the seeds of religious addiction were planted. Family members need help out of those roles. If they do not obtain it, they will almost certainly move on to their own addiction and dependency problems. And while their own problems remain, little support will be available for the recovering religious addict.

Families of religious addicts tend to be very angry. They are angry with the addict and angry with themselves for not being able to change the addict. In treatment, those negative feelings must be expressed and transcended. If they are not resolved, they will lead to alienation and the rejection of the recovering addict. It takes a long time to heal this anger, and everyone needs patience as each member finds a way to express and resolve negative emotions. Once this occurs, the family has the opportunity to re-form and bond into a unified unit of support and love. If treatment does not make every attempt possible to achieve this family recovery, it is not doing what is required.

One young girl in our adolescent unit had been involved in a group that worshiped Satan. Part of her treatment was to help her see why she enjoyed being with such a destructive group and to help her find more positive ways to obtain the same things. The other part of her treatment was to help her family sort through its problems so the girl would have a supportive environment to return to.

The extreme anger of the father became clear in the first session. He was furious at his family and himself. When the counselor mentioned that she saw an extreme amount of anger, he yelled at her and walked out, declaring he did not need to be humiliated in front of his family—a common reaction. The chances of recovery are greatly reduced when a child returns to a family where the father is furious and everyone is a victim of that anger. The family treatment aspects of a program go a long way to provide support for the addict and the opportunity for recovery among the other family members.

WORKING ON NEW FRIENDS: SOCIAL RECOVERY

When the addict abandons the toxic-faith system, many social relationships go with it. If these are not replaced, a terrible void will hamper recovery. The recovery support group provides encouragement and accountability, but it cannot fill this void. New friends and social relationships are needed for the same reasons as the support group, but they are also needed for fun. Recovery is serious business, and too often those involved with it stop having fun. They become so serious that sometimes well-meaning people encourage them to go back to their addiction rather than continue to act so lifeless.

Recovering addicts must seek supportive friends, who are rarely found in bars and nightclubs. They are most likely found in church, at the gym, by a swimming pool, in a club, or in a college course. Making new friends and going new places with them form parts of a comprehensive recovery program. Appropriate treatment shows individuals how to develop new sources of social support.

WORKING ON THE BODY: PHYSICAL RECOVERY

Religious addicts tend to have poor dietary habits, are often overweight, and totally lack physical exercise. They spend so much time on their addiction that they don't have time to exercise. They are so compulsive that they eat everything in sight. They feel drained of energy and feel bad about themselves because they look and feel bad.

Treatment addresses these needs with the same level of importance as the other areas of recovery. The recovering religious addict sees the body as the temple of God and takes care of it accordingly. Rest, exercise, and nutrition are not afterthoughts, but priorities. The moods stabilize as sugar and caffeine consumption decline. Exercise provides a natural form of relaxation. Proper rest reduces stress and irritability. This one area is often the most neglected in a recovery program. As a result, many addicts return to their old compulsive behaviors. They look miserable and feel miserable, so they return to the source of mood alteration that promises to lift them out of their misery.

HOPE FOR RECOVERY

There is great hope for the recovering religious addict, hope that comes in developing a new faith, pure and free of the poison of addiction.

This hope does not spring forth on its own, however. It must be cultivated through a recovery program that encompasses every area of the addict's life and includes the addict's family. The recovering addict must learn to think differently, relate differently, and find different people and places for support and fun. When it all comes together, the recovering addict comes closer to God.

Treatment facilitates the recovery process. It brings the forces of recovery professionals to bear on the addict and the addiction. It is not a cure-all or a quick fix. If it works, it works because the addict decides to make it work with God's help. A person obtains nothing more from it than is put into it. One of its greatest values is the bringing together of fellow strugglers, some sick and some well, to help one another find a new life and new hope in a loving God.

It is my hope and prayer that if you or someone you love needs treatment, you will seek it out and initiate the process of change.

CHAPTER 10

Seventeen Characteristics of Healthy Faith

Healing from religious addiction is the detoxification of faith. Through Bible study, church attendance, prayer, communication with other believers, and time, toxic faith can be purified into a healthy faith.

Through recovery, the addict attains a new knowledge of God and develops a strong, healthy faith. When faith is healthy, the individual's dependency on God becomes a godly dependency. The following discussion provides seventeen key characteristics of a healthy faith. (These characteristics are further developed in our book *More Jesus, Less Religion.*)

FOCUSED ON GOD

Healthy faith focuses completely on God, not on who we want God to be or what we want God to do. Caricatures of God created by our self-obsessed society are replaced with the real God of the Bible.

The Bible is our best link to knowing God. Men and women through the ages have always dreamed up new concepts of who God is and what he does. Inevitably they become very confused in their "make it up as you go" theology, however, since they have no standard or source of authority. If only they would recognize the Bible as the Word of God and that it can be trusted to reveal to us who God is! Through studying it, we can grow in knowledge of God and in faith.

Throughout the Bible, God is shown seeking after his people, persistent in his desire to fellowship with his creation. God loves us and wants a relationship with us, even if we are guilty of many sins. Some of the great men and women of the Bible did many terrible things, and yet God loved those individuals and didn't turn his back on them. This fact should reassure us. People may tell us that God has rejected us, but the loving God of the Bible has gone to a great deal of trouble for all of us.

If you believe the Bible to be the Word of God, you must believe that Christ is his Son. Healthy faith must encompass all of who God is, including the Holy Spirit and Jesus Christ. If people could trust that Jesus died for their sins, it would go a long way toward ridding the world of the shame and guilt of sin. God has taken care of us because he knew we could not be perfect. We feel tremendous relief when we discover that performance can be replaced with the person of Christ.

The common denominator of many popular religions today is a focus on self rather than on God. One man became involved with a Christian cult because of the promises it made, including guarantees of a healthy body, a wonderful family, and enough money to obtain whatever he needed. The man felt complete bliss as long as he focused on what he could obtain to better himself. But eventually he realized how absent God was from his life. He became aware of his constant focus on himself rather than on God. When he discussed this with a church leader, the leader explained it away as a problem with people unwilling to have everything God wanted for them. The man walked away from the church and from his addiction to its false promises. He never returned because his new search focused on God—and he found him.

GROWING

Healthy faith grows and matures over time. Bible study and prayer assist in the process, but the difficulties of life are the greatest faith growers. It is our nature to seek quick relief from pain. In our fear that we will live in pain forever or that the pain will overwhelm us, we run to the closest form of relief available. This does not allow for growth in faith. When we feel pain and stand firm, trusting that God will see us through, we are rewarded with a strengthening of our faith that will make the same crisis less traumatic.

I have watched hundreds of alcoholics go through the detoxification process. They have spent years trusting in a bottle for relief. Then because the pain of drinking becomes greater than the original pain they sought to squelch, they decide to stop. The first three days of detoxification become the most vulnerable time in their lives. They are physically weak and mentally unstable. At any moment they want to tear away and return to a drink, but they persist and make it through the painful process.

Once they make it through this period and regain their physical strength and their mental capacity, they feel clean and pure. Their faith is often all that brings them through. Their first step into sobriety is a big one because if it is the right step, it is a step toward letting God handle things one day at a time. If their focus is correct, they grow spiritually and emotionally. Sometimes they grow more in the first year than they have in the past twenty.

The toxic faithful go through no less a traumatic and painful time when they remove themselves from the addictive behaviors that have captured them. They are vulnerable, left without the old toxic thoughts that made everything instantly better. When they determine to face the storms with only their faith in God and the support of other nontoxic believers, they set themselves up for growth. God will take that little amount of pure faith and from it grow a deep and abiding faith. To start that process of growth, God does not need a lot of faith. He needs only a little seed of healthy faith. Christ described this small faith as being the size of a mustard seed (Matthew 17:20). From that small speck of faith, the impossible can be accomplished.

RESPECTFUL

As faith grows, respect for others grows with it. Too often religious addicts attack others out of their own insecurities. When security depends on God, addicts lose their need to feel threatened. People can be appreciated for their strengths and their weaknesses. Their differing views can be considered a result of different individuals at different places in their growth of faith. Those from different denominations or even from different factions within a denomination are no longer perceived as the enemy.

In the Bible, God instructs us to respect all people. He warns against showing favor to any one group, such as the wealthy. We need to see each person as a wonderful creation of God, with gifts and talents sent directly from God. Faith frees us from the fear of others and allows us to love them. A healthy faith allows us to love them and trust God to work on their problems as we pray for God to do so. First Peter 2:17 tells us to show proper respect for everyone and love all believers alike. When faith grows to reach this level of respect and acceptance of others, we find the freedom to serve God.

FREE TO SERVE

First Peter also addresses the need for God's faithful followers to live in freedom (see chapter 2). This freedom does not allow us to do everything we think is right, but it is a freedom that moves us to serve others. Rather than be locked into a confining role or serve to work our way to heaven, we can be free to serve others as an act of faith to God.

Galatians 5:13 instructs, "You, brethren, have been called to liberty; only do not use liberty as an opportunity for the flesh, but through love serve one another." When most people think of liberty or freedom, they think of having permission to do things that please them. Some feel a liberty to drink; others feel free to drive expensive cars. Healthy faith does not focus on these things. It does not free us to participate in or flirt with evil, but rather it frees us to love one another and to show that love by serving one another.

If our society has gone over the edge on any one point, it is the emphasis on our own needs, desires, and demands. For years, people lived in oppressive relationships where their needs went unmet. We have made great progress in identifying those unhealthy situations and motivating people to grow into healthier ones. We have shown individuals who were plagued with undeserved guilt how to rid themselves of those negative feelings. In the process, however, we have gone too far and gotten people to focus on themselves, not on others. We have driven people into such an obsession with their needs that they are reluctant to love their neighbors as themselves.

Healthy faith reverses this trend and brings balance back to relationships. Where healthy faith exists, people are amazed at the service shown to others. Out of a deep faith in God, we are free, not bound, to serve others.

SELF-WORTHY

The healthier the faith, the more valuable we can feel. Too often we have based our self-worth on what the world considers valuable. The world thinks money measures value, and if we do not have it in great amounts, we feel bad about ourselves. Physical beauty has become almost a religion unto itself, and those without it feel no value in a society that judges worth by the looks on the outside. In this age of technology, IQ is used to determine who is to be esteemed and who is to be snubbed. It is hard for us to measure up. The more we focus on the world's standards and values, the more negative we feel about ourselves.

God has a different system, and if our faith is in him, we can feel tremendous relief. Christ talked about the worth of every individual. His words bring good news to all of us who will never be fashion models, members of a society of geniuses, or holders of Swiss bank accounts. Christ told his followers not to be afraid of those who attack a person physically, because they cannot touch the person's soul. He explained that even though sparrows were sold for about a half-cent apiece, not one sparrow can fall to the ground without God's knowing it—and because we are more valuable than many sparrows, the Savior of the world told us not to worry. God values us so much that he has numbered the very hairs on our heads (see Matthew 10:28-31).

If God knows and cares for all the sparrows, we can feel wonderful about ourselves, knowing he cares much more for us. If our sense of self-worth comes from God, we don't have to worry what the world thinks of us or might do to us. The fact that God sent his Son to die for us should overwhelmingly affirm the worth of each individual. The problem comes when we measure ourselves by the world's standards, take our faith away from God, and place it in our own powers and efforts to measure up. Healthy faith stays focused on God and the value he has given each of us. In this value system of the Creator, no one need feel disappointment over not measuring up to the world. The person with a healthy faith feels valuable to the Creator.

The leader of one of the groups I publish with talks a lot about self-worth. He believes many people make terrible decisions due to low self-worth. I happen to agree. An acquaintance of mine, however, kept bothering me about working with a group that focused on self-esteem. He believed that worth should come from God rather than self. I agreed but explained that many individuals see no worth in people, whether from self or God. Every time we got together, we ended up arguing this point.

Finally I had to confront this man. I told him I had never met anyone with lower self-esteem than him. If his perspective was so great, why did it result in such a negative self-concept?

He reacted as though I had hit him with a pipe. He began to cry and confess that he felt terrible about himself. Though married and a Christian, he masturbated compulsively. He finally admitted that he wanted help.

This man suffered from a common problem. Often those who are most offended about the concept of self-worth are the ones who have the least amount of it.

VULNERABLE

If we believe the words of Christ who tells us not to fear, we are free to be vulnerable. Being vulnerable means being real. It is the ability to risk rejection by laying before others all that we are and are not. If we put our faith in God, we don't need to fear being real. The stronger our faith, the more we are driven to be real. God accepts us, and that is much more important than being accepted by others. Because God accepts us, we can face rejection by others.

So often the toxic-faith system breeds the desire to hide and cover up, as Adam and Eve were driven to do. Healthy faith frees us to come out of hiding and share our imperfect selves with others.

Ephesians 6:16 tells us that we can use our faith as a shield. We don't have to stand behind a facade of materialism or any other earthly creation. We can hold firm to our shield of faith and be vulnerable to others. A true test of faith is how much a person is willing to risk rejection by the world. The mark of the faithful is vulnerability with others due to a complete focus on God.

TRUSTING

Healthy faith grows trust in three areas.

First, trust in God grows the more we give to him. As we give our time, money, and hearts, he rewards us with comfort and peace, and then we trust him with more of what we have and who we are. Every day the recovering religious addict must turn over more and more to God and trust him with greater things. This relieves the addict from the burden of control. As the addict allows God to be in control and trusts his control, the addict is freed to live without being driven.

Some people have lived such terrible lives that they fear God and don't totally trust him. Colossians 1:20-23 addresses this issue. In that passage God speaks to us, telling us that through Christ, he has cleared a path to him. The price Christ paid on the cross has made peace with God possible for the one who trusts in him. He says that many were far away from him, to the point of being his enemy. Evil thoughts and actions separated them from him, but God has brought them back as friends. Through the death of Christ, we are able to stand in the presence of God with nothing held against us. The only requirement is that we fully believe that Christ died to save us; then we can place our total trust in God. If we believe these things, we have no reason not to trust God with all that we have.

Second, we grow to trust others. Although many have deceived us, as we heal we can learn from our mistakes. Eventually, we will be able to trust others again. Placing our trust in God allows us to trust others, because we know that we do not have to allow ourselves to be victimized again.

Third, growing faith helps us trust ourselves. Without a faith anchored in God, we trust in the most convenient object available. As each new object of faith fails, we lose faith in our ability to make good judgments. As our faith in God grows—as we trust him more and rely on him to help us—we find ourselves respecting our judgments because they are anchored in God. We do not trust ourselves more because we have become smarter, but because we have placed our focus more securely on God.

The religious addict has been functioning by trusting in his or her efforts to win favor with God. This futile existence must be forsaken. From Hebrews 4 we learn that all may enter the kingdom of heaven if faith in God is real. Complete trust in him must replace effort and works.

As our faith matures, trust in God will grow with it. We no longer sway with the whims of the day or run from fear of others. Knowing that God will not betray us allows us to trust him, others, and ourselves.

While many have no trouble understanding trust, others find it almost impossible to grasp. One broken woman had been abused sexually by her father. After years of meeting his addictive sexual needs, she lost her ability to trust God or any other human being. People would ask her to trust in Christ, but she could not allow herself to trust any male figure. Finally she began counseling sessions with a gentle man of integrity who had her best interests at heart. He guided her through her fears and showed her that not all men are untrustworthy. He also demonstrated that some are capable of caring with no strings attached. Finally he led her to trust in the God who loved her. An abusive man poisoned her faith, but another man who could be trusted helped her rediscover the joy and fulfillment of trusting fully in God.

Individualized

Religious addiction takes away a person's identity. Where religious addiction abounds, conformity is the order of the day. Rules and roles take priority over the worth and development of each individual. Recovery helps to repair self-identity. Healthy faith allows a person to express faith as an individual, not merely as a conformist to a system.

God has created each person individually in his own image. He does not want to waste the uniqueness of any of us. He has given us many unique gifts that he wants us to develop in service to him. The church is one body of many members. We must continue to come together as a group so that God can use our individual gifts for the benefit of all. As healthy faith grows, shame diminishes, and we delight in finding that we do not have to live in the image of another person—only in the image of God.

Ephesians 4:11 tells us that some individuals have been gifted to preach. Others are better at serving and caring for members of the church. God has made us uniquely for service to one another. When we abandon that uniqueness, we abandon God's will for our lives.

Relationship Oriented

Most toxic-faith systems focus on what people do and how well they conform to the rules of the group. In healthy faith, the focus shifts from rules to relationships. Frequently, the religious addict has abandoned relationships, believing that God is all that matters. But God has shown us that the more we love him, the more we will seek out others and manifest his love through relationships with them. Instead of obeying another's rules, the person with healthy faith strives to develop intimacy. Sharing the faith and loving another in faith build the individual's relationship with God.

Too often people see faith as a hot line to heaven without regard for earthly struggles. Once I discussed toxic faith with a minister. He told me that, three years prior to our conversation, he had been a full-fledged religious addict, obsessed with himself and his knowledge of God. The more his addiction grew, the more isolated he became. He had no time for people, spoke curtly, and most people hated to be around him.

One day a woman who had supported the church for some time came to see him, declaring that she wanted to say only two words to him: "Forget yourself." He asked what she meant, but she said no more. This man thought and thought about this odd message. He became obsessed with learning what she meant. He called her and heard that she was coming for another visit the following week. At that time she would give him another two words.

When she arrived, she looked him in the eye and said two more words: "Serve others." The minister said the woman's words revolutionized his faith. He realized that he had been serving himself and had forgotten the importance of relationships. He began to rebuild what he had torn down, and in so doing his faith became real.

PERSONAL

Religious addicts think of faith as impersonal. They are mere members of the group, not individuals loved and cherished by God. Toxic-faith systems are based on the absence of personal convictions and the acceptance of someone else's definition of faith.

Healthy faith is a personal experience generated internally through trust in God. The Holy Spirit personally leads each individual. Each person can read God's Word individually and hear God speak through his Word. Christ died for each individual.

The healthier one's faith becomes, the more personal it becomes. A personal relationship forms between the believer and God. That relationship becomes so strong that no criticism or system can break the personal bonds formed between God and the believer.

Balanced

Healthy faith is balanced. It does not become so preoccupied with work that it destroys family. It is not so intent on witnessing to people that it fails to meet their needs. It does not become so involved with memorizing Scripture that it forgets the Author of Scripture. Obedience to rules is balanced with freedom to serve others in ways that reflect each person's individuality.

Toxic faith depends on "either/or," "black or white," "us versus them," and "all-or-nothing" thinking. It leaves no room for compromise, no middle ground for others outside the system. Healthy faith accepts that life is not black or white and allows the believer to feel okay about struggling with the gray areas of life. It rejects the us-versus-them mentality. The person with healthy faith sees himself or herself as a part of a greater community, all of whom struggle with their relationships with themselves, their God, and their fellow human beings.

Where healthy faith grows, every area of the believer's life improves. In the balanced practice of faith, families grow closer, friends become stronger, and conflicts get resolved more easily. Believers focus on God, and each individual is seen as a valuable creation of God, worthy of God's attention. Understanding replaces rigidity. Those who grow in the faith find comfort as they regain perspective. They find wholeness in their balanced faith.

Nondefensive

Healthy faith takes a nondefensive position against those who would challenge their beliefs and faith. Healthy faith welcomes critical evaluation and tough questions as opportunities to learn and relate. Those in a healthy system refrain from defining the truth for others and welcome the chance to share what they believe about the truth. Those who question their faith are not considered disobedient but rather are encouraged to explore their doubts.

Those in a toxic-faith system are afraid of every threat to the system.

They feel personally threatened because much of their faith developed from their rules rather than by the Word of God. When God is in charge, we have no reason to feel threatened. He is in control and he will champion the faith.

Healthy faith attracts people to it rather than repels them. Those who become defensive repel other people—they forget how attractive Christ was as he drew people to himself. What a relief it is not to have to defend every criticism made by everyone outside the faith!

NONJUDGMENTAL

In the beautiful Sermon on the Mount, Christ gives us specific instructions about judging others. In Matthew 7:1-2 he instructs us not to judge others or we will be judged in the same way.

All too often we are guilty of the very things we point out as wrong in others. Recovering religious addicts stop judging people and start listening to them. When this occurs, compassion and empathy develop. This overcomes a major flaw of the toxic-faith system, which so heavily focuses on the system that it forgets the needs of people.

Healthy believers don't judge what people say; they listen to what others have to offer. They evaluate it; they do not judge it. When we judge people, we accept them only under certain conditions. Healthy faith removes the conditions and the need to judge. Healthy believers look for similarities of experience to establish a relationship. They see each person as a fellow struggler in different stages of the struggle. Healthy believers are so busy developing a personal relationship with God, they have no time to judge where others might be in developing their own relationship.

REALITY BASED

The toxic believer denies reality. His or her faith is not based on a belief in the supernatural power of God but rather on a desire to see magical solutions that stop pain. Toxic hope is found in a servant-God intent on making life easy.

The healthy believer embraces reality. Healthy faith acknowledges the supernatural power of God and does not need miraculous intervention to believe God is real. The healthy believer does not look for God to change circumstances magically but looks to him in the midst of trials.

When faith grows strong, there is no need to deny reality. Believing that God is faithful to help them through their trials and tribulations, healthy believers have no need to walk away from reality. They see the problems before them, do what they can to resolve them, and trust God to do the rest.

The Nature of Mature Faith

A study researching faith came up with eight core dimensions that indicate the maturity of one's faith. A mature believer:

1. Trusts in God's saving grace and believes firmly in the humanity and divinity of Jesus
2. Experiences a sense of personal well-being, security, and peace
3. Integrates faith and life, seeing work, family, social relationships, and political choices as part of one's religious life
4. Seeks spiritual growth through study, reflection, prayer, and discussion with others
5. Seeks to be part of a community of believers in which people give witness to their faith and support and nourish one another
6. Holds life-affirming values, including commitment to racial and gender equality, affirmation of cultural and religious diversity, and a personal sense of responsibility for the welfare of others
7. Advocates social and global change to bring about greater social justice
8. Serves humanity consistently and passionately through acts of love and justice

PETER L. BENSON AND CAROLYN H. EKLIN[1]

Able to Embrace Our Emotions

Healthy faith gives a person the ability to embrace his or her emotions. The Christian must recognize that Christ did not deny his emotions; he embraced them. As he walked the earth, he revealed his love, anger, sorrow, and many other emotions. His grief became so great that he admitted his soul was full of sorrow unto death (see Mark 14:34). What depths of emotion he felt!

Healthy faith has no need to hide its feelings. We should rejoice that God has given us emotions to experience the extremes of life. We must acknowledge them, confess them when they are self-centered, and express them as they develop. Too many religious addicts are filled with hidden anger and fear. As they find healthy faith, they feel the freedom to release those emotions bound by the religious addiction.

Able to Embrace Our Humanity

Healthy faith allows us to embrace humanity. It acknowledges the capacity to sin and make mistakes. It gives no illusion of perfection and has no driven need to be perfect (or hide when we are not). Healthy faith allows us to experience God's mercy and grace.

The toxic believer obeys God out of a fear of divine anger or a terror of rejection by the system. The mercy and grace of God are lost to a superficial existence of living up to another's standards. Performance for acceptance overpowers the knowledge that no one can act good enough to get to God.

Healthy faith knows that mercy and grace are gifts, freely given. If they were to be earned, they would not be gifts. Healthy believers follow God out of gratitude for mercy and grace, accepting that everyone will fail and that God's infinite wisdom has already made a provision for that failure. We do not need to deny who we are to be acceptable to God. He made us and loves us anyway.

Loving

Healthy faith and the healthy believer are able to love and be loved. Healthy faith allows a person to love self, God, and others. The healthy believer is able to extend to God and others the characteristics outlined in 1 Corinthians 13. The exercise of healthy faith allows a person to be patient with God, to trust that God will never abandon or reject his beloved children.

Healthy believers are patient with others and themselves as they allow God to correct their character defects. Such patience is seen only in the hearts of the healthy faithful. If faith does not move persons to love more, it is not healthy.

As believers mature in love, they grow in kindness toward others. Healthy believers are also kind to themselves and find no need to punish themselves when they miss the mark. This kindness is so attractive that others come into the faith because of it.

The love of healthy faith is also humble. Pride vanishes where believers focus totally on God. The healthy believer turns away from rejection, rudeness, and self-seeking. He or she forgives freely; grudges and healthy faith cannot coexist. Healthy believers rejoice in truth and grieve over evil.

Healthy believers grow full of love. In fact, love is the predominant characteristic of those with a healthy faith. Their love heals and helps them bear up under every trial. It provides the foundation for a future with God and growing relationships with others. If believers have all the talents in the world but do not have a deep and abiding love, their faith is worthless. But where love is present, faith grows, and people are attracted to God.

Growing in Faith

Developing a healthy faith in God is the achievement of a lifetime. It is a never-ending process with seasons of tremendous growth and times of near stagnation. At times God seems to direct every step we take; at other times he feels as distant as another solar system.

God wants us to seek him as he seeks us. As we trust him more, we find him more loving and accepting of who we are. He desires that we grow and remains patient with us even when we stubbornly refuse to do so. He is always there for us, and those with a healthy faith return to him quickly after each relapse into sin.

I pray that you will grow strong in your faith. I hope that your search for profit, power, pleasure, and/or prestige will end as you find God to be your source of fulfillment. The wounds of addiction do not heal quickly. Be patient with yourself and give yourself time to heal through God's love. As you heal, remember that you are still susceptible to falling back into your addiction. You are vulnerable to false teachers and false teachings. I encourage you to consider the words of Paul in 1 Thessalonians 5:21: "Test all things; hold fast what is good." As you grow in faith, test the faith and teachings of others so you will no longer be led astray.

God loves you and wants you for his own. The more you give of yourself to him, the more joy you will have. God bless you on your journey of faith as you seek to find God as he is.

Do You Have Toxic Faith?

Yes   No

❏   ❏   1. Has your family complained that you are always going to a church meeting rather than spending time with them?

❏   ❏   2. Do you feel extreme guilt for being out of church just one Sunday?

❏   ❏   3. Do you sense that God is looking at what you do, and if you don't do enough, he might turn on you or refuse to bless you?

❏   ❏   4. Do you often tell your children what to do without explaining your reasons, since you know you are right?

❏   ❏   5. Do you find yourself with little time for the pleasures of earlier years because you are so busy serving on committees and attending other church groups?

❏   ❏   6. Have people complained that you use so much Scripture in your conversation that it is hard to communicate with you?

❏   ❏   7. Are you giving money to a ministry because you believe God will make you wealthy if you give?

❏   ❏   8. Have you ever been involved sexually with a minister out of wedlock?

❏   ❏   9. Is it hard for you to make a decision without consulting your minister? Even over the small issues?

Yes	No		
❏	❏	10.	Do you see your minister as more powerful than other humans?
❏	❏	11.	Has your faith led you to lead an isolated life, making it hard for you to relate to your family and friends?
❏	❏	12.	Have you found yourself looking to your minister for a quick fix to a lifelong problem?
❏	❏	13.	Do you feel extreme guilt over the slightest mistakes or inadequacies?
❏	❏	14.	Is your most significant relationship deteriorating over your strong beliefs, compared to those of a "weaker partner"?
❏	❏	15.	Do you ever have thoughts of God wanting you to destroy yourself or others in order to go and live with him?
❏	❏	16.	Do you regularly believe God is communicating with you in an audible voice?
❏	❏	17.	Do you feel God is angry with you?
❏	❏	18.	Do you believe you are still being punished for something you did as a child?
❏	❏	19.	Do you feel if you work a little harder, God will finally forgive you?
❏	❏	20.	Has anyone ever told you a minister was manipulating your thoughts and feelings?

If you answered yes to at least three of the above questions, call:
1-800-NEW-LIFE
or e-mail us at
www.newlife.com

Twelve Steps to Overcoming Toxic Faith

The twelve steps have provided a path to recovery for millions of people for over half a century. Here they have been adapted to apply to those recovering from religious addiction. Working through these steps could be your means of escape from religious addiction and into a real faith in God.

1. We admitted that we were powerless over our compulsive religious behaviors and toxic faith—that our lives had become unmanageable.
2. We came to believe that a Power greater than ourselves could restore us to sanity.
3. We made a decision to turn our will and our lives over to the care of God.
4. We made a searching and fearless moral inventory of ourselves.
5. We admitted to God, to ourselves, and to another human being the exact nature of our wrongs.
6. We were entirely ready to have God remove all these defects of character.
7. We humbly asked him to remove our shortcomings.
8. We made a list of all the individuals we had harmed and became willing to make amends to them all.
9. We made direct amends to such individuals whenever possible, except when to do so would injure them or others.

10. We continued to take personal inventory and when we were wrong, promptly admitted it.
11. We sought through meditation and prayer to improve our conscious contact with God, praying only for knowledge of his will and the power to carry that out.
12. Having enjoyed a spiritual awakening as a result of these steps, we tried to carry this message to other religious addicts and to practice these principles in all our affairs.

Notes

Introduction

1. Rosemary Radford Ruether, "Don't Fall for Every Spirit Lurking Under the Name of Spirituality," *National Catholic Reporter,* 4 October 1988, 15.

Chapter 1: The Extremes of Toxic Faith

1. Jerry and Steve Arterburn, *How Will I Tell My Mother?* (Nashville: Oliver-Nelson, 1988).
2. "Baptists Kidnap Girl, Raise As Slave/Sex Toy," Associated Press, 23 March 2000, wysiwyg://http://www.postfun.com/pfp.news.wel.
3. "Cops Chase Car, Find 20 Nude People," and "Naked Preacher Accepts Gift of RV from God," based on reports in the Associated Press, 20 August 1993, http://www.airspeed.com/~shydavid/ca-04.html.
4. "Reggie White's Pastor Gets 10 Years," based on reports in the *Milwaukee Journal Sentinel,* 27 March 2000, wysiwyg://8/http://www.postfun.com/pfp.news.wel.
5. Mark Fritz, "A Mystery of the Cloth," *Los Angeles Times*, 16 November 1998, Home Edition, A-1.
6. "Faith Healer Molests Children," Reuters, 16 May 2000.
7. "Ten Commandments Claim 900+ Victims," Reuters, 31 March 2000; "Cult Killings Exceed Jonestown Toll," *Los Angeles Times*, 1 April 2000, A-14; Margaret Ramirez, "Tie to Death Cult Stuns Those Who Knew Priest," *Los Angeles Times*, 8 April 2000, B-5; "55 More Victims of Uganda Doomsday Cult Discovered," *Los Angeles Times*, 28 April 2000, A-15.

Chapter 4: When Religion Becomes an Addiction

1. Adrian Van Kaam, "Addiction: Counterfeit of Religious Addiction," *Studies in Formative Spirituality* 8 (May 1987): 243.

2. Van Kaam, "Addiction: Counterfeit of Religious Addiction," 246-7.

Chapter 10: Seventeen Characteristics of Healthy Faith

1. Peter L. Benson and Carolyn H. Eklin, *Effective Christian Education: A National Study of Protestant Congregations* (Minneapolis: a research project of Search Institute, March 1990), 10.

Stephen Arterburn is the creator of Women of Faith, whose conferences have been attended by over one million women. He is also the founder and chairman of New Life Clinics, the largest provider of Christian counseling in the United States, and he hosts the daily *New Life Live!* radio program. A nationally known speaker and a licensed minister, he is the best-selling author of more than thirty-five books, including *More Jesus, Less Religion; The Seven Keys to Spiritual Renewal;* and *Every Man's Battle.* He resides with his family in Laguna Beach, California. He can be reached at SArterburn@newlife.com.

Jack Felton is a licensed therapist, an ordained minister at New Hope Christian Counseling Center, and president and founder of Compassion Move Ministries. Felton is a frequent lecturer in the southern California area and has numerous local and national television and radio appearances to his credit. He and his wife, Robin, and their children, Jack III and Christy, live in Huntington Beach, California. He can be reached at jackfelton@jps.net.